Yanmar

YANMAR MARINE DIESEL ENGINE 2QM15

Service Manual

Yanmar

YANMAR MARINE DIESEL ENGINE 2QM15

Service Manual

ISBN/EAN: 9783954272747
Erscheinungsjahr: 2013
Erscheinungsort: Bremen, Deutschland

© *maritimepress in Europäischer Hochschulverlag GmbH & Co. KG, Fahrenheitstr. 1, 28359 Bremen. Alle Rechte beim Verlag und bei den jeweiligen Lizenzgebern.*
www.maritimepress.de | office@maritimepress.de

Bei diesem Titel handelt es sich um den Nachdruck eines historischen, lange vergriffenen Buches. Da elektronische Druckvorlagen für diese Titel nicht existieren, musste auf alte Vorlagen zurückgegriffen werden. Hieraus zwangsläufig resultierende Qualitätsverluste bitten wir zu entschuldigen.

YANMAR
SERVICE MANUAL

MARINE DIESEL ENGINE

MODEL **2QM15**

FOREWORD

This service manual has been compiled for engineers engaged in the sales, service, inspection and maintenance of the 2QM15 marine diesel engine. Accordingly, descriptions of the construction and functions of the engine are emphasized in this manual while items which should already be common knowledge are omitted.

One characteristic of a marine diesel engine is that its performance in a vessel is governed by the applicability of the vessel's hull construction and its steering system.

Engine installation, fitting out and propeller selection have a substantial effect on the performance of the engine and the vessel. Moreover, when the engine runs unevenly or when trouble occurs, it is essential to check a wide range of operating conditions—such as installation to the hull and suitability of the ship's piping and propeller—and not just the engine itself. To get maximum performance from this engine, you should completely understand its functions, construction and capabilities, as well as proper use and servicing.

Use this manual as a handy reference in daily inspection and maintenance, and as a text for engineering guidance.

Model 2QM15

CHAPTER 1 GENERAL
1. Exterior Views 1-1
2. Specifications 1-2
3. Principal Construction 1-3
4. Performance Curves 1-4
5. Features.. 1-5
6. Sectional Views 1-6
7. Exterior Views 1-7
8. System Diagrams................................. 1-8
9. Standard Accessories 1-15
10. Optional Accessories............................ 1-16

CHAPTER 2 BASIC ENGINE
1. Cylinder Block 2-1
2. Cylinder Liner.................................... 2-2
3. Cylinder Head 2-5
4. Piston.. 2-15
5. Connecting Rod.................................. 2-19
6. Crankshaft 2-22
7. Camshaft.. 2-26
8. Timing Gear 2-29

CHAPTER 3 FUEL SYSTEM
1. Construction 3-1
2. Injection Pump................................... 3-2
3. Injection Nozzle.................................. 3-11
4. Fuel Filter 3-14
5. Fuel feed pump 3-15
6. Fuel Tank 3-16

CHAPTER 4 GOVERNOR
1. Governor 4-1
2. Injection Limiter 4-6
3. No-Load Maximum Speed Limiter................. 4-7
4. Engine Stop Spring 4-8

CHAPTER 5 INTAKE AND EXHAUST SYSTEMS
1. Intake and Exhaust Systems 5-1
2. Intake Silencer................................... 5-2
3. Exhaust System.................................. 5-3
4. Breather Pipe.................................... 5-4

CHAPTER 6 LUBRICATION SYSTEM
1. Lubrication System 6-1
2. Oil Pump 6-3
3. Oil Filter... 6-5
4. Oil Pressure Regulator Valve...................... 6-6
5. Oil Pressure Measurement 6-7

CHAPTER 7 COOLING SYSTEM
1. Cooling System 7-1
2. Water Pump..................................... 7-3
3. Thermostat...................................... 7-7
4. Anticorrosion Zinc 7-8
5. Kingston Cock 7-9
6. Bilge Strainer 7-10

CHAPTER 8 REDUCTION AND REVERSING GEAR
1. Construction 8-1
2. Installation....................................... 8-5
3. Operation and Maintenance....................... 8-6
4. Inspection and Servicing 8-7
5. Disassembly 8-12
6. Reassembly 8-16

CHAPTER 9 REMOTE CONTROL SYSTEM
1. Construction 9-1
2. Clutch Regulator One-handle Remote Control...... 9-2
3. Decompression Remote Control................... 9-4
4. Engine Stop Remote Control...................... 9-5

CHAPTER 10 ELECTRICAL SYSTEM
1. Composition..................................... 10-1
2. Battery.. 10-3
3. Starter Motor 10-6
4. Alternator....................................... 10-13
5. Alarm Circuit 10-23

CHAPTER 11 INSTALLATION AND FITTING OUT
1. Propeller Selection............................... 11-1
2. Engine Installation............................... 11-2
3. Stern Equipment 11-6
4. Interior Piping and Wiring........................ 11-10
5. Front Power Take-Off 11-15

CHAPTER 12 OPERATING INSTRUCTIONS
1. Fuel Oil And Lubricating Oil...................... 12-1
2. Engine Operating Instructions.................... 12-8
3. Troubleshooting And Repair 12-12

CHAPTER 13 DISASSEMBLY AND REASSEMBLY
1. Disassembly And Reassembly Precautions 13-1
2. Disassembly And Reassembly Tools............... 13-2
3. Other... 13-6
4. Disassembly..................................... 13-7
5. Reassembly..................................... 13-15
6. Tightening Torque............................... 13-24
7. Packing Supplement and Adhesines 13-26

CHAPTER 14 INSPECTION AND SERVICING
1. Periodic Inspection and Servicing................. 14-1

CHAPTER 1
GENERAL

1. Exterior Views 1-1
2. Specifications 1-2
3. Principal Construction 1-3
4. Performance Curves 1-4
5. Features....................................... 1-5
6. Sectional Views 1-6
7. Exterior Views 1-7
8. System Diagrams................................ 1-8
9. Standard Accessories 1-15
10. Optional Accessories........................... 1-16

Chapter 1 General
1. Exterior Views
SM/2QM15

1. Exterior Views

1-1 Intake side viewed from stern

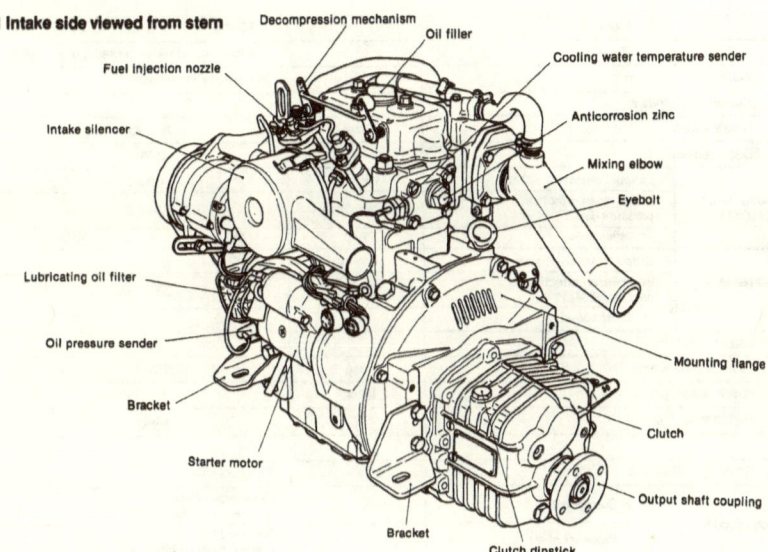

1-2 Exhaust side viewed from bow

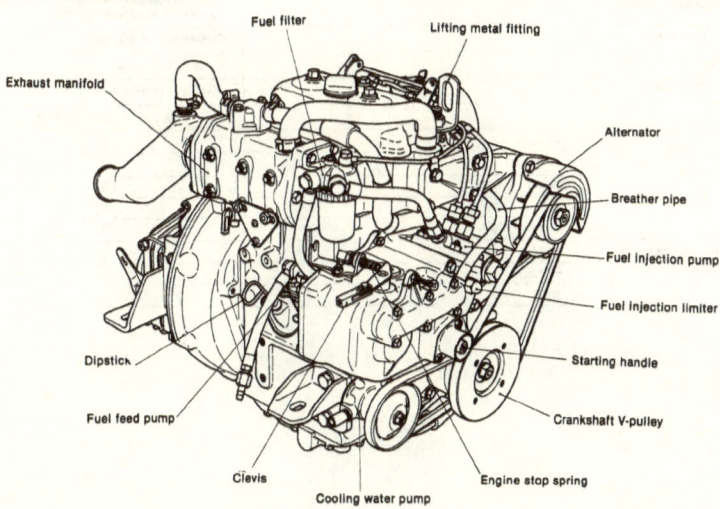

Chapter 1 General
2. Specifications

2. Specifications

Model				2QM15	2QM15G
Type				Vertical 4-cycle water-cooled diesel engine	
Combustion chamber				Precombustion type	
Number of cylinders				2	
Bore × stroke			mm	75 × 75	
Displacement			l	0.662	
Continuous rated output (DINA)	Output/crankshaft speed		HP/rpm	14/3000	
	Brake mean effective pressure (BMEP)		kg/cm²/m/s	6.34/7.5	
	Propeller speed		rpm	1400	1060
One hour rating (DINB)	Output/crankshaft speed		HP/rpm	15/3000	
	Brake mean effective pressure (BMEP)		kg/cm²/m/s	6.80/7.5	
	Propeller speed		rpm	1400	1060
Compression ratio				23:1	
Fuel injection timing			deg	bTDC 27	
Fuel injection pressure			kg/cm²	160 ±10	
Engine weight (dry)			kg	145	
Power takeoff position				Flywheel side	
Direction of rotation	Crankshaft			Counterclockwise (viewed from clutch side)	
	Propeller shaft			Clockwise (viewed from clutch side)	
Cooling system				Sea water forced cooling (rubber impeller water pump)	
Lubrication system				Closed forced lubrication	
Starting system				Electric and manual	
Reduction gear system				Spur gear constant-mesh system	
Clutch				Wet multi-disc mechanical type	
Reduction ratio	Ahead			2.14	2.83
	Astern			2.50	2.50
Engine size	Overall length		mm	698	
	Overall width		mm	452	
	Overall height		mm	553	
Lubricating oil capacity (rake angle 8°)	Total		l	2.5	
	Effective		l	1.0	
Clutch	Total		l	0.7	

3. Principal Construction

Group	Part	Construction
Engine block	Cylinder block	Integrally-cast water jacket and crankcase
	Cylinder liner	Wet type coated with anticorrosion paint
	Main bearing	Metal housing type
	Oil sump	Oil pan
Intake and exhaust systems and valve mechanism	Cylinder head	Integrated two-cylinder
	Intake and exhaust valves	Poppet type, seat angle 90°
	Exhaust manifold	Integral water-cooled type
	Exhaust silencer	Water-cooled mixing elbow type (optional)
	Valve mechanism	Overhead valve push rod, rocker arm system
	Intake silencer	Round polyurethane sound absorbing type
Main moving elements	Crankshaft	Stamped forging
	Flywheel	Attached to crankshaft by flange, with ring gear
	Piston	Oval type
	Piston pin	Floating type
	Piston rings	3 compression rings, 1 oil ring
Lubrication system	Oil pump	Trochoid pump
	Oil filter	Full-flow cartridge type, paper element
	Oil level gauge	Dipstick
Cooling system	Water pump	Rubber impeller type
	Thermostat	Wax pellet type
Bilge system	Bilge pump	Rubber impeller (tandem type) combined with C.W. pump (optional)
Fuel system	Fuel injection pump	Bosch integral 2-cylinder type
	Fuel injection valve	530 semi-throttle valve
	Fuel strainer	Filter paper
Governor	Governor	Centrifugal all-speed mechanical type
Starting system	Electric	Pinion ring gear type starter motor
	Manual	Camshaft starting
Electrical system	Charger	Alternator (with built-in IC regulator)
Reduction reversing	Reduction gear	Spur gear constant-mesh system
Clutch system	Clutch	Wet multi-disc mechanical type

4. Performance Curves

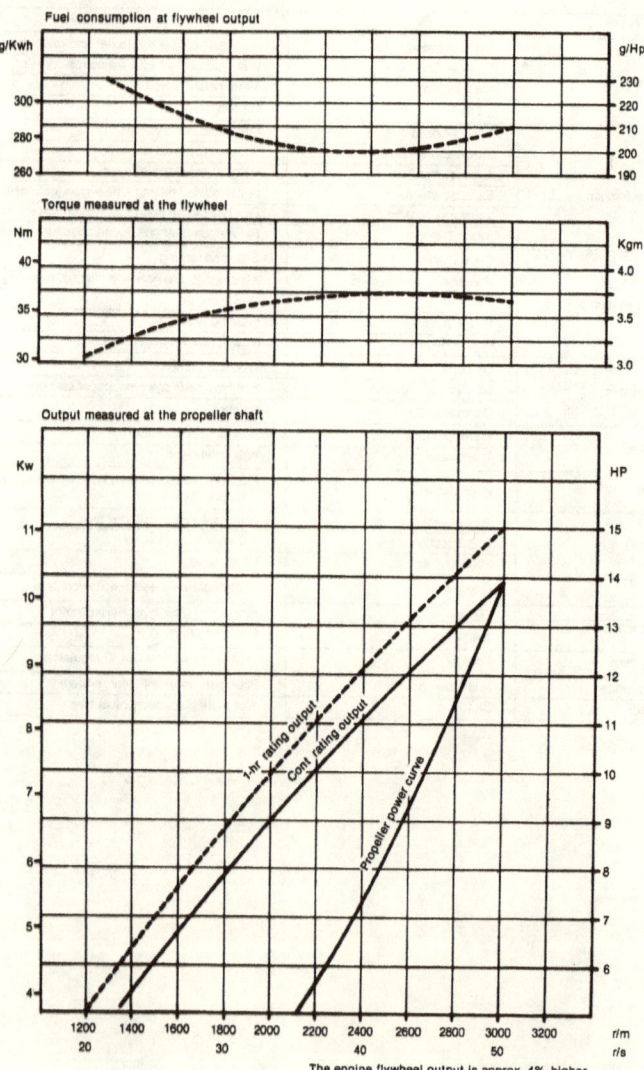

The engine flywheel output is approx. 4% higher.

Chapter 1 General
5. Features
SM/2QM15

5. Features

1. Superior combustion performance
The unique Yanmar swirl precombustion chamber combustion system and new cooling system display superior combustion performance in all types of operation. Low-speed, low-load combustion performance, especially demanded for marine applications, is also superb, and stable performance is maintained over a wide range of speeds. Since starting characteristics are also excellent and warm-up is fast, full engine performance can be obtained within a short time.

2. Low operating costs
Excellent combustion and low friction reduce fuel costs, while the optimized piston shape and ring configuration and improved cooling system reduce oil consumption. Continuous operating time has been extended and operating costs reduced through improved durability.

3. Compact, lightweight
The cylinder head is an integrally-cost two cylinder type, and the crankshaft is the housing type without an intermediate bearing. Minimum weight has been pursued for each engine part, and a reduction reversing gear employing a special new mechanism has been incorporated to obtain revolutionary engine lightness.

4. Long term continuous operation
Improved durability has been achieved by adopting special construction and materials for main moving parts and the valve mechanism, which are the areas most subject to trouble in high-speed engines. Moreover, a bypass system with a thermostat maintains the cooling water at a stable high temperature, resulting in reduced cylinder liner and piston ring wear, reduced thermal load around the combustion chamber, and substantially improved durability. Long-term continuous operation is possible by correct operation and proper attention to fuel and lubricating oil.

5. Low vibration
Vibration has been reduced by minimizing the weights of the pistons, connecting rods, and other sources of vibration, stringent weight management at assembly, and balancing of the flywheel, V-pulley, etc. Vibration has also been suppressed through the adoption of a special cylinder block rib construction and improved rigidity. Rubber shock mounts are available when the engine is to be used under conditions which may lead to severe vibration.

6. Quiet operation
Intake and exhaust noises have been lowered by adopting an intake silencer, water-cooled exhaust manifold and water mixing elbow type exhaust system.
The precombustion chamber system and semi-throttle type injection valve suppress combustion noise substantially.
Moreover, gear noise has been reduced by the use of helical gears around the gear train and clutch gear, and by the buffering effect of a damper disc.
In addition, noise prevention measures have also been taken at the control valve mechanism and other parts.

7. Superior matching to the hull
(1) Four-point support engine installation feet make installation easy.
(2) Mist intake system prevents contamination of the engine room.
(3) Since the fuel pump is mounted to the engine, the fuel tank can be installed anywhere.
(4) Water-cooled manifold prevents a rise in the engine temperature.
(5) Independent type instrument panel can be installed wherever it is easiest to see.
(6) Speed, clutch forward and reverse, decompression and engine stop can all be remotely controlled.
(7) The use of rubber and vinyl hoses for ship interior piping not only facilitates piping work, but also eliminates brazing faults caused by vibration.
(8) Tandem type cooling water/bilge pump is available as an option.

8. Easy to operate
(1) Cooling water temperature switch and lubricating oil pressure switch are provided, and alarm lamps and buzzer are mounted on the instrument panel.
(2) Threaded hole in the V-pulley permits front power take-off.
(3) Hole for manual starting handle permits manual starting.
(4) Positive clutch engagement and disengagement; propeller shaft does not rotate when clutch is placed in Neutral position.

Printed in Japan
2F015A

Chapter 1 General
6. Sectional Views

6. Engine Cross-section

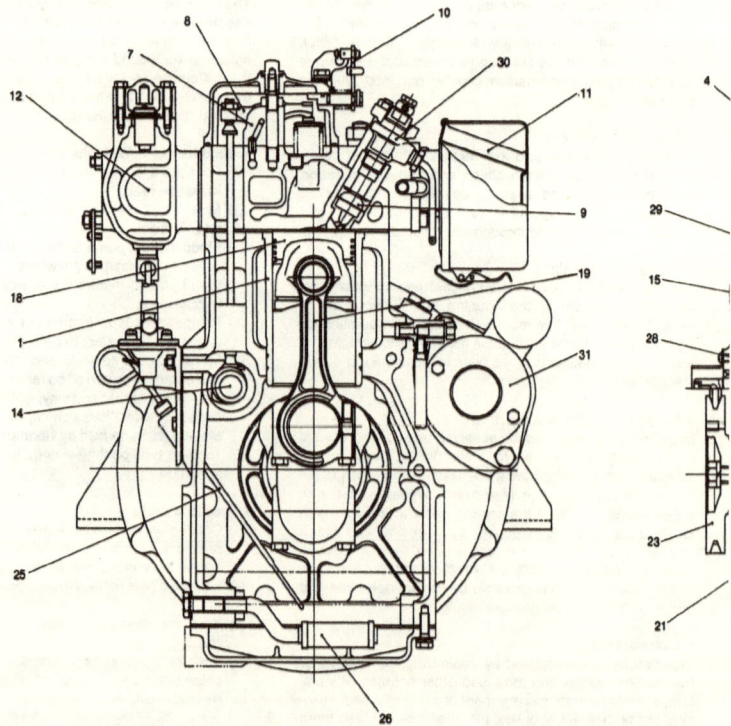

1. Cylinder liner
2. Main bearing housing
3. Cylinder head
4. Exhaust valve
5. Intake valve
6. Valve spring
7. Valve rocker arm support
8. Valve rocker arm
9. Precombustion chamber
10. Decompression lever
11. Intake
12. Exhau
13. Mixin
14. Cams
15. Cams
16. Tappe
17. Push
18. Piston
19. Conn
20. Crank

SM/2QM15

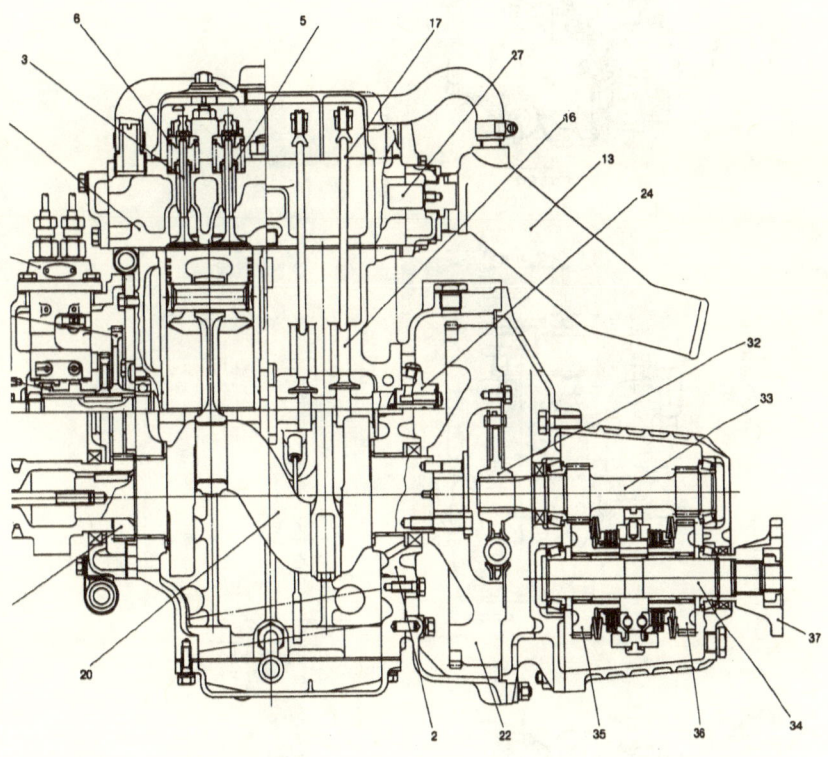

silencer	21. Crankshaft gear	31. Alternator
st manifold	22. Flywheel	32. Damper disc
g elbow	23. Crankshaft V-pulley	33. Input shaft
haft	24. Lubricating oil pump	34. Output shaft
haft gear	25. Dipstick	35. Forward large gear
t	26. Lubricating oil inlet pipe	36. Reverse large gear
rod	27. Anticorrosion zinc	37. Output shaft coupling
	28. Fuel injection pump cam	
cting rod	29. Fuel injection pump	
shaft	30. Fuel injection nozzle	

Chapter 1 General
7. Exterior Views

SM/2QM15

7. Exterior Views

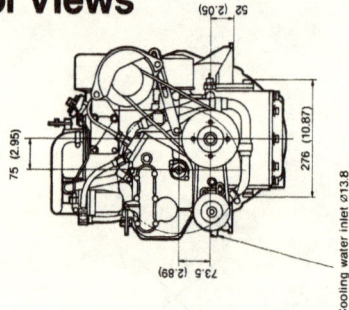

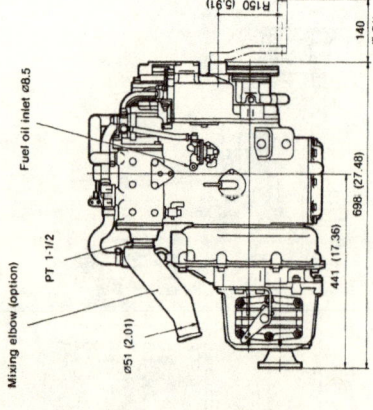

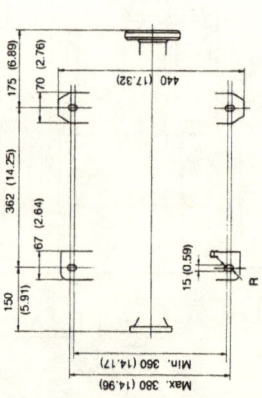

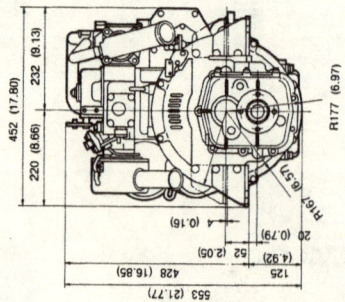

8. System Diagrams

8-1 Cooling system

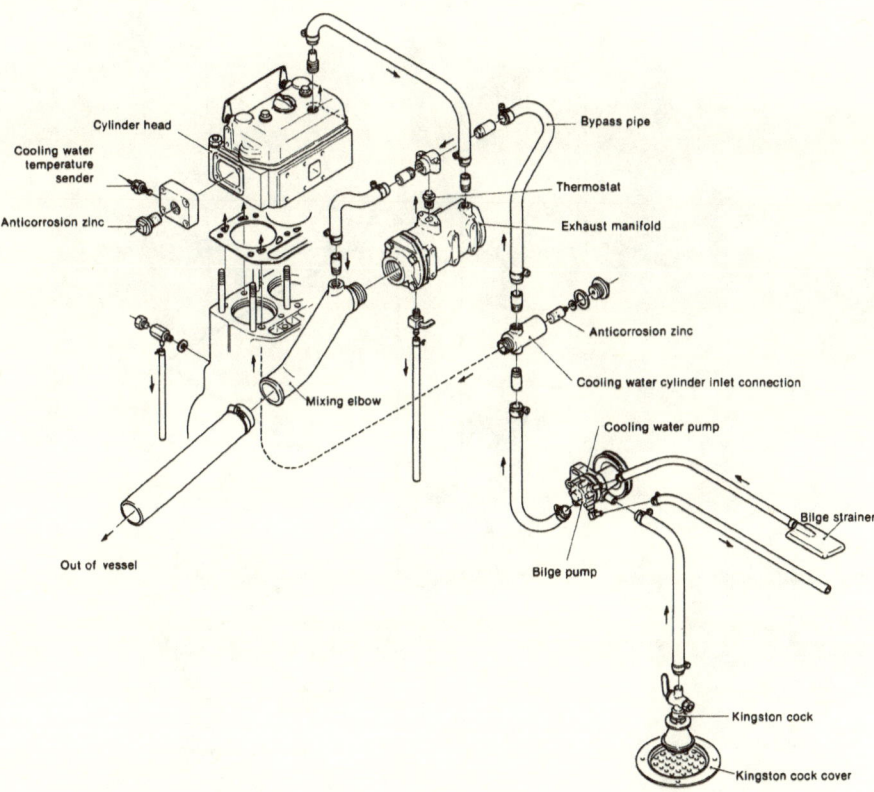

Chapter 1 General
8. System Diagrams
SM/2QM15

8-2 Lubrication system

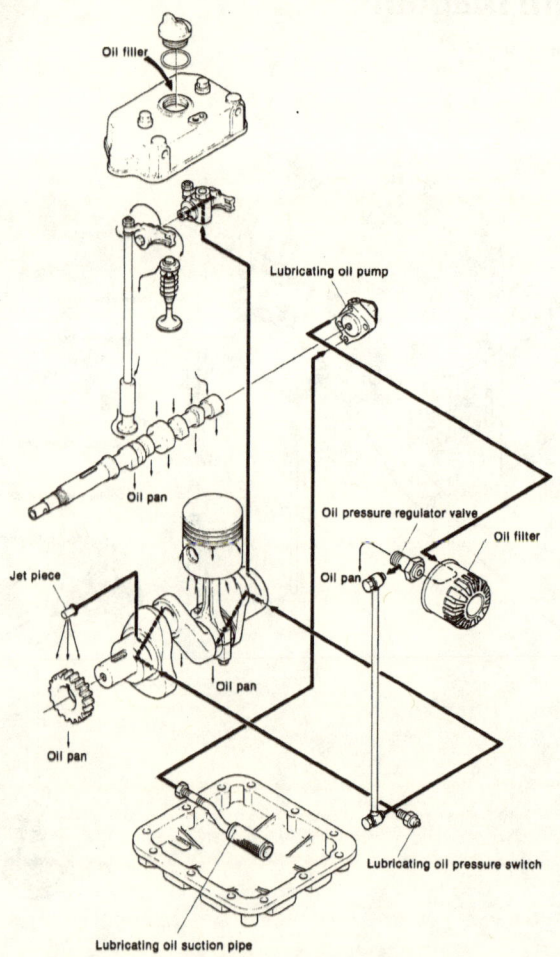

Chapter 1 General
8. System Diagrams — SM/2QM15

8-3 Fuel system

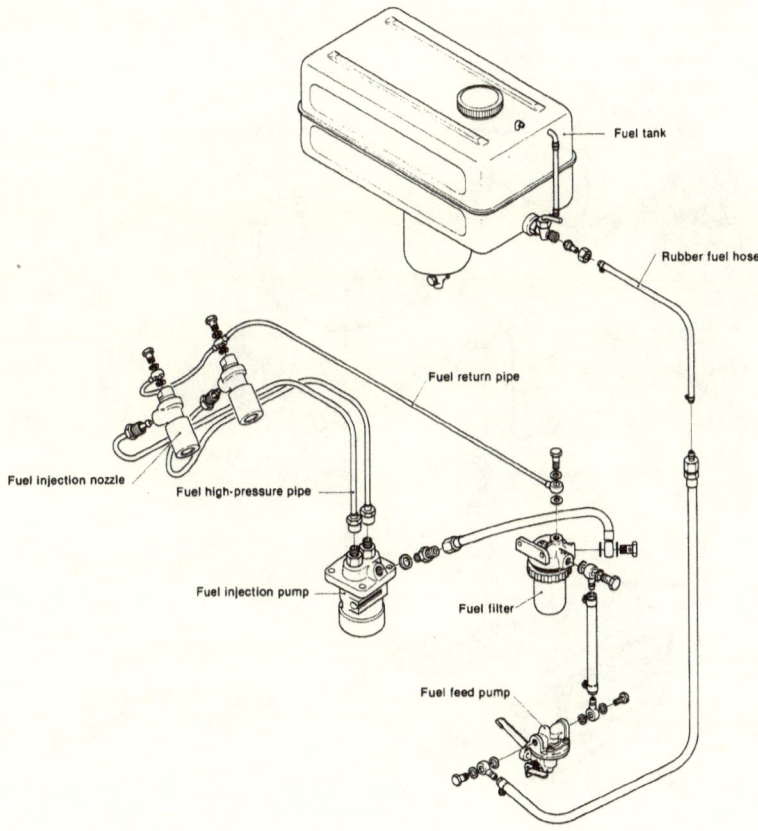

Chapter 1 General
8. System Diagrams
SM/2QM15

8-4 Electrical system

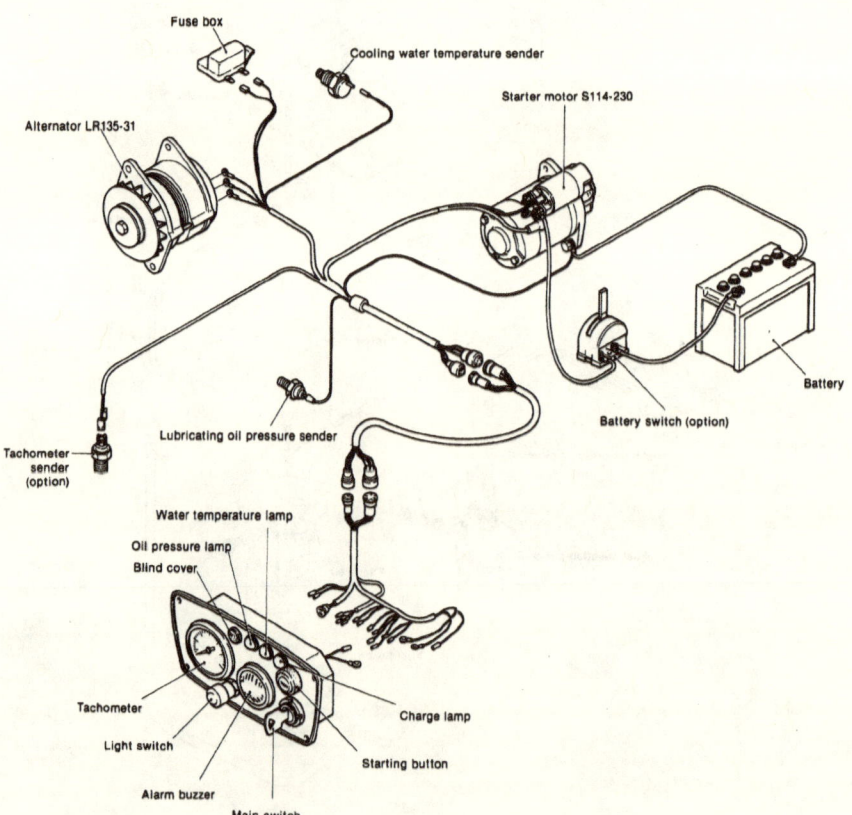

Chapter 1 General
8. System Diagrams

SM/2QM15

8-5 Timing gear train

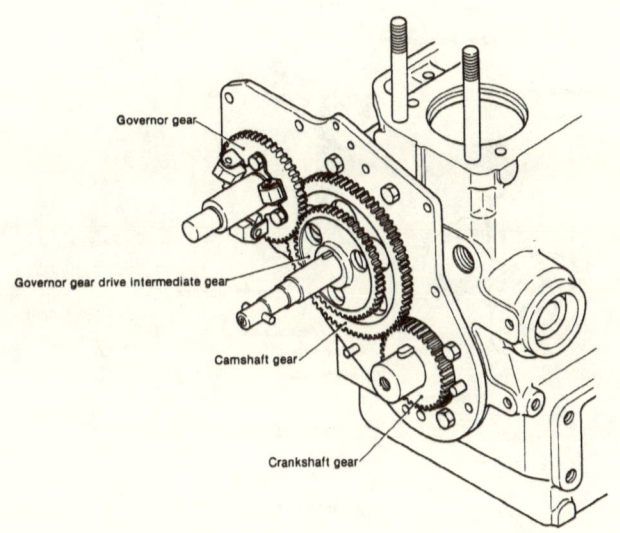

8-6 Reduction reversing power transmission system

Forward

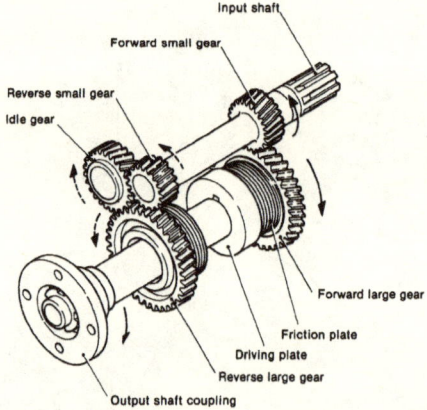

Reverse

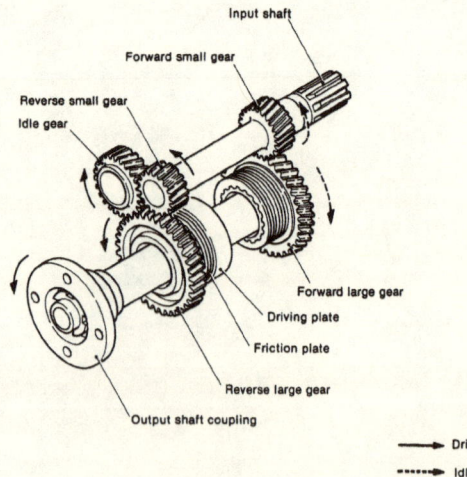

→ Driving
------▶ Idling

Chapter 1 General
8. System Diagrams _____ *SM/2QM15*

8-7 Remote control system

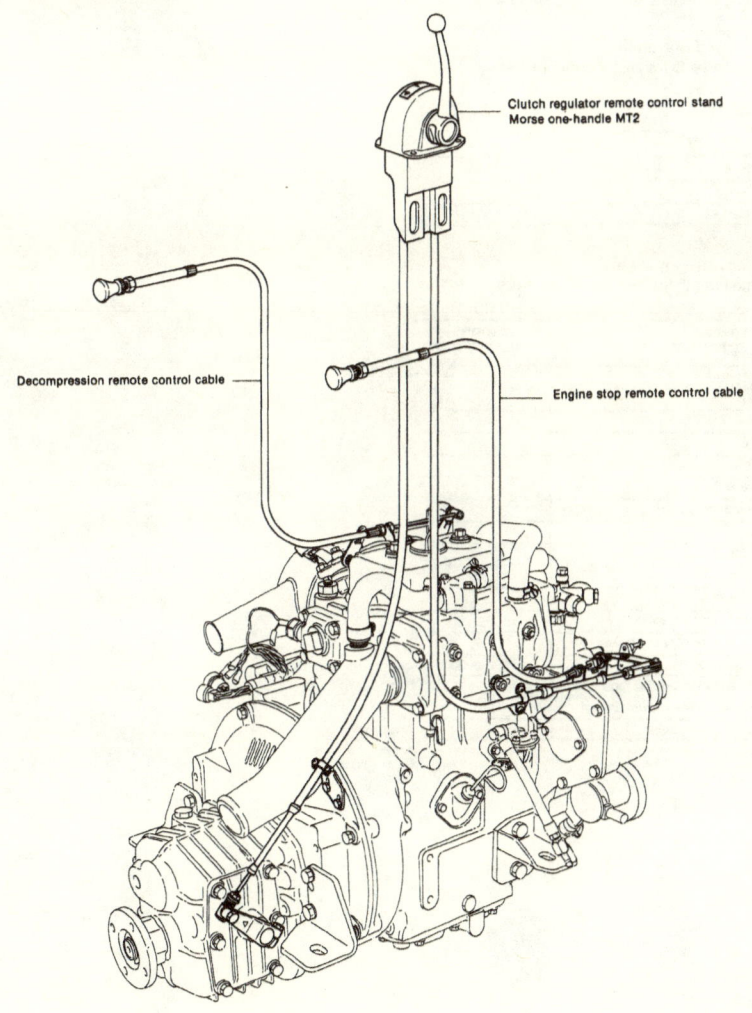

9. Standard Accessories

9-1 Parts packed with engine
The parts packed with the engine are listed below.

Part name	Remarks
Instrument panel ass'y	
Starting handle	
Tool box	
Operating manual	

9-2 Parts mounted on engine
The parts mounted to the engine are listed below.

Part name	Remarks
Intake silencer	
Exhaust manifold	
Water pump	
Feed pump	
Fuel strainer	
Oil strainer	
Oil pressure switch	
Water temperature switch	
Thermostat	
Starter motor	
Alternator (with ICR)	
Wiring harness	
Speed remote control bracket	
Engine stop remote control bracket	
Engine stop device	
Clutch remote control bracket (bow)	
Decompression remote control bracket	
Fuse box	

Chapter 1 General
10. Optional Accessories   *SM/2QM15*

10. Optional Accessories

10-1 Parts mounted to engine
The parts mounted to the engine are listed below.

Part name	Remarks
Tachometer sender	Hex plug M18 unnecessary
Bilge pump	
Mixing elbow	
U-type mixing elbow	
Alternator (with ICR) 55A	Alternator 35A unnecessary

10-2 Parts packed with engine
The parts packed with the engine are listed below.

Part name	Remarks
Decompression remote control cable ass'y	
Rubber shock mounts (fixed type), flexible coupling	
Rubber shock mounts (adjustable type), flexible coupling	
Fuel tank ass'y	
Evacuation pump	
Bilge strainer and accessories	
Kingston cock and accessories	
Battery switch	
Shaft coupling (solid type) and accessories	
Shaft coupling (slit type) and accessories	
Extension wiring harness, 3m	
Extension wiring harness, 6m	
Tachometer	
Stop remote control cable ass'y	
Clutch remote control bracket (stern)	
Morse one handle control	Need remote control cable, 4m × 2
Open wire	
Special disassembly tools	
Spare parts kit	
Packing kit	

CHAPTER 2
BASIC ENGINE

1. Cylinder Block 2-1
2. Cylinder Liner 2-2
3. Cylinder Head 2-5
4. Piston 2-15
5. Connecting Rod 2-19
6. Crankshaft 2-22
7. Camshaft 2-26
8. Timing gear 2-29

1. Cylinder Block

1·1 Construction
The cylinder block is a high-quality cast iron casting, with integral cylinders and deep skirt crankcase construction. As a result of stress analyses, the shape and thickness of each part has been optimized, and special ribs employed which not only increase the strength and rigidity of the block, but also reduce noise.

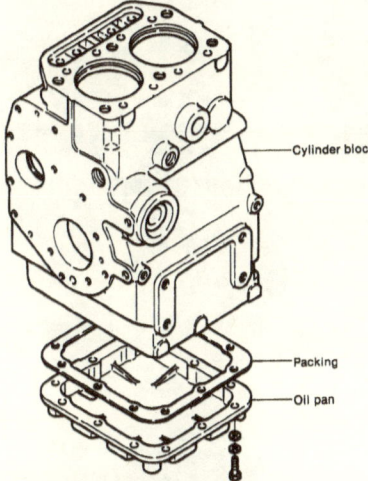
Cylinder block
Packing
Oil pan

1·2 Cylinder block inspection
1·2.1 Inspecting each part for cracks
If the engine has been frozen or dropped, visually inspect it for cracks and other abnormalities before disassembling. If there are any abnormalities or the danger of any abnormalities occurring, make a color check.

1·2.2 Inspecting the water jacket of the cylinders for corrosion
Inspect the cooling water passages and cylinder liner contact parts for sea water corrosion, scale, and rust. Replace the cylinder body if corrosion, scale or rust is severe.
Cylinder body jacket corrosion depth limit: 1.5mm

1·2.3 Cylinder head bolts
Check for loose cylinder head bolts and for cracking caused by abnormal tightening, either by visual inspection or by a color check.
Replace the cylinder block if cracked.

1·2.4 Oil and water passages
Check the oil and water passages for clogging and build-up of foreign matter.

1·2.5 Cylinder bore and ledge
Perform a color check on the ledge at the top of the cylinder head bore, and replace the cylinder if any cracks are detected.

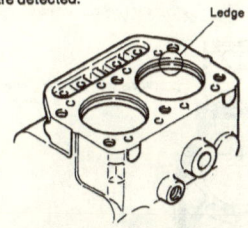
Ledge

1·2.6 Color check flaw detection procedure
(1) Clean the inspection point thoroughly.
(2) Procure the dye penetration flaw detection agent. This agent comes in spray cans, and consists of a cleaner, penetrant, and developer in one set.

(3) Pretreat the inspection surface with the cleaner. Spray the cleaner directly onto the inspection surface, or wipe the inspection surface with a cloth moistened with the cleaner.
(4) Spray the red penetration liquid onto the inspection surface. After cleaning the inspection surface, spray the red penetrant (dye penetration flaw detection agent) onto it and allow the liquid to penetrate for 5-10 minutes.
If the penetrant fails to penetrate the inspection surface because of the ambient temperature or other conditions, allow it to dry and respray the inspection surface.
(5) Spray the developer onto the inspection surface. After penetration processing, remove the residual penetrant from the inspection surface with the cleaner, and then spray the developer onto the inspection surface. If the inspection surface is flawed, red dots or lines will appear on the surface within several minutes. When spraying the developer onto the inspection surface, hold the can about 30—40cm from the surface and sweep the can slowly back and forth to obtain a uniform film.
(6) Reclean the inspection surface with the cleaner.

Chapter 2 Basic Engine
1. Cylinder Block

SM/2QM15

NOTE: Before using the dye penetration flaw detection agent, read its usage instructions thoroughly.

1-3 Cylinder bore measurement

Measure the inside diameter of the part which contacts the cylinder liner, and repair or replace if it is severely distorted.

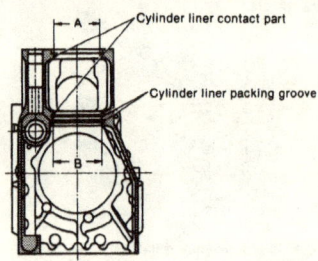

mm (in.)

	Maintenance standard	Roundness	Maximum allowable distortion
Top A	$88 \,^{+0.035}_{0}$ (3.4646 ~ 3.4659)	0.02 (0.0008)	0.1 (0.0039)
Bottom B	$86 \,^{+0.035}_{0}$ (3.3858 ~ 3.3872)	0.02 (0.0008)	0.1 (0.0039)

Printed in Japan
2F015A

2. Cylinder Liner

2-1 Construction
High-quality special high-phosphorous cast iron wet type cylinder liners are used. The outside of the cylinder liner is machined to a uniform thickness to prevent local heat expansion and improve durability. Two O-rings (rubber packing) are installed at the cylinder liner skirt to prevent cylinder liner deformation and distortion, and to keep cooling water from leaking into the crankcase.

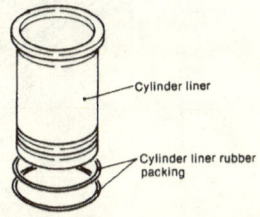

2-2 Inspection
Since the piston and piston rings constantly slide against the cylinder liner while the engine is in operation, and side pressure is applied to the cylinder liner by the movement of the crankshaft, eccentric wear occurs easily.
Moreover, if lubrication and cooling are insufficient, the inner surface will be damaged or rusted. Inspect the inner surface and replace the cylinder liner if the surface is noticeably damaged or rusted.

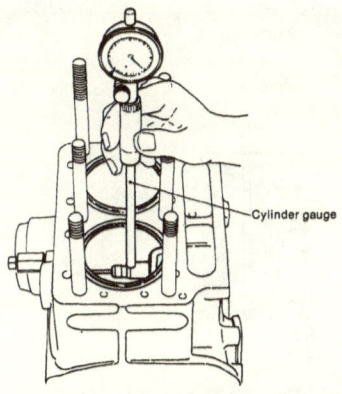

2-3 Cylinder liner bore diameter measurement
Measure the bore diameter of the cylinder liner with a cylinder gauge at the positions shown in the figure.
Replace the cylinder liner when the measured value exceeds the wear limit.

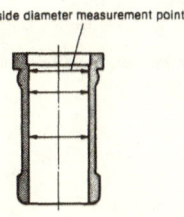

Inside diameter measurement points

mm (in.)

	Maintenance standard	Clearance at assembly	Maximum allowable clearance	Wear limit
Cylinder liner diameter	⌀75 (2.9528)	0.079 ~ 0.139 (0.0031 ~ 0.0055)	0.3 (0.0118)	⌀75.17 (2.9594)
Piston outside diameter	⌀75 (2.9528)			
Cylinder liner circularity	0.02 (0.0008)	—	—	0.1 (0.0039)

2-4 Cylinder liner replacement

(1) Pull the cylinder liner to the top of the cylinder block as shown in the figure, using the special cylinder liner puller tool.

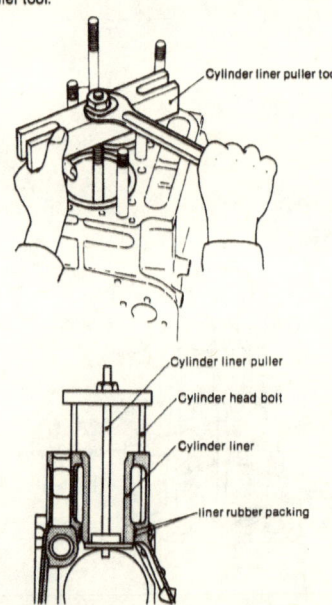

(2) Remove the rust from the area where the cylinder liner contacts the cylinder block.
(3) Install new O-rings in the two O-ring grooves of the cylinder liner.
(4) Coat the outside of the cylinder liner with waterproof paint or grease.
(5) Push the cylinder liner into the cylinder liner hole of the cylinder block.
(6) After inserting the liner, measure its bore diameter.
(7) Measure the amount of liner projection.

2-5 Measuring cylinder liner projection

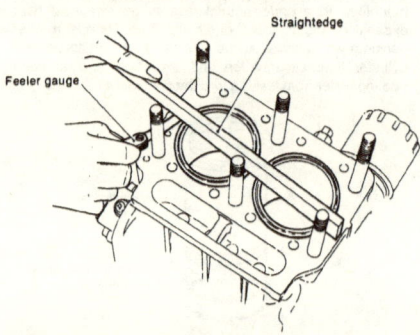

If the cylinder liner projects too far from the block, the torque reactance will increase, causing the compression ratio to drop and the gasket packing to be damaged. Excessive cylinder liner projection is frequently caused by incomplete removal of the rust at the ledge (part A of figure) of the cylinder block.

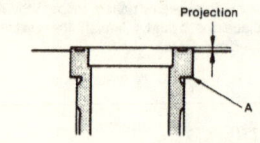

mm (in.)

Cylinder liner projection	0.05 ~ 0.13 (0.00197 ~ 0.00512)

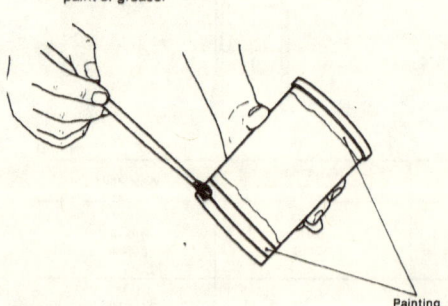

Chapter 2 Basic Engine
3. Cylinder Head
SM/2QM15

3. Cylinder Head

3-1 Construction

The cylinder head is an integral two cylinder type which is bolted to the block with 6 bolts.

The unique Yanmar swirl type precombustion chambers are at an angle in the cylinder head, and form the combustion chambers, together with the intake and exhaust valves.

Large diameter intake valves and smoothly shaped intake and exhaust ports provide high intake efficiency and superior combustion performance.

Special consideration has also been given to the shape of the cooling water passages so that the combustion surface and precombustion chamber are uniformly cooled by an ample water flow.

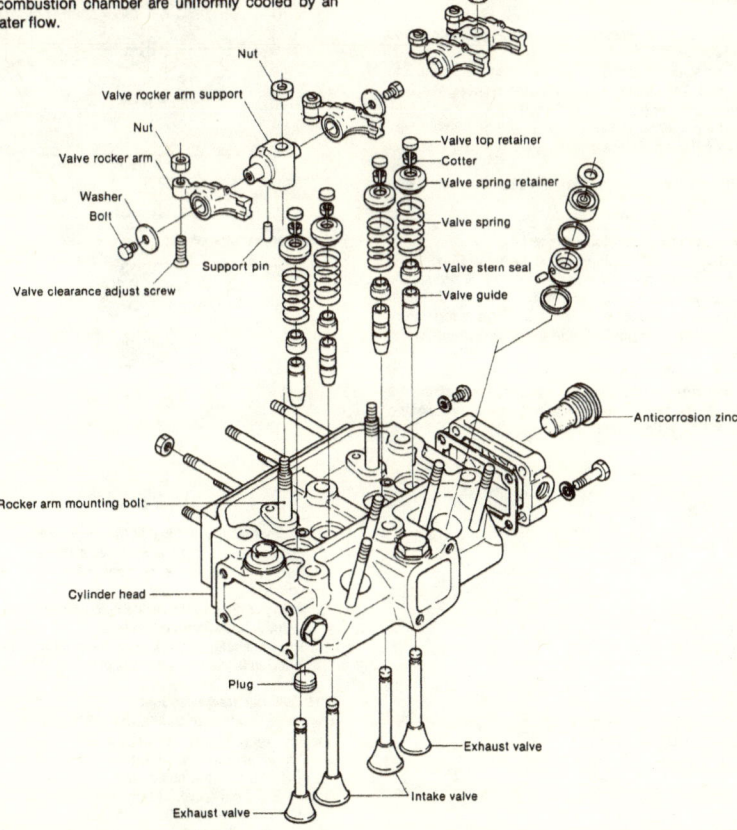

Chapter 2 Basic Engine
3. Cylinder Head

_____ SM/2QM15

3-2 Cylinder head inspection and measurement

3-2.1 Measurement of carbon build-up at combustion surface and intake and exhaust ports
Visually check for carbon build-up around the combustion surface and the port near the intake and exhaust valve seats, and remove any build-up.
When a large amount of carbon has been built up, check the top of the chamber combustion for oil flow at the intake and exhaust valve guides, and take suitable corrective action.

3-2.2 Scale build-up at water passages
Check for build-up of scale at the water passages, and remove any scale with a scale remover. When a large amount of scale has been built up, check each part of the cooling system.

3-2.3 Inspection of corrosion at water passages and anticorrosion zinc
Inspect the state of corrosion of the water passages, and replace the cylinder head when corrosion is severe.
  Corrosion pitting limit: 2mm (0.0787in.)
Inspect the anticorrosion zinc on the cylinder head cover, and replace the zinc when it has been worn over the wear limit.
  Anticorrosion zinc wear limit: Volumetric ratio with new zinc = 2/3

3-2.4 Cracking of combustion surface
The combustion surface is exposed to high temperature, high pressure gas and low pressure air, and is repeatedly flexed during operation. Moreover, it is used under extremely severe conditions, such as high temperature gradient of the combustion surface and cooling water passages.
Inspect the combustion surface for cracking by the color check, and replace the cylinder head if any cracking is detected. At the same time, check for signs of overloading and check the cooling water flow.

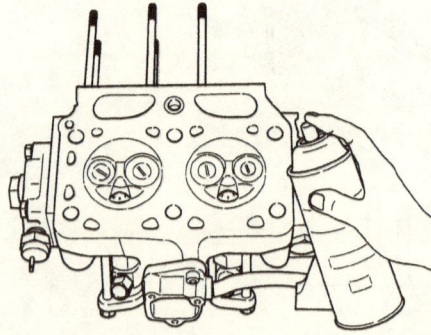

3-2.5 Cylinder head distortion
Distortion of the cylinder head causes gasket packing damage, compression leakage, change in compression, etc.
Measure the distortion as described below, and replace the cylinder head when the wear limit is exceeded. Since distortion of the cylinder head is caused by irregular tightening forces, faulty repair of the mounting face, and gasket packing damage, these must also be checked.

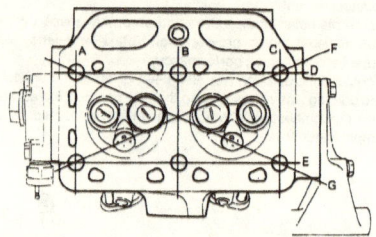

mm (in.)

	Maintenance standard	Wear limit
Cylinder head distortion	0.03 (0.00118)	0.07 (0.00275)

Measurement procedure

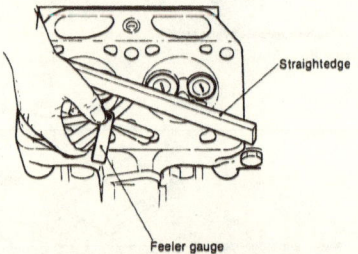

Straightedge

Feeler gauge

1. Clean the cylinder head tightening surface.
2. Place a straightedge across two symmetrical points at the four sides of the cylinder head, as shown in the figure.
3. Insert feeler gauges between the straightedge and the cylinder head combustion face.
4. The thickness of the largest feeler gauge that can be inserted is the amount of distortion.

3-2.6 Cylinder head valve seat
The valve seats become wider with use. If the seats become wider than the maintenance standard, carbon build-up at the seats will cause compression leakage. On the other hand, if the seats are too narrow, they will wear quickly and heat transmission efficiency will deteriorate. Clean the carbon and other foreign matter from the valve seats, and check that the seats are not scored or dented.

Chapter 2 Basic Engine
3. Cylinder Head

Measure the seat width with a vernier calipers, and repair or replace the seat when the wear limit is exceeded.
When the valves have been lapped and/or ground, measure the amount of valve recess, and replace the valve when the wear limit is exceeded.

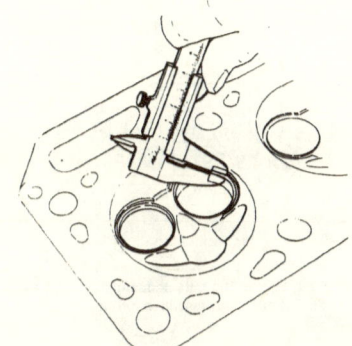

	Maintenance standard	Wear limit
Seat width	1.77 (0.0696)	2.2 (0.0866)
Seat angle	90°	—

mm (in.)

(1) Lapping the valve seat.
When scoring and pitting of the valve seat is slight, coat the seat with valve compound mixed oil, and lap the seat with a lapping tool.
At this time, be sure that the compound does not flow to the valve stem and valve guide.

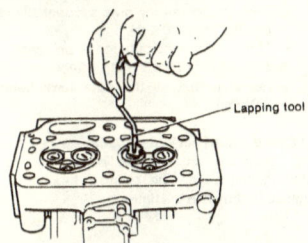
Lapping tool

(2) Correcting valve seat width.
When the valve seat is heavily pitted and when the seat width must be corrected, repair with a seat grinder.
 1) Repair pitting of the seat face with a 45° grinder.
 2) Since the valve seat is larger than the initial value, correct the seat width to the maintenance standard by grinding the inside face of the seat with a 70° grinder.
 3) Grind the outside face of the valve seat with a 15° grinder, and finish the seat width to the standard value.

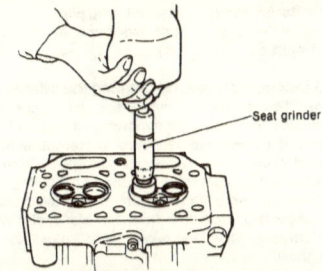
Seat grinder

4) Mix the compound with oil, and lap the valve.
5) Finally, lap with oil.

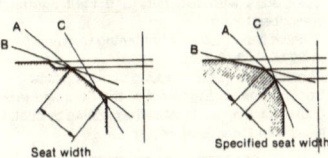
Before correction   After correction

(A) Grind with a 45° grinder
(B) Grind with a 15° grinder
(C) Grind with a 65° ~ 75° grinder

NOTE: When the valve seat has been corrected with a seat grinder, insert an adjusting shim between the valve spring and cylinder head.

3-2.7 Measuring valve recess
When the valve has been lapped many times, the valve will be recessed and will adversely affect the combustion performance. Therefore, measure the valve recess, and replace the valve and cylinder head when the wear limit is exceeded.

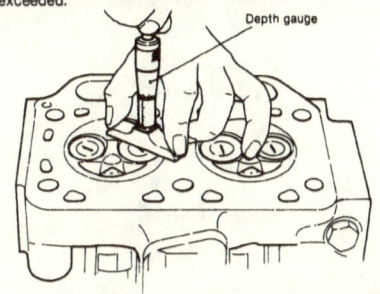
Depth gauge

mm (in.)

	Maintenance standard	Wear limit
Valve recess	1.25 (0.0492)	1.55 (0.0610)

Chapter 2 Basic Engine
3. Cylinder Head

_____ SM/2QM15

3-2.8 Rocker arm support positioning pin
Check if the guide pin is damaged or if the hole is clogged, and replace the pin if faulty.

3-3 Dismounting and remounting the cylinder head
When dismounting and remounting the cylinder head, the mounting bolts must be removed and installed gradually and in the prescribed sequence to prevent damaging the gasket packing and to prevent distortion of the cylinder head. Since the tightening torque and tightening sequence of the mounting bolts when remounting the cylinder head are especially important from the standpoint of engine performance, the following items must be strictly observed.

3-3.1 Cylinder head stud bolt assembly sequence
(1) Check for loose cylinder head stud bolts, and lock any loose bolts with two nuts and then tighten to the prescribed torque.
Cylinder head stud bolt tightening torque: 4.5 ~ 6.0 kg-m (32.55 ~ 43.40 ft-lb)
(2) Checking the gasket packing mounting face.
Confirm correct alignment of the front and rear of the gasket packing, and install the packing by coating both sides with Three Bond 50.

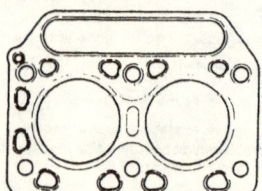

The side between cylinders is the cylinder head side.

(3) Installing the cylinder head ass'y.
Position the cylinder head ass'y parallel to the top of the cylinder block, and install the ass'y to the block, being careful that the cylinder head ass'y does not touch the threads of the cylinder head bolts.

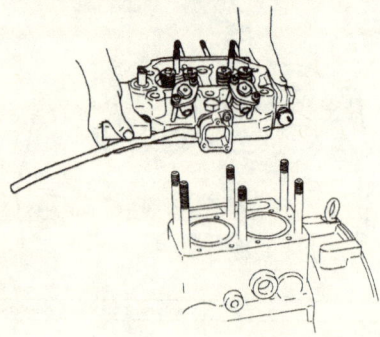

3-3.2 Tightening the cylinder head tightening nuts
(1) Cylinder head nut tightening sequence
1) Coat the threads of the cylinder head bolts with lubricating oil, and screw the cylinder head nuts onto the bolts.

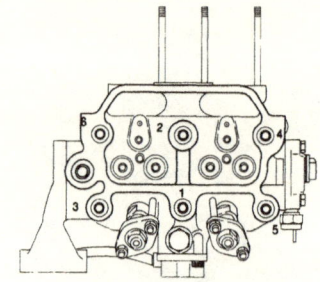

2) First, tighten the nuts sequentially to 1/3 (6kg-m, 43.40 ft-lb) of the prescribed torque.

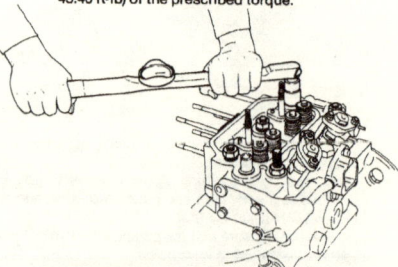

3) Second, tighten the nuts sequentially to a torque of 12kg-m (86.80 ft-lb).
4) Third, tighten the nuts to the prescribed torque of 15 ~ 16kg-m. (108.5 ~ 115.7 ft-lb).
5) Recheck that all the nuts have been properly tightened.

3-3.3 Cylinder head nut loosening sequence
When loosening the cylinder head nuts, reverse the tightening sequence. The cylinder head nut loosening sequence is shown in the figure.

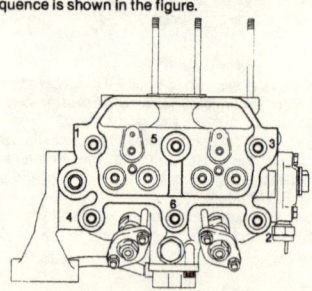

Chapter 2 Basic Engine
3. Cylinder Head

3-4 Intake and exhaust valves, valve guide and valve spring

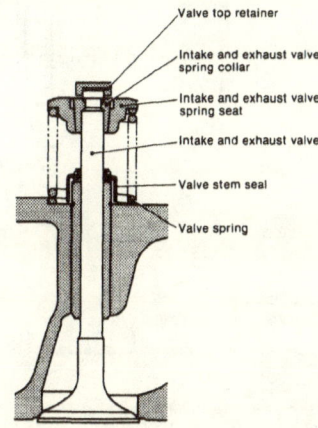

3-4.1 Inspecting and measuring the intake and exhaust valves

(1) Valve seat wear and contact width.
Inspect valve seats for carbon build-up and heavy wear.
Also check if each valve seat contact width is suitable.
If the valve seat contact width is narrower than the valve seat width, the seat angle must be checked and corrected.

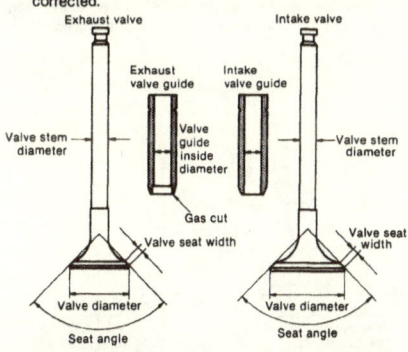

Intake valve diameter	Ø32 (1.2598)
Exhaust valve diameter	Ø27 (1.063)
Valve seat width	3.04 (0.1197)
Valve seat angle	90°

NOTE: Note that the intake valve and exhaust valve have a different diameter.

(2) Valve stem bending and wear.
Check for valve stem wear and staining, and repair when such damage is light. Measure the outside diameter and bend, and replace the valve when the wear limit is exceeded.

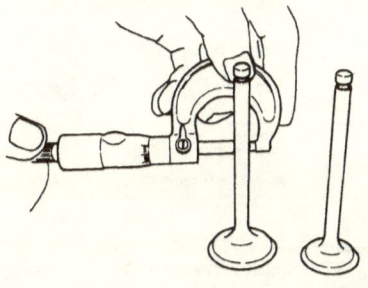

mm (in.)

	Maintenance standard	Wear limit
Valve stem outside diameter	Ø7 (0.2755)	Ø6.9 (0.2716)
Valve stem bend	—	0.03 (0.00118)

(3) Valve seat hairline cracks.
Inspect the valve seat by the color check, and replace the seat if cracked.

3-4.2 Inspecting and measuring valve guides

The valve guide is different for the intake valve and exhaust valve in that the inner face of the exhaust valve has a gas cut.
Be sure that the correct guide is used when replacing the guides.

(1) Floating of the intake and exhaust valve guides.
Check for intake and exhaust valve guide looseness and floating with a test hammer, and replace loose or floating guides with guides having an oversize outside diameter.

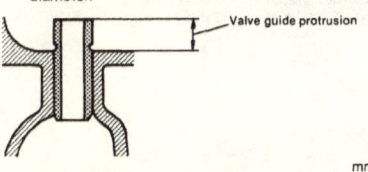

mm (in.)

Valve guide protrusion	7 (0.2756)

Chapter 2 Basic Engine
3. Cylinder Head

SM/2QM15

(2) Measuring the valve guide inside diameter.
Measure the valve guide inside diameter and clearance, and replace the guide when wear exceeds the wear limit.

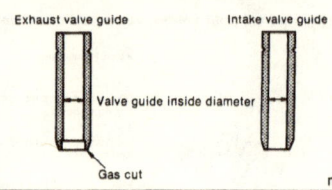

mm (in.)

		Maintenance standard	Clearance at assembly	Maximum allowable clearance	Wear limit
Intake	Valve guide inside diameter (after assembly)	ø7 (0.2756)	0.040 ~ 0.065 (0.0016 ~ 0.0026)	0.15 (0.0059)	ø7.08 (0.2787)
	Stem outside diameter	ø7 (0.2756)			ø6.90 (0.2717)
Exhaust	Valve guide inside diameter (after assembly)	ø7 (0.2756)	0.050 ~ 0.075 (0.002 ~ 0.003)	0.15 (0.0059)	ø7.08 (0.2787)
	Stem outside diameter	ø7 (0.2756)			ø6.90 (0.2717)

(3) Intake and exhaust valve guide fitting.
Always fit the intake and exhaust valve guides with a press. Never tap with a hammer.

mm (in.)

Tightening allowance	0.015 ± 0.014 (0.00004 ~ 0.00114)

Fit the intake and exhaust valve guides until the bottom of the groove around the outside of the valve guide is flush with the end of the cylinder head.

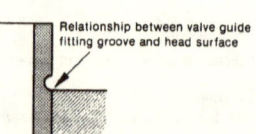

Relationship between valve guide fitting groove and head surface

3-4.3 Valve spring

(1) Valve spring inclination.
Since inclination of the valve spring is a direct cause of eccentric contact of the valve stem, always check it at disassembly.
Stand the valve upright on a stool, and check if the entire spring contacts the gauge when a square gauge is placed against the outside diameter of the valve spring.
If there is a gap between the gauge and spring, measure the gap with a feeler gauge.
When the valve spring inclination exceeds the wear limit, replace the spring.

(2) Valve spring free length.
Measure the free length of the valve spring, and replace the spring when the wear limit is exceeded.

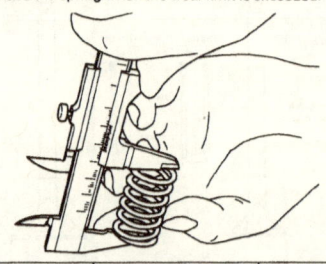

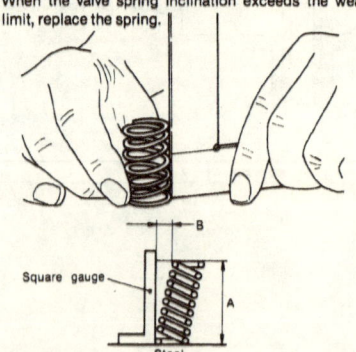

	Maintenance standard	Wear limit
Valve spring free length	36.5 mm (1.44in.)	35.0mm (1.38in.)
Valve spring inclination	—	1.22 mm (0.048in.)
Mounted valve spring load 8.5mm (0.33in.) compression	11.1 kg (24.4 lb.)	10.6 kg (23.3 lb.)

NOTE: Valve spring inclination (perpendicularity): B/A within 0.03 (B = 36.5mm) (B = 1.437in.)

Chapter 2 Basic Engine
3. Cylinder Head

3-4.4 Valve stem seal
A valve stem seal is assembled at the top of the valve guide and the valve stem chamber oil is sucked to the combustion chamber through the valve guide (oil down) to prevent an increase in oil consumption.
The valve stem seal must always be replaced whenever it has been removed.
When assembling, coat the valve stem with engine oil before inserting.

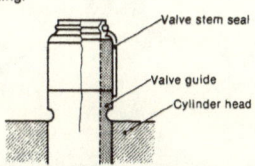

3-4.5 Spring retainer and spring cotter pin
Inspect the inside face of the spring retainer and the outside surface of the spring cotter pin, and the contact area of the spring cotter pin inside surface and the notch in the head of the valve stem. Replace the spring retainer and spring cotter pin when the contact area is less than 70% or when the spring cotter pin has been recessed because of wear.

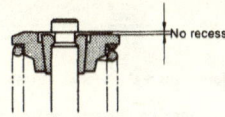

3-5 Precombustion chamber and top clearance
3-5.1 Precombustion chamber
Remove the packing and insulation packing at the precombustion chamber's front and rear chambers, and inspect.
Check for burning at the front end of the precombustion chamber front chamber, acid corrosion at the precombustion chamber rear chamber, and for burned packing.
Replace if faulty.

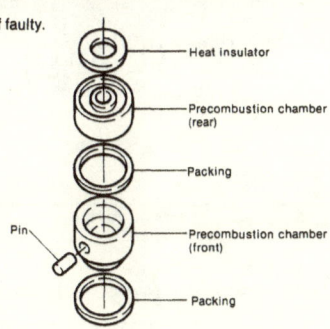

3-5.2 Insulation packing
The insulation packing prevents transmission of heat from the precombustion chamber to the nozzle valve and serves to improve the nozzle's durability.
Always put in a new insulation packing when it has been disassembled.

3-5.3 Top clearance
Top clearance is the size of the gap between the cylinder head combustion surface and the top of the piston at top dead center.
Since top clearance has considerable effect on the combustion performance and the starting characteristic of the engine, it must be checked periodically.

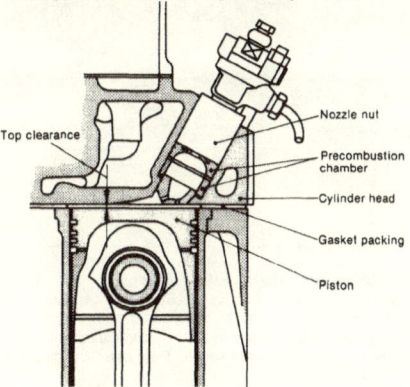

(1) Top clearance measurement
1) Check the cylinder head mounting bolts and tightening torque.
2) Remove the fuel injection valve and precombustion chamber.
3) Lower the piston at the side to be measured.
4) Insert quality fuse wire (Ø1.2mm, 0.472in.) through the nozzle holder hole. (Be careful that the wire does not enter the intake and exhaust valve and the groove in the combustion surface.)
5) Crush the fuse wire by moving the piston to top dead center by slowly cranking the engine by hand.
6) Lower the piston by hand cranking the engine and remove the crushed fuse wire, being careful not to drop it.

Chapter 2 Basic Engine
3. Cylinder Head

7) Measure the thickness of the crushed part of the fuse wire with vernier calipers or a micrometer.

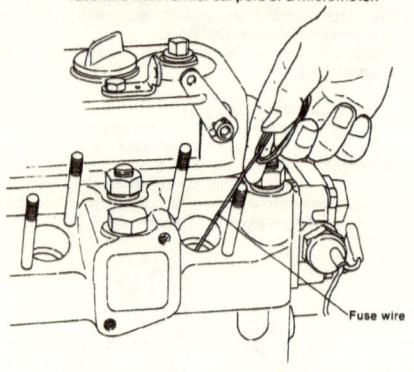

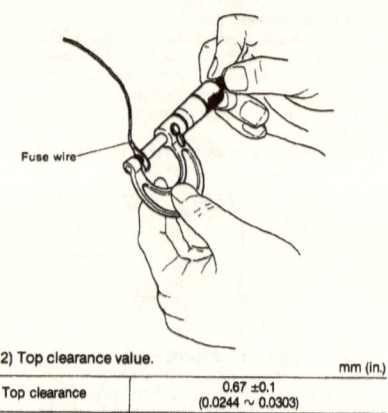

(2) Top clearance value.

mm (in.)

Top clearance	0.67 ±0.1 (0.0244 ~ 0.0303)

When the top clearance value is not within the above range, check for damaged gasket packing, distortion of the cylinder head combustion surface, or other abnormal conditions.

3-6 Intake and exhaust valve rocker arm
Since the intake and exhaust valve rocker arm shaft and bushing clearance and valve head and push rod contact wear are directly related to the valve timing, and have an effect on engine performance, they must be carefully serviced.

3-6.1 Measuring the valve rocker arm shaft and bushing clearance
Measure the outside diameter of the valve rocker arm shaft and the inside diameter of the bushing, and replace the rocker arm or bushing if the measured value exceeds the wear limit.
Replace a loose valve rocker arm shaft bushing with a new bushing. However, when there is no tightening allowance, replace the valve rocker arm.

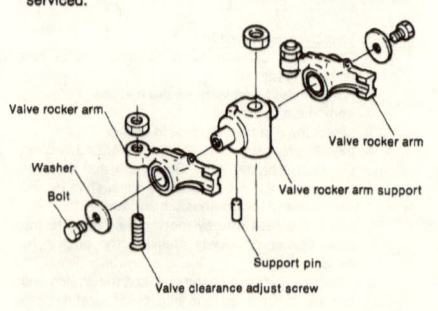

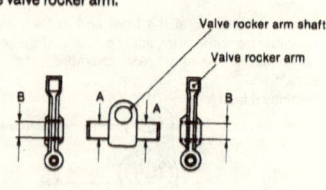

mm (in.)

		Maintenance standard	Clearance at assembly	Maximum allowable clearance	Wear limit
Intake and exhaust valve rocker arm shaft outside diameter	A	Ø14 (0.5512)	0.016 ~ 0.052 (0.0006 ~ 0.0020)	0.15 (0.0059)	Ø13.9 (0.5472)
Intake and exhaust valve rocker arm bushing inside diameter (assembled)	B	Ø14 (0.5512)			Ø14.1 (0.5551)

Chapter 2 Basic Engine
3. Cylinder Head
_____SM/2QM15

3-6.2 Valve rocker arm and valve head contact and wear
Check the valve rocker arm and valve head contact, and replace when there is any abnormal wear or peeling.

3-6.3 Valve clearance adjusting screw
Inspect the valve clearance adjusting screw and push rod contact, and replace when there is any abnormal wear or peeling.

3-6.4 Classification of the intake and exhaust valve rocker arms
Since the intake and exhaust valve rocker arms have different shapes, care must be exercised in service and assembly.

3-7 Adjusting intake and exhaust valve head clearance
Adjustment of the intake and exhaust valve head clearance governs the performance of the engine, and must be performed accurately. The intake and exhaust valve head clearance must always be checked and readjusted, as required, when the engine is disassembled and reassembled, and after every 300 hours of operation. Adjust the valve head clearance as described below.

3-7.1 Adjustment
Make this adjustment when the engine is cold.
(1) Remove the valve rocker arm cover.
(2) Crank the engine and set the No. 1 (flywheel side) piston to top dead center (TDC) on the compression stroke.
NOTE: Set to the position at which the valve rocker arm shaft does not move even when the crankshaft is turned to the left and right, centered around the TD mark.
(3) Check and adjust the intake and exhaust valve head clearances of the No. 1 piston.
Loosen the valve clearance adjusting screw lock nut, adjust the clearance to the maintenance standard with a feeler gauge, and retighten the lock nut.

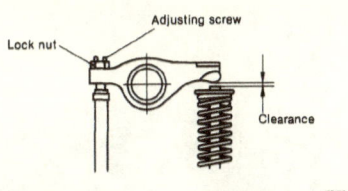

	mm (in.)
Intake and exhaust valve head clearance:	0.20 (0.00787)

(4) Adjust the valve head clearance of the No. 2 cylinder in the same manner. (After turn the crankshaft 180°)
NOTE: If you adjust the valve head clearance of the No. 2 cylinder first, turn the crankshaft 540°. Adjust the clearance of the No. 1 cylinder in the same manner.

3-7.2 Adjusting without a feeler gauge
Set the head clearance to zero by tightening the adjusting screw, being careful not to tighten the screw too tight.
Then adjust the valve clearance to the maintenance standard by backing off the adjusting screw by the angle given below.

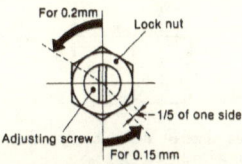

Valve clearance adjusting screw	M8 × 1.25
Adjusting screw backoff angle	Approx 58°

NOTE: Calculating the backoff angle.
Calculate the 0.2mm advance angle from 1.25mm advance at one turn = 360°
0.2/1.25 × 360° = 57.6° ≒ 58°
One side (60°) of the hexagonal nut should be used to measure.

3-8 Decompression mechanism
The decompression mechanism is used when the starter motor fails to rotate sufficiently because the battery is weak, and to facilitate starting in cold weather.
When the decompression lever is operated, the valve is pushed down, the engine is decompressed, the engine turns over easily and the flywheel inertia increases, thus making starting easy.

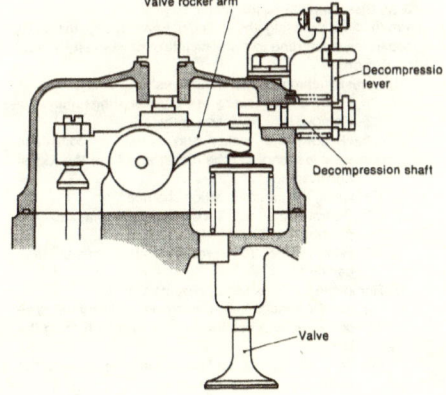

Chapter 2 Basic Engine
3. Cylinder Head

SM/2QM15

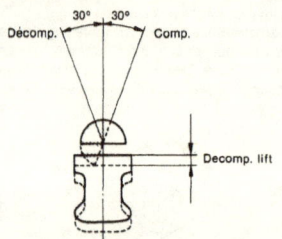

With this engine, there is no need to adjust the decompression lift.

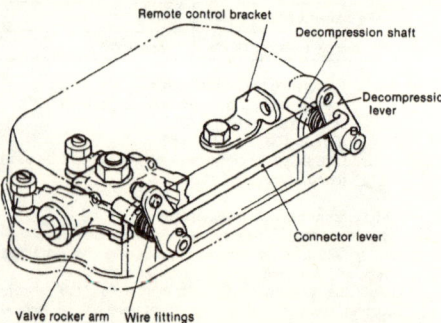

5) Pull the valve from the cylinder head.
6) Remove the valve stem seal.
7) Remove the valve guide.

3-9.2 Reassembling the cylinder head
Before reassembling the cylinder head, wash all the parts, inspect and measure the dimensions of each part, and repair or replace any parts that are abnormal. Be careful not to confuse the parts grouped by cylinder number and intake or exhaust.
(1) Assembling the intake and exhaust valves
  1) Press the valve guide into the cylinder head.
  2) Install the valve stem seal. (Always replace the valve stem seal with a new seal.)
  3) Install the valve in the cylinder head.
  4) Install the valve spring and valve spring seat.
  5) Install the split collar.
     • Using the special tool
     • Using a wrench
(2) Installing the valve arm ass'y
  1) Install the rocker arm support on the cylinder head and tighten the supporting nuts.
  2) Install the intake and exhaust rocker arms to the rocker arm support and set the bolts.
(3) Installing the precombustion chamber
  1) Install the front chamber and packing.
  2) Install the rear chamber and packing.
     (Always replace the insulation packing.)

3-9 Disassembling and reassembling the cylinder head
3-9.1 Disassembling the cylinder head
When disassembling the cylinder head, group the parts separately according to cylinder, intake or exhaust to avoid confusion.
(1) Disassembling the rocker arm ass'y
  1) Remove the rocker arm ass'y mounting nuts.
  2) Remove the rocker arm ass'y.
  3) Remove the rocker arm mounting bolts and washers, and pull the rocker arm from the rocker arm mount.
(2) Removing the precombustion chamber
  1) Remove the rear precombustion chamber and packing.
  2) Remove the front precombustion chamber and packing.
(3) Removing the intake and exhaust valve ass'y
  1) Set the special tool at the intake and exhaust valve ass'y and depress the valve spring by turning the lever.
  2) When the special tool is not available, depress the valve spring with a wrench.
  3) Remove the spring cotter pin.
  4) Turn the lever of the special tool in the loosening direction, release the valve spring retainer, and remove the valve spring retainer and valve spring.

Chapter 2 Basic Engine
4. Piston
_____ SM/2QM15

4. Piston

4-1 Piston ass'y construction

The pistons are made of LO-EX (AC8A-T7) for lightness and are designed for reduced vibration. The outside of the piston is machined to a special oval shape. During operation, thermal expansion is small, the optimum clearance between the piston and cylinder liner is maintained, and a stable supply of lubricating oil is assured.

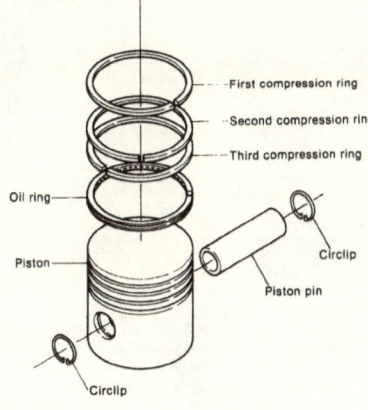

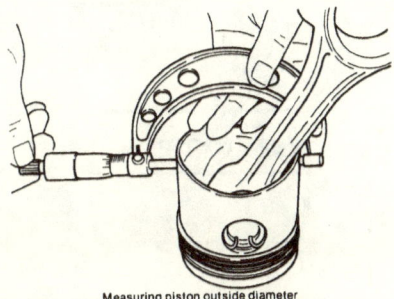

Measuring piston outside diameter

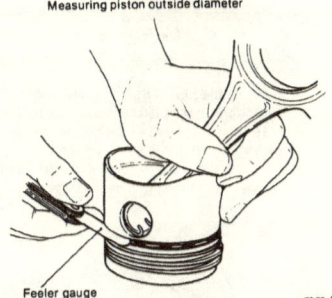

Feeler gauge

4-2 Piston

4-2.1 Inspection

(1) Measuring important dimensions

Measure each important dimension, and replace the piston when the wear limit is exceeded.

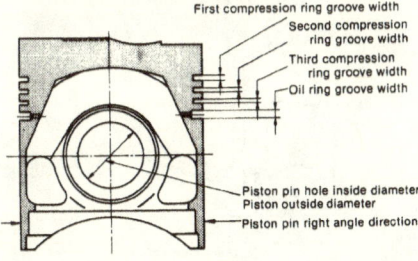

	Maintenance standard	Wear limit
Piston outside diameter (axial direction)	⌀75 (2.9527)	⌀74.8 (2.9448)
Piston pin hole inside diameter	⌀23 (0.9055)	—
First compression piston ring-to-groove clearance	0.050 ~ 0.080 (0.00196 ~ 0.00314)	0.2 (0.00787)
Second and third compression piston ring-to-groove clearance	0.020 ~ 0.055 (0.00078 ~ 0.00216)	0.2 (0.00787)
Oil ring-to-groove clearance	0.020 ~ 0.055 (0.00078 ~ 0.00216)	0.2 (0.00787)

mm (in.)

(2) Piston pin outside contact and ring groove carbon build-up.

Check if the piston ring grooves are clogged with carbon, if the rings move freely, and for abnormal contact around the outside of the piston. Repair or replace the piston if faulty.

4-2.2 Replacing a piston

If the dimension of any part is worn past the wear limit or outside of the piston is scored, replace the piston.

(1) Replacement

1. Install the piston pin circlip at one side only.

Chapter 2 Basic Engine
4. Piston

2. Immerse the piston in 80°C oil for 10 ~ 15 minutes.

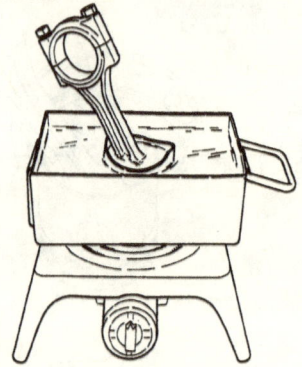

3. Remove the piston from the hot oil and place it on a bench with the piston head at the bottom.
4. Insert the small end of the connecting rod into the piston, insert the piston pin with a rotating motion, and install the other piston pin circlip. Use wooden hammer if necessary.

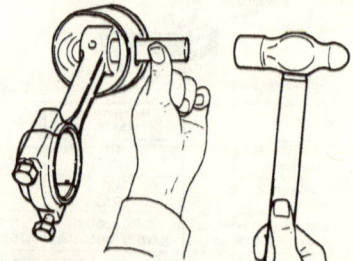

(2) Precautions
1. Before inserting, check whether the piston pin is in the connecting rod.
2. Coat the piston pin with oil to facilitate insertion.
3. Check that the connecting rod and piston move freely.
4. Insert the pin quickly, before the piston cools.

4-3 Piston pin and piston pin bushing
4-3.1 Piston pin
Measure the dimensions of the piston pin, and replace the pin if it is worn past the wear limit or severely scored.

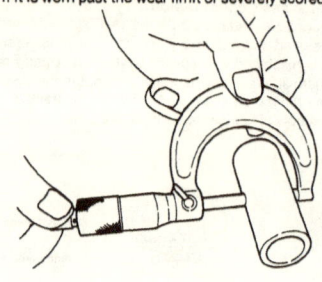

mm (in.)

	Maintenance standard	Wear limit
Piston pin outside diameter	Ø23 (0.9055)	Ø22.98 (0.9047)
Piston pin hole and piston pin tightening allowance	−0.004 ~ +0.008 (−0.000157 ~ 0.00314)	—

4-3.2 Piston pin bushing
A copper alloy wound bushing is pressed onto the piston pin.
Since a metallic sound will be produced if the piston pin and piston pin bushing wear is excessive, replace the bushing when the wear limit is exceeded.
The piston pin bushing can be easily removed and installed with a press. However, when installing the bushing, be careful that it is not tilted.

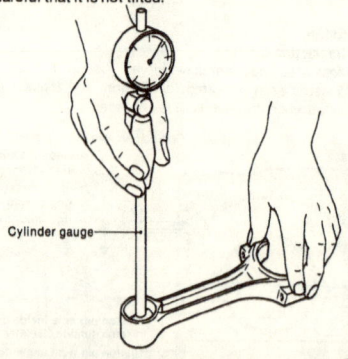

Cylinder gauge

mm (in.)

	Maintenance standard	Wear limit
Piston pin bushing inside diameter	Ø23 (0.9055)	Ø23.1 (0.9094)

NOTE: "Piston pin bushing inside diameter" is the dimension after pressing onto the connecting rod.

Chapter 2 Basic Engine
4. Piston
_____SM/2QM15

4-4 Piston rings
4-4.1 Piston ring configuration
(1) The first compression ring is a barrel face ring that effectively prevents abnormal wear caused by engine loading and combustion gas blowby at initial run-in.

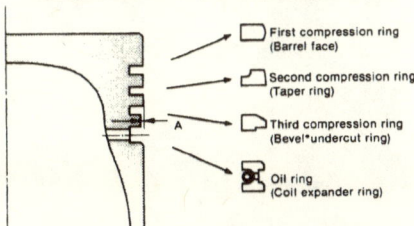

(2) The second compression ring is a taper ring having a sliding face taper of 30' ~ 1°30'. Since the cylinder liner is straight, and the contact area at initial operation is small, it is easily seated to the cylinder liner. Moreover, the bottom of the sliding face is sharp, and oil splash is excellent and air-tightness is superb.
(3) Since the third compression ring has a cross-section that combines the shape of a bevel ring and undercut ring, oil splash is superb and oil upflow control is excellent.
The land (A in figure) between the third compression ring and the oil ring has a small 1.0mm outside diameter that effectively improves oil collection and reduces oil consumption.
(4) The oil ring is a chrome-plated coil expander having a small contacting face, and exerts high pressure against the cylinder liner wall. Oil splash at the bottom of the sliding face is excellent, and its oil control effect is high.

4-4.2 Inspection
(1) Piston ring contact
Inspect the piston ring contact, and replace the ring when contact is faulty. Since the oil ring side contact is closely related to oil consumption, it must be checked with particular care.

(2) Measuring the piston ring gap
Insert the piston ring into the cylinder liner by pushing the piston ring at the head of the piston as shown in the figure, and measure the piston ring gap with a feeler gauge. Measure the gap at a point about 150mm from the top of the cylinder liner.

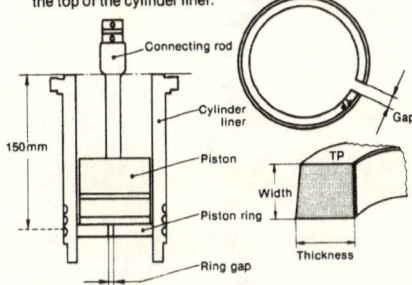

mm (in.)

		Maintenance standard	Wear limit
Piston ring (1, 2, 3)	Thickness	3.3 ±0.1 (0.1259 ~ 0.1338)	—
	Width	$2^{-0.01}_{-0.03}$ (0.0775 ~ 0.0783)	1.90 (0.0748)
Oil ring	Thickness	2.6 ±0.2 (0.0945 ~ 0.1102)	—
	Width	$4.0^{-0.01}_{-0.03}$ (0.1562 ~ 0.1570)	3.90 (0.1535)
Piston ring gap (1, 2, 3)		0.2 ~ 0.4 (0.00787 ~ 0.01574)	1.5 (0.059)
Oil ring gap		0.2 ~ 0.4 (0.00787 ~ 0.01574)	1.5 (0.059)

(3) Piston ring replacement precautions
1) Clean the ring grooves carefully when replacing the rings.
2) When installing the rings, assemble the rings so that the manufacturer's mark near the gap is facing the top of the piston.
3) After assembly, check that the rings move freely in the grooves.
4) The rings must be installed so that the gaps are 180° apart. At this time, be careful that the ring gap is not lined up with the piston side pressure part.

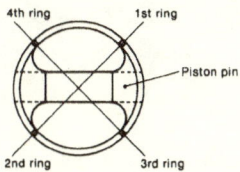

Chapter 2 Basic Engine
4. Piston
SM/2QM15

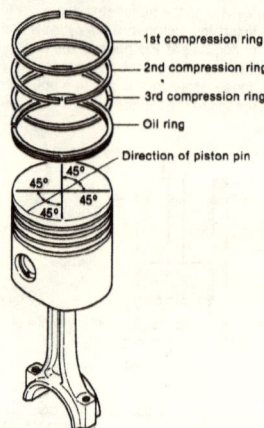

Chapter 2 Basic Engine
5. Connecting Rod — SM/2QM15

5. Connecting Rod

5-1 Connecting rod ass'y construction

The connecting rod connects the piston pin and crank pin and transmits the explosive force of the piston to the crankshaft. It is a stamp forging designed for extreme lightness and ample strength against bending. A kelmet bushing split at right angles is installed to the large end of the rod, and a round copper alloy is pressed onto the small end.

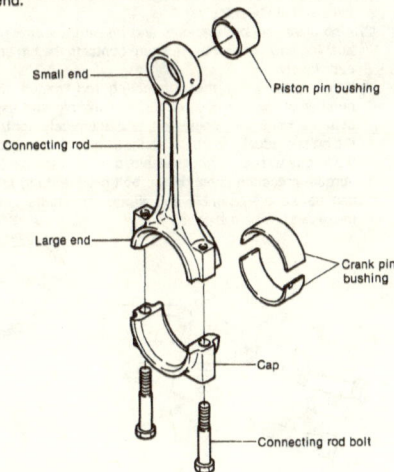

5-2 Inspection
5-2.1 Large and small end twist and parallelity

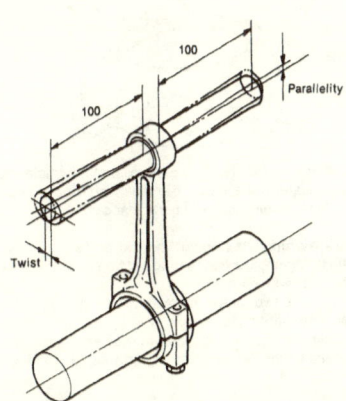

Pass a test bar through the large end and small end holes of the connecting rod, place the bars on a V-block on a stool and center the large end test bar. Then set the sensor of a dial indicator against the small end test bar and measure twist and parallelity. When the measured value exceeds the wear limit, replace the connecting rod. Twisting and poor parallelity will cause uneven contact of the piston and bushing and shifting of the piston rings, resulting in compression leakage.

Connecting rod twist and parallelity   mm (in.)

Maintenance standard	0.03/100 or less (0.00118/3.937)
Limit	0.08/100 or less (0.00315/3.937)

5-3 Crank pin bushing

Since the crank pin bushing slides while receiving the load from the piston, an easy-to-replace kelmet bushing with a wear-resistant overlay is used.

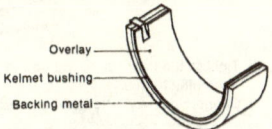

5-3.1 Crank pin bushing inside diameter

Tighten the large end of the connecting rod to the prescribed torque with the connecting rod bolts, and measure the inside diameter of the crank pin bushing. Replace the bushing if the inside diameter exceeds the wear limit or the clearance at the crank pin part exceeds the wear limit.

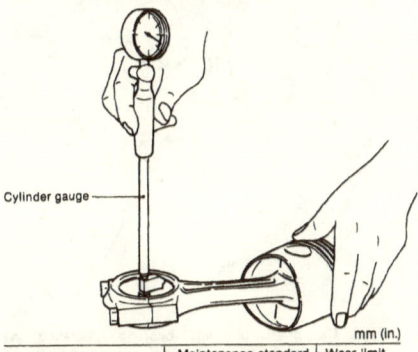

mm (in.)

	Maintenance standard	Wear limit
Crank pin bushing inside diameter	Ø47 (1.8503)	Ø47.1 (1.854)
Crank pin and bushing oil clearance	0.036 ~ 0.092 (0.00141 ~ 0.00362)	0.15 (0.0059)
Connecting rod bolt tightening torque	4.75kg-m (34.4 ft-lb)	

Chapter 2 Basic Engine
5. Connecting Rod

_SM/2QM15_

NOTE: The crank pin bushing inside diameter must always be measured with the connecting rod bolts tightened to the prescribed torque.

5-3.2 Crank pin and bushing clearance (oil clearance)
Since the oil clearance affects both the durability of the bushing and lubricating oil pressure, it must always be the prescribed value. Replace the bushing when the oil clearance exceeds the wear limit.

(1) Measurement
1) Thoroughly clean the inside surface and crank pin section of the crank pin bushing.
2) Install the connecting rod on the crank pin section of the crankshaft and simultaneously fit a Plasti gauge on the inside surface of the crank pin bearing.

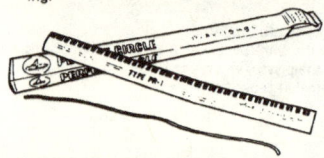

3) Tighten the connecting rod bolt to the prescribed tightening torque.
Connecting rod tightening torque: 4.75kg-m (34.4 lb-ft)
4) Loosen the connecting rod bolt and slowly remove the connecting rod big end cap, then measure the crushed Plasti gauge with a gauge.

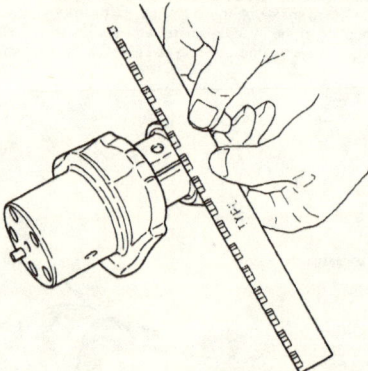

5) The crank pin and bushing clearance (oil clearance) may also be measured with a micrometer, in addition to measurement with a Plasti gauge. With this method, the outside diameter of the crankshaft crank pin section and the inside diameter of the connecting rod's big end bushing, when the connecting rod bolt has been tightened to the prescribed torque, are measured, and the difference between the large end bushing inside diameter and crank pin outside diameter is set as the oil clearance.

(2) Measurement precautions
1) Be careful that the Plasti gauge does not enter the crank pin oil hole.
2) Be sure that the crankshaft does not turn when tightening the connecting rod bolt.

5-3.3 Crank pin bushing replacement precautions
(1) Thoroughly clean the crank pin bushing and the rear of the crank pin bushing.
(2) Also clean the big end cap, and install the crank pin bushing and check if the bushing contacts the big end cap closely.
(3) When assembling the connecting rod, match the number of the big end section and the big end cap, coat the bolts with engine oil, and alternately tighten the bolts gradually to the prescribed tightening torque. If a torque wrench is not available, put matching marks (torque indication lines) on the bolt head and big end cap before disassembly and tighten the bolts until these two lines are aligned.

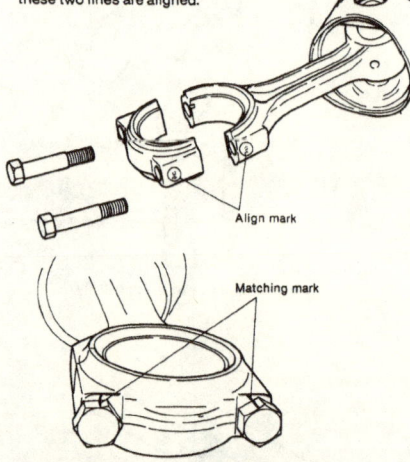

Align mark

Matching mark

(4) Check that there is no sand or metal particles in the lubricating oil and that the crankshaft is not pitted. Clean the oil holes with particular care.

5-4 Tightening the connecting rod bolts
When tightening the connecting rod bolts, coat the threads of the bolts with engine oil.
Tighten the two bolts alternately and gradually to the prescribed tightening torque. If a torque wrench is not available, make matching marks (torque indication lines) on the head of the bolt and the big end cap and tighten the bolts until these two marks are aligned.
Connecting rod tightening torque: 4.75kg-m (34.4 lb-ft)

Chapter 2 Basic Engine
5. Connecting Rod

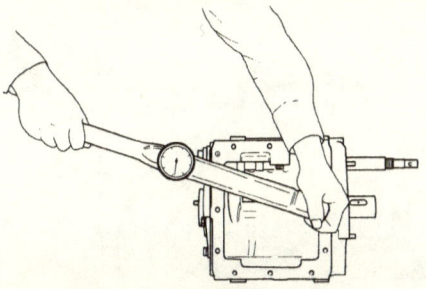

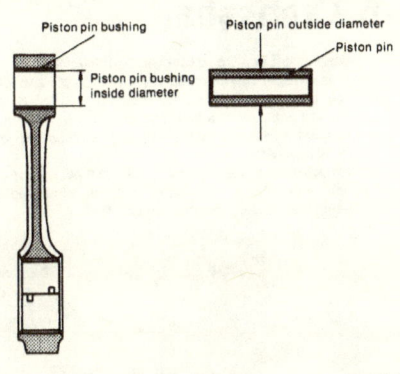

5-5 Connecting rod side clearance
After installing the connecting rod on the crankshaft, push the rod to one side and measure the side clearance by inserting a feeler gauge into the gap produced at the other side.
The connecting rod bolts must also be tightened to the prescribed tightening torque in this case.

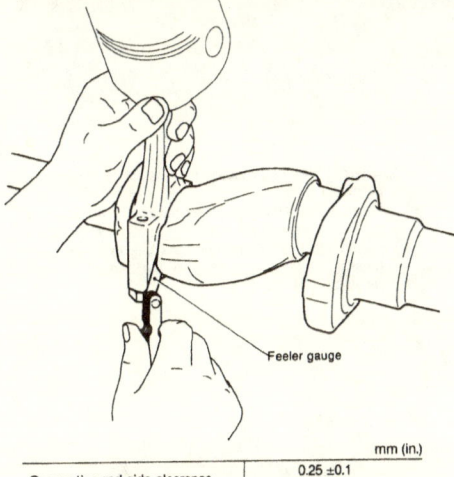

Feeler gauge

	mm (in.)
	Maintenance standard	Wear limit
Piston pin outside diameter	ø23 (0.9055)	ø22.98 (0.9047)
Piston pin bushing inside diameter	ø23 (0.9055)	ø23.1 (0.9094)
Piston pin and bushing clearance	0.025 ~ 0.047 (0.00098 ~ 0.00185)	0.11 (0.00433)

NOTE: The piston pin bushing can be easily removed and installed with a press. However, be careful that throttling is not produced by tilting the bushing during installation.

	mm (in.)
Connecting rod side clearance	0.25 ±0.1 (0.0059 ~ 0.0137)

5-6 Piston bushing and piston pin
The piston bushing is a round copper alloy bushing driven onto the small end of the connecting rod. During use, the piston pin bushing and piston pin will wear. If this wear becomes excessive, a metallic sound will be produced and the engine will become noisy.

Chapter 2 Basic Engine
6. Crankshaft

SM/2QM15

6. Crankshaft

6-1 Crankshaft ass'y and bearing construction

The crankshaft is stamp-forged, and the crank pin and journal sections are high-frequency induction hardened and ground and polished to a high precision finish. Therefore, the contact surface with the bushing is excellent and durability is superb.

The crankshaft is a balance weight integral type. Engine unbalance, which causes vibration, has been minimized by balancing the V-pulley, flywheel, and crankshaft.

Engine length has been reduced and serviceability improved by eliminating the intermediate bearing between the two cylinders and adopting a metal housing type flywheel bearing.

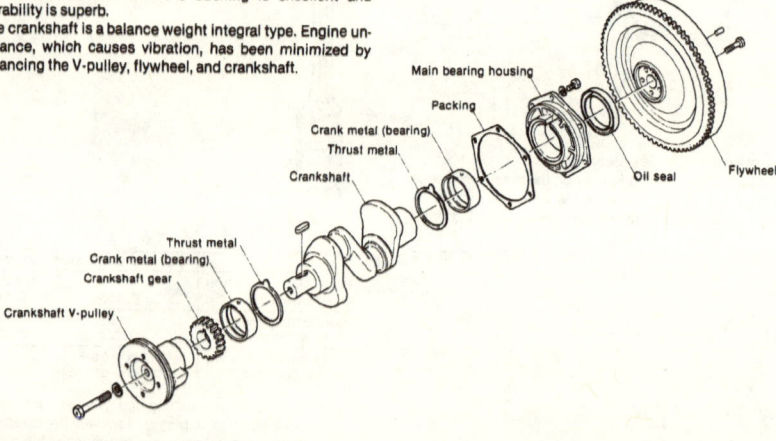

6-2 Inspection
6-2.1 Crank journal and crank pin
(1) Cracking

If cracking of the crank journal or crank pin is suspected, thoroughly clean the crankshaft and perform a color check on the shaft, or run a candle flame over the crankshaft and look for oil seepage from cracks. If any cracks are detected, replace the crankshaft.

(2) Crank pin and crank journal outside diameter measurement.

When the difference between the maximum wear and minimum wear of each bearing section exceeds the wear limit, replace the crankshaft. Also check each bearing section for scoring. If the scoring is light, repair it with emery cloth.

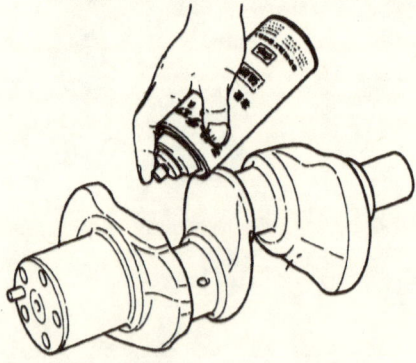
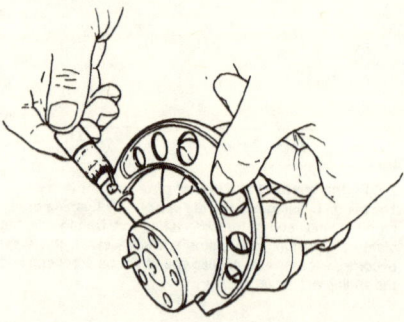

Chapter 2 Basic Engine
6. Crankshaft
_____ SM/2QM15

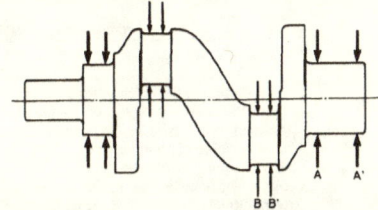 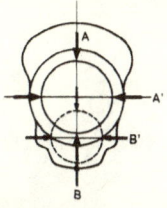

mm (in.)

		Maintenance standard	Wear limit
Crankshaft journal wear	A, A'	ø65 (2.5590)	ø64.9 (2.5551)
Crank pin wear	B, B'	ø47 (1.8503)	ø46.92 (1.8472)
Crank journal/pin eccentric wear		—	0.01 (0.00039)
Crank journal and bushing oil clearance	Gear side	0.036 ~ 0.099 (0.0014 ~ 0.0038)	0.15 (0.0059)
	Flywheel side	0.036 ~ 0.099 (0.0014 ~ 0.0038)	0.15 (0.0059)
Crank pin and crank pin bushing oil clearance		0.036 ~ 0.099 (0.0014 ~ 0.0038)	0.15 (0.0059)

6-3 Crankshaft side gap
6-3.1 Side gap
The clearance in the axial direction after the crankshaft has been assembled is called the side gap.
If the side gap is too large, contact with pistons will be uneven, the clutch disengagement position will change, and other troubles will occur. If it is too small, the crankshaft sliding resistance will increase and cranking will become stiff.
Adjust the side gap to the maintenance standard by the thickness of the crankshaft thrust washer and the thickness of the main bearing shell paper packing.
The main bearing shell packing thicknesses are 0.1mm (0.00394in.) and 0.2mm (0.00788in.).

6-3.2 Measuring side gap
Set a dial indicator against the end of the crankshaft (or end of the flywheel) and measure the amount of movement of the crankshaft in the axial direction. If the measured value exceeds the wear limit, replace the crankshaft thrust washer. Main bearing housing packing of the prescribed thickness must be used.

6-3.3 Side gap maintenance standard and wear limit

	Maintenance standard	Wear limit
Crankshaft side gap	0.10 ~ 0.20 (0.00394 ~ 0.00788)	0.40 (0.01575)

6-4 Main bearing
6-4.1 Construction
The main bearing consists of a crank bearing and thrust metal. The crank bearing is a round copper-leak sintered alloy bearing featuring superior durability.
The crank bearing and thrust metal are installed at the bearing housing and cylinder block, respectively.

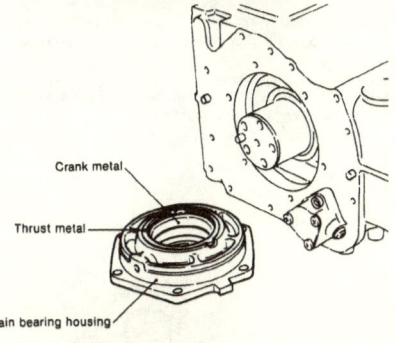

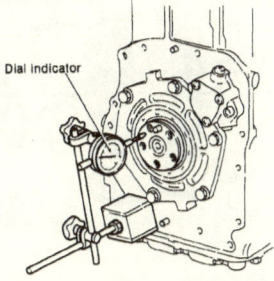

6-4.2 Inspecting the crank bearing
(1) Crank bearing inside diameter
Measure the inside diameter of the crank bearing and replace the bearing when wear exceeds the wear limit. Crank bearing replacement is described in 6-4.4.

Chapter 2 Basic Engine
6. Crankshaft

___SM/2QM15___

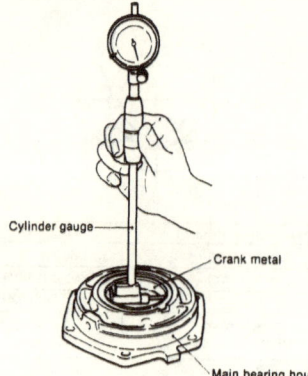

Cylinder gauge
Crank metal
Main bearing housing

NOTE: Measure the crank bearing at the four points shown in the figure and replace the bearing if the wear limit is exceeded at any of these points.

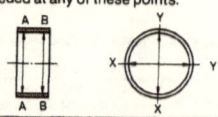

	Maintenance standard	Wear limit
		mm (in.)
Flywheel side crank bearing inside diameter	ø65 (2.559)	ø65.12 (2.5631)
Gear side crank bearing inside diameter	ø65 (2.559)	ø65.12 (2.5631)

(2) Crank bearing contact and scoring
Inspect the crank bearing for contact scoring, and replace the bearing if uneven contact is severe or the bearing is heavily scored. Check all the parts which may be the cause of uneven contact and take suitable corrective action.

6-4.3 Inspecting the thrust metal
Measure the thickness of the thrust metal and replace the metal when wear exceeds the wear limit.

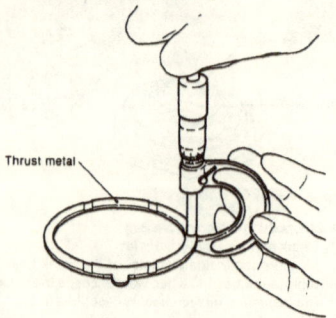

Thrust metal

	Maintenance standard	Wear limit
		mm(in.)
Thrust metal thickness	2.95 (0.1161)	2.75 (0.1082)

6-4.4 Replacing the crank bearing
Since the crank bearings at both ends of the crankshaft are pressed to the cylinder block and bearing housing with a press, a force of approximately 1.0 ~ 1.5 tons (2200 ~ 3300 lbs) is required to remove them.
Moreover, since the crankshaft will not rotate smoothly and other trouble may occur if the bearing is distorted, it must always be installed with the special tool.

(1) Removal
Assemble the spacer and plate A as shown in the figure, place the puller/extractor against the bearing from the opposite end and pull the bearing by tightening the nut of the special tool. Remove the oil seal before pulling the bearing pressed to the bearing housing.

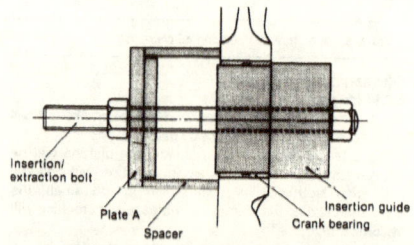

Insertion/extraction bolt
Plate A
Spacer
Insertion guide
Crank bearing

(2) Installation
Coat the outside of the bearing with oil and align the positions of the bearing oil holes. Then press in plate B until it contacts the cylinder block or bearing housing, using the puller/extractor as a guide, as shown in the figure.
After inserting the bearing, measure its outside diameter. If the bearing is distorted, remove it again and replace it with a new bearing.

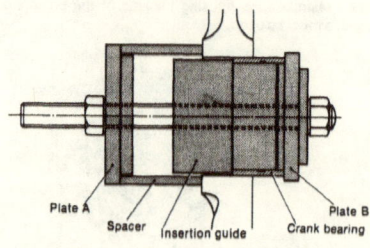

Plate A
Spacer
Insertion guide
Plate B
Crank bearing

Chapter 2 Basic Engine
6. Crankshaft

(3) Crank bearing installation precautions
1) Pay careful attention to the crank bearing insertion direction. Insert the bearing so that the side with the outside fillet is at the outside.
2) Align the oil hole of the crank bearing with the oil holes of the cylinder block and bearing housing.
3) After inserting the crank bearing, check that the crankshaft rotates easily with the thrust metal and bearing housing installed.
4) Be careful that the bearing is not tilted during insertion.

6-5 Crankshaft oil seal
6-5.1 Oil seal type and size
Spiral oil seals are employed at both ends of the crankshaft. This type of oil seal is pulled toward the oil pan by pump action while the engine is running so that there is no oil leakage.
Since the viscous pump action will be lost if the lip of the seal is coated with grease, coat the lip with oil when assembling.

(4) Insert the oil seal with a press. However, when unavoidable, the seal may be installed by tapping the entire periphery of the seal with a hammer, using a block. In this case, be careful that the oil seal is not tilted.
Never tap the oil seal directly.

GOOD

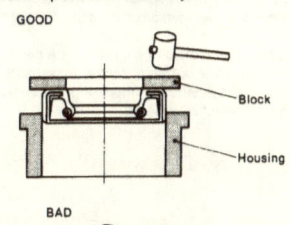

BAD

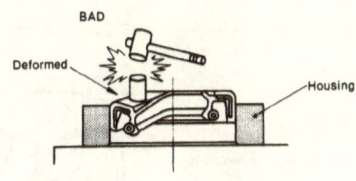

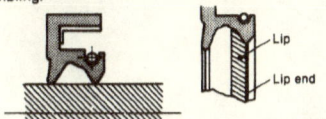

mm(in.)

	Manufacturer	Size	Spiral	Part No. (Yanmar)
Gear side	NOK	58.80.12	YES	124450-01800
Flywheel side (Bearing housing side)	NOK	65.88.9	YES	124060-02220

6-5.2 Oil seal insertion precautions
(1) Clean the inside of the housing hole, ascertaining that the hole was not dented when the seal was removed.
(2) Be sure that the insertion direction of the oil seal is correct. Insert so that the main lip mounting the spring is on the inside (oil side).

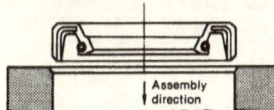

(3) Since the direction of rotation of the shaft is specified on a spiral oil seal, be sure that the rotating direction is correct.

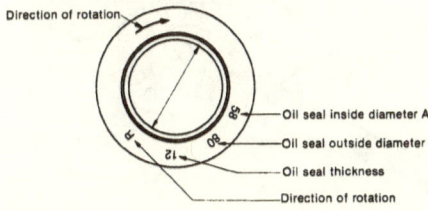

7. Camshaft

7-1 Construction

The camshaft is an integral camshaft with intake and exhaust cams for two cylinders on the flywheel side. The camshaft gear and fuel cam are mounted on the gear side by keys.

Since the intake and exhaust cam profile is a parabolic acceleration cam with a buffering curve, movement of the valve at high speed is smooth, improving the durability of the intake and exhaust valve seats.

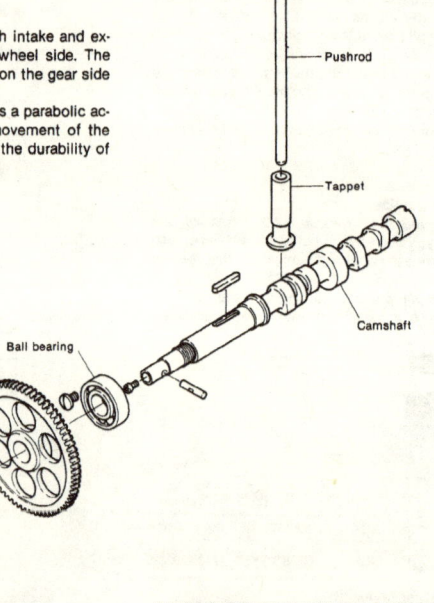

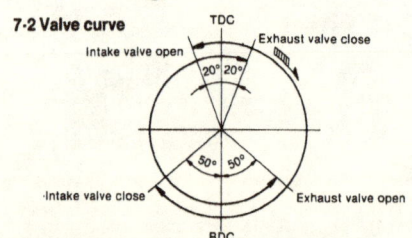

7-2 Valve curve

Intake and exhaust valve head clearance	0.20mm (0.00787in.)
intake valve open b. TDC	20°
Intake valve close a. BDC	50°
Exhaust valve open b. BDC	50°
Exhaust valve close a. TDC	20°

7-3 Inspection

Since the cam surface is tempered and ground, there is almost no wear. However, measure the height of the intake and exhaust cams, and replace the camshaft when the measured value exceeds the wear limit.

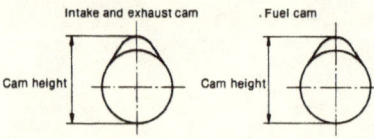

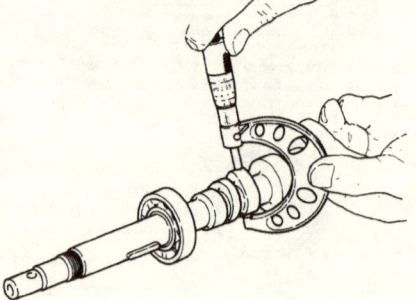

Chapter 2 Basic Engine
7. Camshaft
SM/2QM15

mm (in.)

		Maintenance standard	Clearance at assembly	Maximum allowable clearance
Flywheel side	Shaft bearing section outside diameter	ø30 (1.1811)	0.040 ~ 0.081 (0.0016 ~ 0.0032)	0.15 (0.0059)
	Bearing inside diameter	ø30 (1.1811)		
Center	Bearing section outside diameter	ø42 (1.6535)		
	Bearing inside diameter	ø42 (1.6535)		

mm (in.)

		Maintenance standard	Wear limit
Camshaft height	Intake and exhaust cam	35 (1.377)	34.7 (1.3661)
	Fuel cam	45 (1.771)	44.9 (1.7677)
Camshaft side clearance		0	—

7-4 Camshaft ball bearing
The camshaft bearing is a single row deep groove ball bearing. The construction and material of this ball bearing such that it can withstand the radial load, thrust loads in both directions, and a combination of both these loads. When the ball bearing does not rotate smoothly, or when the axial direction play is large, replace the bearing.
(Ball bearing type: 6205)

7-5 Tappets
These mushroom type tappets feature a special iron casting with chill-hardened contact surfaces for high wear resistance. The center of the cam surface width and the center of the tappet are offset to prevent eccentric wear of the contact surface.

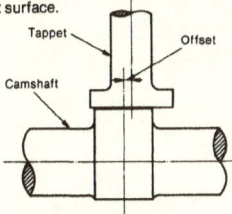

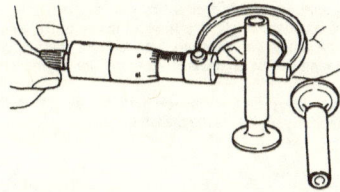

7-5.3 Tappet and cam contact surface
Since the tappet and cam are offset, the tappet rotates in an up and down movement during operation, so there is no uneven contact.
Since eccentric wear will occur if cam tappet contact is poor, replace the tappet if there is any uneven contact or deformation.

7-5.1 Tappet disassembly precautions
The cylinder number and intake and exhaust must be clearly indicated when disassembling the camshaft and tappets.

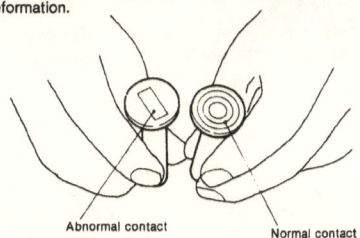

Abnormal contact   Normal contact

7-5.2 Tappet stem wear and contact
Measure the outside diameter of the tappet stem, and replace the tappet when the wear limit is exceeded or contact is uneven.

mm (in.)

	Maintenance standard	Wear limit
Tappet stem outside diameter	ø10 (0.4330)	ø9.95 (0.3917)
Tappet stem and guide hole clearance	0.005 ~ 0.035 (0.00019 ~ 0.00137)	0.10 (0.0039)

7-6 Push rods
The push rods are sufficiently rigid and strong to prevent bending.
Place the push rod on a stool or flat surface and measure the clearance between the center of the push rod and the flat surface, and replace the push rod if the wear limit is exceeded.

Chapter 2 Basic Engine
7. Camshaft

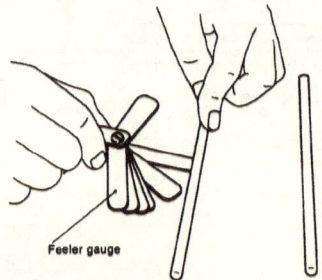

Check both ends for wear and peeling, and replace the push rod if faulty.

mm(in.)

	Maintenance standard	Wear limit
Push rod bend	0.03 or less (0.00118 or less)	0.3 (0.0118)

7-7 Fuel cam assembly precautions
Install the fuel cam by aligning it with the key of the camshaft. If the installation direction is not correct, the fuel injection timing will be considerably off and the engine will not start.
When assembling the fuel cam, be sure that the "0" mark side of the cam is opposite the camshaft gear.

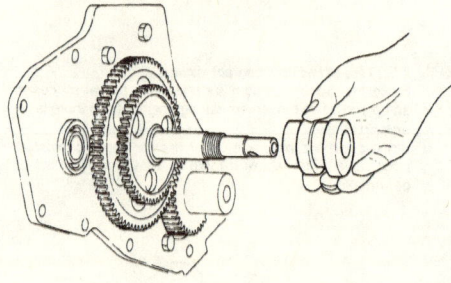

8. Timing Gear

8-1 Timing gear train construction

The timing gear chamber gear train consists of a crankshaft gear, camshaft gear, governor gear, and an intermediate gear that drives the governor gear.

The governor gear drive intermediate gear is attached to the camshaft, together with the camshaft gear, and has the same number of teeth as the governor gear to rotate the governor gear at the same speed as the camshaft.
All gears are spur gears.

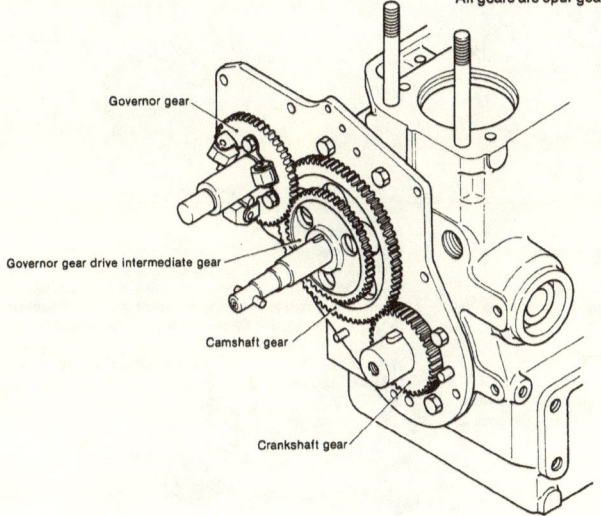

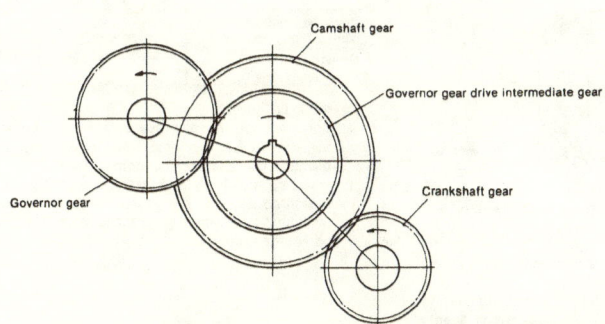

mm(in.)

	Module m	Number of teeth	Width of teeth	Center distance	
Camshaft gear	2.0	35	19 (0.748)	105 $^{+0.062}_{0}$	(4.1339~4.1363)
Crankshaft gear	2.0	70	10 (0.394)		
Governor gear	2.0	48	8 (0.315)	96 $^{+0.048}_{0}$	(3.7795~3.7814)
Governor intermediate gear	2.0	48	8 (0.315)		

Chapter 2 Basic Engine
8. Timing Gear

8-2 Disassembly and reassembly
8-2.1 Disassembly

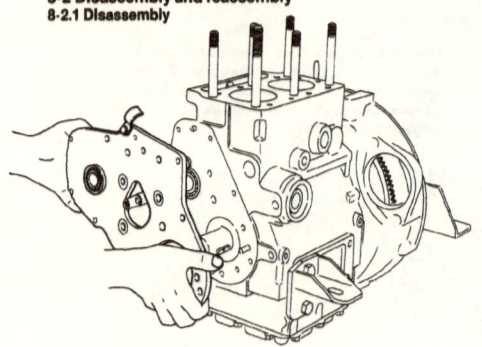

(1) Remove the crankshaft pulley and V-belt.
(2) Remove the regulator spring chamber cover.
(3) Remove the fuel injection pump.
(4) Remove the governor bearing blind plug.
(5) Remove the timing gear chamber while tapping the governor shaft lightly.
(6) Pull the gears using a puller.

8-2.2 Reassembly
Reassemble in the reverse order of disassembly. However, assemble the governor and install the timing gear case as described below.

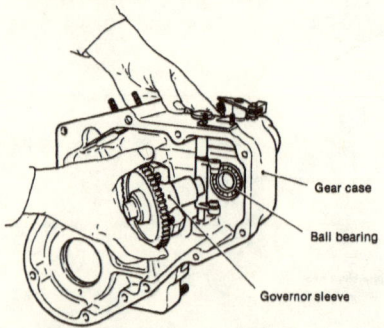

Gear case
Ball bearing
Governor sleeve

8-2.3 Disassembly and reassembly precautions
(1) Timing mark
A timing mark is provided on the crankshaft gear and camshaft gear to adjust the timing between opening and closing of the intake and exhaust valves and fuel injection when the piston is operated.
Always check that these timing marks are aligned when disassembling and reassembling the timing gear.

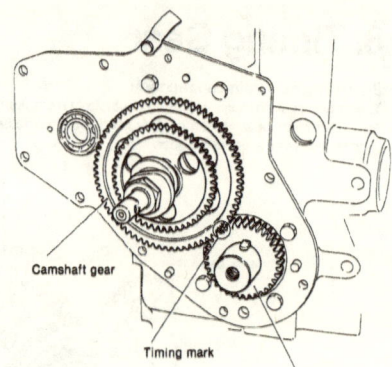

Camshaft gear
Timing mark
Crankshaft gear

8-3 Inspection
8-3.1 Backlash
Unsuitable backlash will cause excessive wear or damage at the tooth top and abnormal noise during operation. Moreover, in extreme cases, the valve and fuel injection timing will deviate and the engine will not run smoothly.

When the backlash exceeds the wear limit, repair or replace the gears as a set.

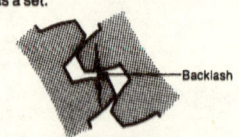
Backlash

	Maintenance standard	Wear limit
Crankshaft gear and camshaft gear backlash	0.08 ~ 0.16 (0.0031 ~ 0.0062)	0.3 (0.0118)
Governor gear and intermediate gear backlash		

mm(in.)

Measuring backlash
(1) Lock one of the two gears to be measured and measure the amount of movement of the other gear by placing a dial gauge on the tooth surface.
(2) Insert a piece of quality solder between the gears to be measured and turn the gears. The backlash can be measured by measuring the thickness of the crushed part of the solder.

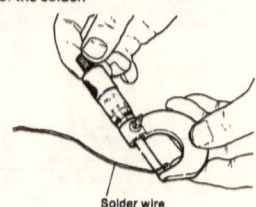
Solder wire

8-3.2 Inspecting the gear tooth surface

Check the tooth surface for damage caused by pitching and check tooth contact. Repair if the damage is light. Also inspect the gears for cracking and corrosion.
When gear noise becomes high because of wear or damage, replace the gears as a set.

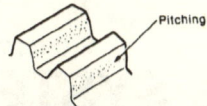
Pitching

8-3.3 Inspecting the gear boss

Check for play between each gear and the gear shaft, burning caused by play, key damage, and for cracking at the edge of the key groove. Replace the gears when faulty.

CHAPTER 3
FUEL SYSTEM

1. Construction 3-1
2. Injection Pump 3-2
3. Injection Nozzle 3-11
4. Fuel Filter 3-14
5. Fuel Feed Pump 3-15
6. Fuel Tank 3-16

Chapter 3 Fuel System
1. Construction

1. Construction

The fuel system consists mainly of an injection pump, injection pipe, and an injection nozzle, plus a fuel tank, feed pump, fuel filter and other associated parts. The injection pump is driven by a fuel cam mounted on one end of the camshaft and is controlled by a governor. Fuel stored in the fuel tank is fed to the fuel filter through the feed pump. (The feed pump is indispensable when the fuel tank is installed lower than the injection pump.)
Dirt and other impurities in the fuel are removed by the filter and the clean fuel is sent to the injection pump, which applies the necessary pressure for injection to the fuel and atomizes the fuel by passing it through the injection nozzle. The injection pump also controls the amount of fuel injected and the injection timing according to the engine load and speed by means of a governor.
The injection pump feeds the fuel to the injection nozzle through a high pressure pipe. The pressurized fuel is atomized and injected by the injection nozzle into the precombustion chamber.
Fuel that overflows the injection nozzle is returned to the fuel filter through the fuel return pipe. The quality of the equipment and parts comprising the fuel injection system directly affects combustion performance and has a considerable effect on engine performance. Therefore, this system must be inspected and serviced regularly to ensure top performance.

1-1 Fuel system diagram

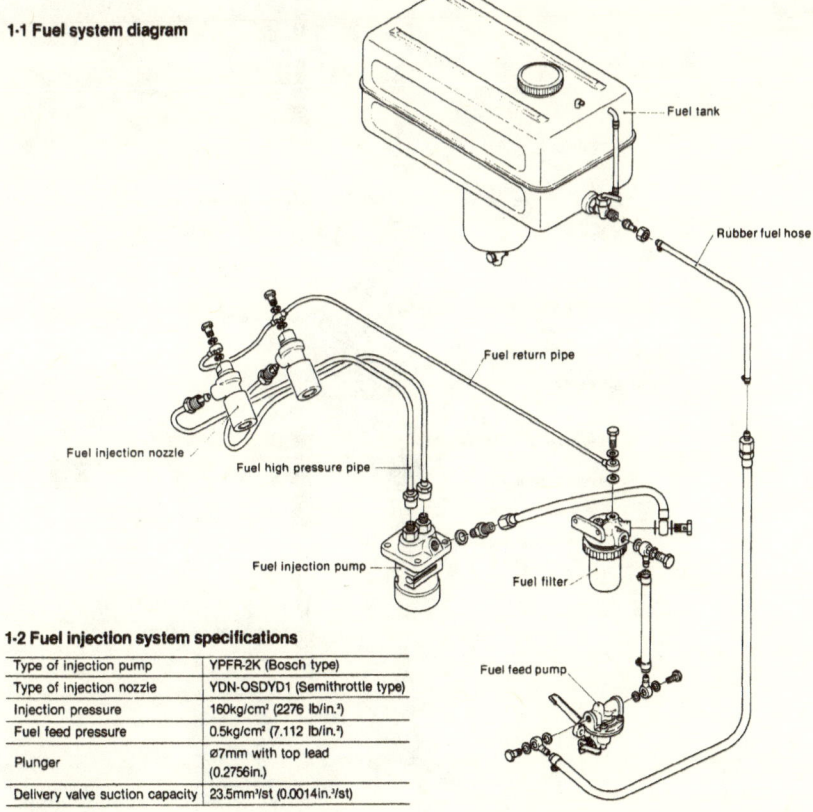

1-2 Fuel injection system specifications

Type of injection pump	YPFR-2K (Bosch type)
Type of injection nozzle	YDN-OSDYD1 (Semithrottle type)
Injection pressure	160kg/cm² (2276 lb/in.²)
Fuel feed pressure	0.5kg/cm² (7.112 lb/in.²)
Plunger	⌀7mm with top lead (0.2756in.)
Delivery valve suction capacity	23.5mm³/st (0.0014in.³/st)

Chapter 3 Fuel System
2. Injection Pump

SM/2QM15

2. Injection Pump

The injection pump is the most important part of the fuel system. This pump feeds the proper amount of fuel to the engine at the proper time in accordance with the engine load.

This engine uses a Bosch integral type injection pump for two cylinders. It is designed and manufactured by Yanmar, and is ideal for the fuel system of this engine.

Since the injection pump is subjected to extremely high pressures and must be accurate as well as deformation—and wear-free, stringently selected materials are used and precision finished after undergoing heat treatment.

The injection pump must be handled carefully. Since the delivery valve and delivery valve holder and the plunger and plunger barrel are lapped, they must be changed as a pair.

2-1 Construction

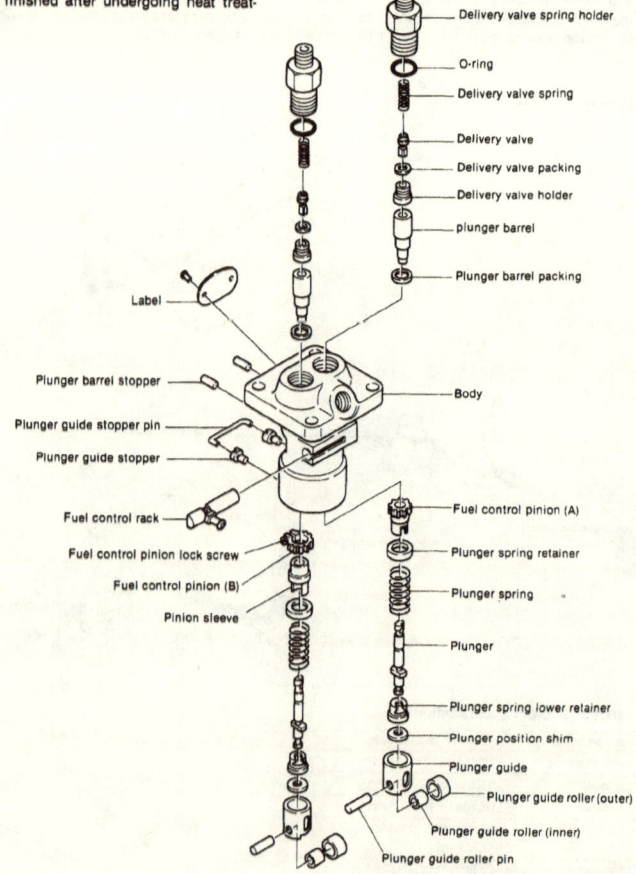

- Delivery valve spring holder
- O-ring
- Delivery valve spring
- Delivery valve
- Delivery valve packing
- Delivery valve holder
- plunger barrel
- Plunger barrel packing
- Label
- Plunger barrel stopper
- Plunger guide stopper pin
- Plunger guide stopper
- Body
- Fuel control rack
- Fuel control pinion (A)
- Fuel control pinion lock screw
- Plunger spring retainer
- Fuel control pinion (B)
- Plunger spring
- Pinion sleeve
- Plunger
- Plunger spring lower retainer
- Plunger position shim
- Plunger guide
- Plunger guide roller (outer)
- Plunger guide roller (inner)
- Plunger guide roller pin

Chapter 3 Fuel System
2. Injection Pump

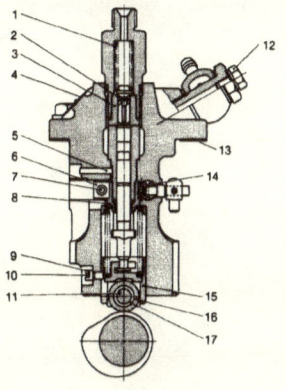
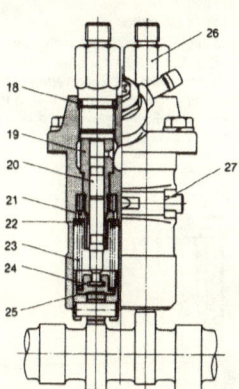

1. Delivery valve spring
2. Delivery valve
3. Delivery valve holder
4. Label
5. Plunger barrel stopper
6. Fuel control pinion (B)
7. Fuel control pinion lock screw
8. Pinion sleeve
9. Plunger guide stopper
10. Plunger guide stopper pin
11. Plunger guide roller pin
12. Air bleeding bolt
13. Injection timing shim
14. Fuel control rack
15. Plunger guide
16. Plunger guide roller (outer)
17. Plunger guide roller (inner)
18. O-ring
19. Plunger barrel
20. Plunger
21. Fuel control pinion (A)
22. Plunger spring retainer
23. Plunger spring
24. Plunger spring lower retainer
25. Plunger position shim
26. Delivery valve spring holder
27. Reference face

2-2 Operation of plunger

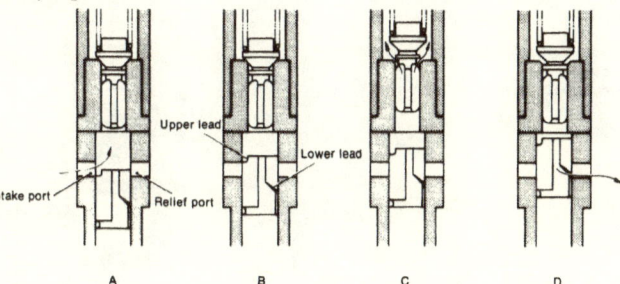

A. When the plunger reaches its lowest position (when the fuel cam reaches base circle), the top and vertical grooves of the plunger are filled with fuel through the intake port.
B. When the plunger rises to the position at which the upper lead closes the intake port, the fuel begins to push the delivery valve upward.
C. As the plunger rises further, the delivery valve is pushed up and the fuel is sent to the injection nozzle through the delivery valve and high pressure pipe.
D. The plunger continues to rise until the lower lead closes the discharge port. At this point the fuel is discharged through the relief port from the vertical groove, the delivery valve is pushed back, and fuel feed is halted. The amount of fuel and the injection timing are adjusted by rotation of the plunger with the control sleeve and by changing the relative positions of the upper lead, lower lead, and ports. In other words, the amount of fuel and the injection timing are adjusted by changing the plunger stroke from the closing of the intake port by the upper lead to the opening of the relief port by the lower lead.

Chapter 3 Fuel System
2. Injection Pump _____ SM/2QM15

2-3 Delivery valve fuel suction collar
The delivery valve of this engine is equipped with a piston (collar), as shown in the figure. This collar prevents injection cutting and dripping—caused by a lowering of the pressure inside the pipe—by sucking back the fuel in the high pressure pipe when the delivery valve drops due to the stopping of the effective stroke of the plunger.

(3) Remove the No. 2 plunger guide.

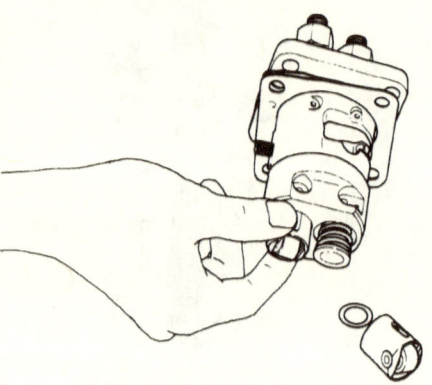

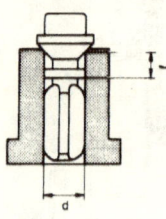

Amount of fuel sucked back: $\pi/4 \ d^2 l = 23.5 \text{mm}^3/\text{stroke}$
$(0.0014 \text{in}^3./\text{st.})$

2-4 Disassembly
As a rule, the injection pump should not be disassembled, but when disassembly is unavoidable, proceed as described below.
The injection pumps are arranged in No. 1 cylinder and No. 2 cylinder order, from right to left, as viewed from the name plate installed at the top of the pump body.
When disassembling the pumps, divide the parts into No. 1 cylinder and No. 2 cylinder groups, using two disassembly plates.
If these parts are mixed together, reassembly becomes impossible without a pump tester.
  (1) Remove the plunger guide stopper pin with needle nose pliers.

(4) Remove the No. 2 plunger and plunger spring lower retainer and plunger shim; be careful not to damage the plunger.
(5) Remove the No. 2 plunger spring.

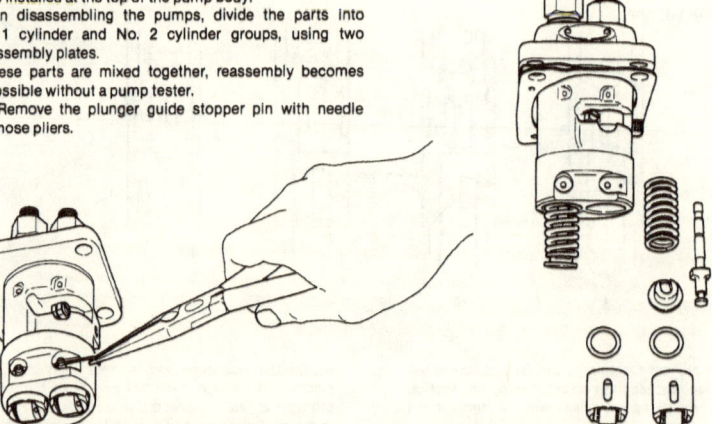

(6) Remove the No. 2 plunger spring upper retainer, using your fingers or tweezers.

(2) Remove the No. 2 plunger guide stopper.
The stopper can be removed by pushing the plunger guide down with the palm of your hand.

Chapter 3 Fuel System
2. Injection Pump

SM/2QM15

(7) Remove the No. 2 control sleeve (A).

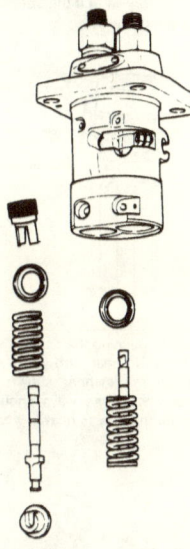

(8) Remove the No. 2 delivery valve holder; be careful not to damage the O-ring.
(9) Remove the No. 2 delivery valve spring.
(10) Remove the No. 2 delivery valve, delivery valve seat and packing.

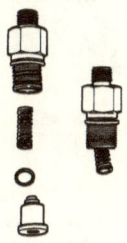

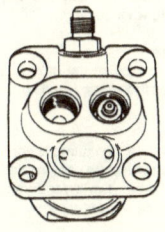

(11) Remove the No. 2 plunger barrel; be careful not to damage the face that matches the delivery valve seat.
(12) Since the No. 1 fuel adjusting gear is separated into a control sleeve (B) and a pinion, scribe matching marks on both parts with a scribe; otherwise, reassembly may be impossible.

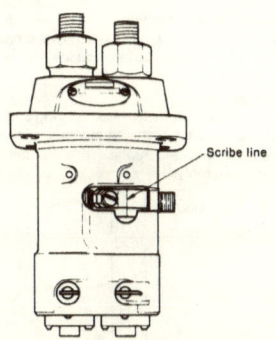

Scribe line

(13) Loosen the No. 1 fuel adjusting set screw.
(14) Perform steps (2)—(6) above on the No. 1 cylinder pump.
(15) Remove the No. 1 control sleevel (B) using tweezers so that the sleeve does not drop into the gears.
(16) Perform steps (8)—(11) above on the No. 1 cylinder pump.
(17) Remove the No. 1 pinion.
(18) Remove the control rack.
(19) Remove the No. 1 and No. 2 plunger barrel packings.

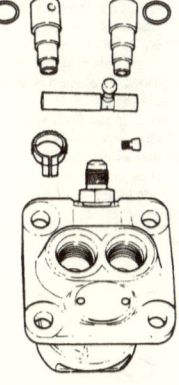

2-5 Inspecting injection pump parts

2-5.1 Tappet
Inspect the cam sliding surface of the tappet roller for wear, scoring and peeling; replace the tappet and roller assembly when the total tappet and roller play exceeds 0.3mm.

2-5.2 Control rack and pinion
When the control rack does not move smoothly when a force of within 60g is applied, replace the rack and pinion assembly.

2-5.3 Plunger
(1) Inspect the plunger for wear, scoring and discoloration around the lead. If any problems are found, conduct a pressure test and replace the plunger and plunger barrel assembly.

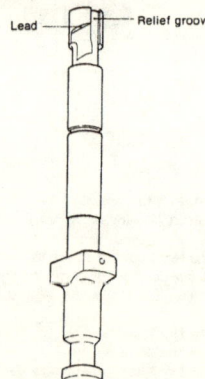

(2) Inspect the outside sliding surface of the plunger with a magnifying glass. Lap or replace the plunger and plunger barrel assembly when corrosion, hairline cracks, staining and/or scoring are detected.
(3) Check the clearance between the plunger collar and control sleeve groove. Replace these parts when wear exceeds the specified limit.
(4) After cleaning the plunger, tilt it approximately 60°, as shown in the figure, and slowly slide it down. Repeat this several times while rotating the plunger. The plunger should slide slowly and smoothly. If it slides too quickly, or binds along the way, repair or replace it.

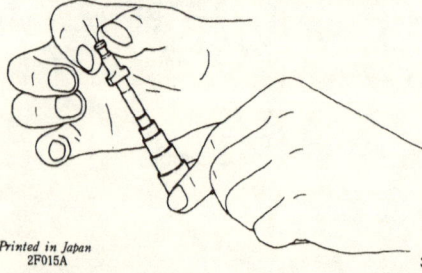

2-5.4 Delivery valve
(1) Replace the delivery valve if the return collar and seat are scored, dented or worn.

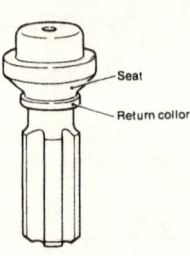

(2) After thoroughly washing the delivery valve, block the bottom of the valve seat with your finger, push the valve lightly in the manner shown in the figure. Remove your finger. The valve should return. If it doesn't, the return collar is heavily worn and must be replaced.

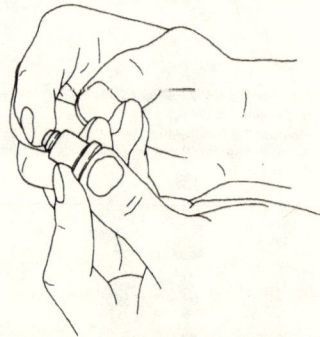

2-5.5 Plunger spring and delivery valve spring
Inspect the plunger spring and delivery valve spring for fractured coils, rust, inclination and permanent strain. Replace the spring when faulty.

2-5.6 Plunger guide
Inspect the sliding face of the plunger guide for damage and wear. Replace the spring when faulty.

2-6 Reassembly
To ensure that the injection pump is correctly reassembled, the following points must be kept in mind:
- The parts for the No. 1 cylinder pump and No. 2 cylinder pump must not be mixed together.

Chapter 3 Fuel System
2. Injection Pump

- When parts are replaced, the parts for the No. 1 cylinder pump and No. 2 cylinder pump must always be replaced at the same time.
- When assembling, parts must be washed in fuel oil and matching marks and scribe lines must be lined up.

(1) Install the No. 2 plunger barrel packing.
(2) Insert the No. 2 plunger barrel by aligning the groove of the barrel lock pin.

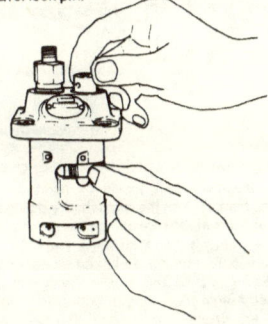

(3) Install the No. 2 delivery valve, delivery valve seat and packing.

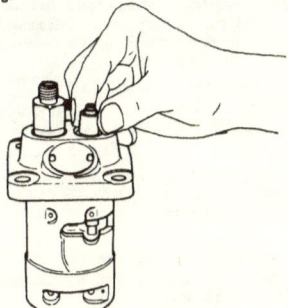

(4) Insert the No. 2 delivery valve spring.
(5) Tighten the No. 2 delivery valve holder.
  Tightening torque: 4—4.5kg-m (29—32.6 lb-ft)

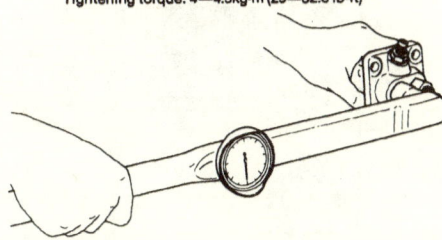

(6) Insert the control rack, making sure that it is inserted in the proper direction.

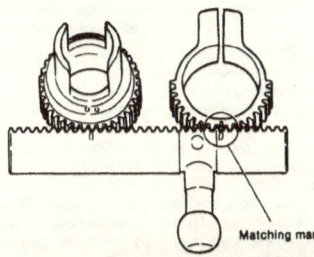

Matching mark

(7) Insert the No. 2 control sleeve (A). The matching marks on the sleeve must line up with those on the rack.
(8) Insert the No. 2 plunger spring upper retainer. Make sure that it is not inserted backwards.
(9) Insert the No. 2 plunger spring.
(10) Insert the No. 2 plunger; line up the matching marks.

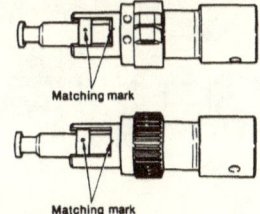

Matching mark

Matching mark

(11) Install the No. 2 plunger spring lower retainer. Make sure that it is not installed backwards.
(12) Insert the plunger shim.
(13) Insert the No. 2 plunger guide.
(14) Insert the No. 2 plunger guide stopper.
  Insert the stopper, while pushing the plunger guide with your hand. While moving the rack, push the plunger guide so that the plunger collar fits into the groove of the pinion.
(15) Insert the No. 1 pinion into the pump body.
(16) Perform steps (1)—(5) above on the No. 1 cylinder pump.
(17) Insert the No. 1 control sleeve and tighten with the set screw.
  Align the scribe marks of the sleeve and pinion.
(18) Perform steps (8)—(14) above on the No. 1 cylinder pump.
(19) Install the plunger guide stopper.

NOTE: When the tightening torque of the delivery valve holder exceeds the prescribed torque, the plunger will be distorted, the sliding resistance of the control rack will increase, and proper performance will not be obtained. Moreover, excessive tightening will damage the pump body and delivery valve gasket, and cause a variety of other problems.

Chapter 3 Fuel System
2. Injection Pump

2-7 Inspection after reassembly

When the engine runs roughly and the injection pump is suspected as being the cause, or when the pump has been disassembled and parts replaced, always conduct the following tests.

2-7.1 Control rack resistance test

After reassembling the pump, wash it in clean fuel, move the rack and check resistance as follows:
(1) This test is performed to determine the resistance of the control rack. When the resistance is large, the engine will run irregularly or race suddenly.
(2) Place the pump on its side, hold the control rack up and allow it to slide down by its own weight. The rack should slide smoothly over its entire stroke. Place the pump on end and perform the above test again; check for any abnormalities.
(3) Since a high sliding resistance is probably a result of the following, disassemble the pump and wash or repair it.

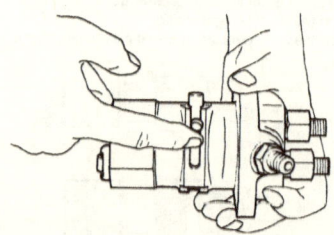

(a) Resistance of the rotating and sliding parts of the plunger assembly is too high.
(b) Delivery valve holder is too tight (plunger barrel distorted).
(c) Control rack or control sleeve teeth and control rack outside circumference are dirty or damaged.
(d) Injection pump body control rack hole is damaged.
(e) Plunger barrel packing is not installed correctly and the barrel is distorted. (Since in this case fuel will leak into the crankcase and dilute the lubricating oil, special care must be taken).

2-7.2 Fuel injection timing

Fuel injection timing is adjusted by timing shims inserted between the pump body and gear case pump mounting seat.
When deviation of the No. 1 cylinder and No. 2 cylinder injection interval occurs at the pump, the injection timing of one of the pumps is incorrect even though the other is properly set. Therefore, the injection pump must be mounted to the engine, and the No. 1 cylinder and No. 2 cylinder injection timing adjusted.
Adjusting the injection timing
(1) Remove the injection pipe from the pump.
(2) Install a measuring pipe if the injection pump does not have a nipple on the delivery side.

(3) Bleed the air from the injection pump.

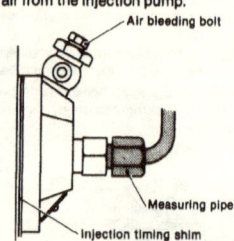

(4) Set the control rack to the middle fuel injection position.
(Pull the lever when setting the accelerator lever.)
(5) Turn the crankshaft slowly by hand, and read the timing mark (TD) on the crankshaft V-pulley the instant fuel appears at the measuring pipe or pipe joint nipple. (FID + Fuel injection from delivery valve.)
(6) If the injection timing is off, add plunger shims when the timing is slow, and remove shims when the timing is fast. Adjust the timing of both pumps in the same manner. (Refer to item, "Plunger head gap adjustment".)
(7) After the injection timing of both the No. 1 cylinder pump and No. 2 cylinder pump has been matched, recheck the injection timing as described in item (5) above. If the injection timing is not properly set, adjust it with the timing shims.

Fuel injection timing	b.TDC 27° ±2°
Injection timing shim	Thickness 0.1mm (0.004in.)
Plunger shim	Injection timing change 1° (crankshaft)

(8) Finally, turn the crankshaft slowly and confirm that it turns easily. If it is stiff or does not rotate, the plunger head gap is too small.

2-8 Injection pump adjustment

The injection pump is adjusted with an injection pump tester after reassembly.

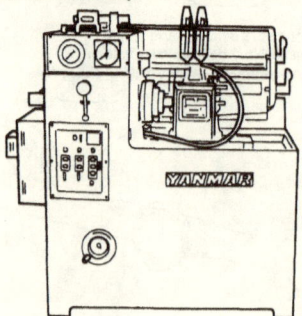

Chapter 3 Fuel System
2. Injection Pump

2-8.1 Setting pump on tester
(1) After the injection pump has been disassembled and reassembled, install it on a pump tester (cam lift: 7mm (0.276in.).
(2) Confirm that the control rack slides smoothly. If it does not, inspect the injection pump and repair it so that the rack slides smoothly.

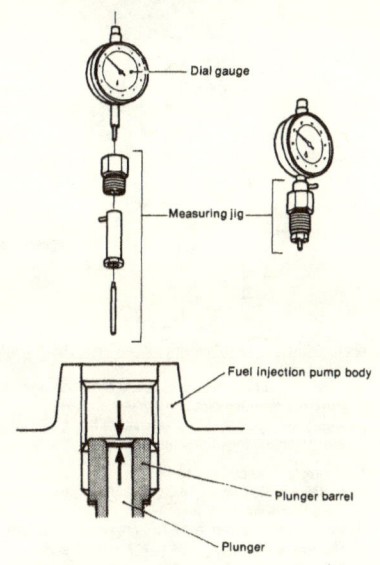

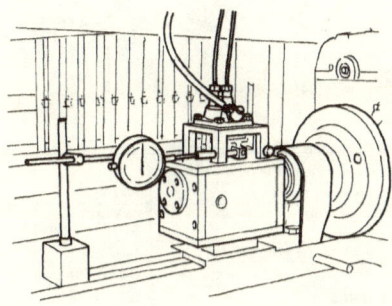

(3) Run the pump tester at low speed, loosen the air bleeder screw, and bleed the air from the injection pump.

2-8.2 Adjusting the plunger head gap
(1) Set the pump installation dimension (end of plunger barrel when the roller is on the cam base cycle) at 83mm (3.268in.), remove the delivery valve holder and delivery valve, and set the plunger to top dead center by turning the camshaft. Measure the difference in height (head gap) between the end of the plunger and the end of the plunger barrel using a dial gauge.

mm(in.)

Plunger head gap	0.5 ±0.05 (0.0177 ~ 0.0217)

(2) Using the plunger head gap measuring jig
  1) Install a dial gauge on the measuring jig.
  2) Stand the measuring jig on a stool and set the dial gauge pointer to O.
  3) Remove the pump delivery valve and install the measuring jig.
  4) Turn the camshaft to set the plunger to top dead center and read the dial gauge at this time. This value is the plunger head gap.

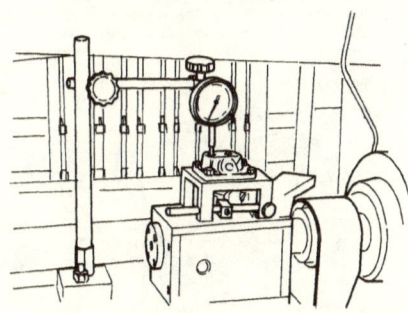

(3) When the plunger head gap is larger than the prescribed value, remove the plunger guide and insert plunger shims between the plunger spring lower retainer and the plunger guide. Adjust both pumps in the same manner.
Plunger shim thickness: 0.1mm (0.004in.), 0.2mm (0.008in.)
(4) After rechecking adjustment, install the delivery valve.
Delivery valve holder tightening torque: 4.0 ~ 4.5kg-m (29. ~ 32.6 lb-ft)

2-8.3 Checking the cylinder injection interval
(1) Align the control rack punch mark with the pump reference face.

Chapter 3 Fuel System
2. Injection Pump

2-8.6 Measuring the fuel injection volume

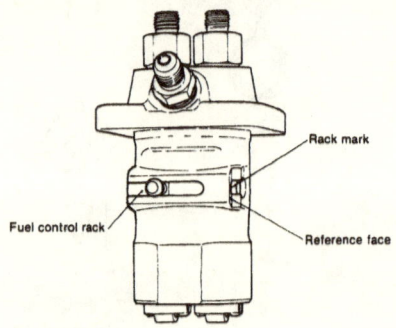

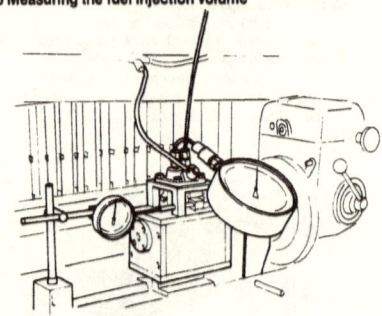

(2) Turn the pump by hand to check the No. 1 cylinder injection timing.
(3) Turn the pump in the prescribed direction and check the No. 2 cylinder injection timing.
(4) Using the plunger shims, adjust the No. 1 cylinder and No. 2 cylinder injection timing interval to 180°.

2-8.4 Delivery valve oil-tight test
(1) Install a 1,000kg/cm² (14,223 lb/in.²) pressure gauge to the delivery valve holder.
(2) Drive the fuel pump to apply a pressure of approximately 120kg/cm² (1,707 lb/in.²) and measure the time required for the pressure to drop from 100kg/cm² (1,422 lb/in.²) to 10kg/cm² (142.2 lb/in.²).

Pump speed	200 rpm
Pressure drop limit	.5 sec. or less

2-8.5 Plunger pressure test

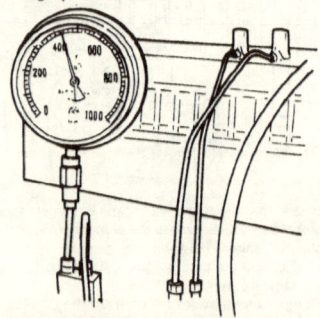

(1) Install a 1,000kg/cm² (14,223 lb/in.²) pressure gauge to the delivery valve holder.
(2) Check that there is no oil leaking from the delivery valve holder and high pressure pipe mountings, and that the pressure does not drop suddenly when the pressure has been raised to 500kg/cm² (7,112 lb/in.²) or higher.
Pressure gauge AVT 1/2 × 150 × 1,000kg/cm².

(1) Set the fuel pump camshaft speed.
(2) Check the injection nozzle.

Camshaft speed	1500 rpm
Plunger diameter x stroke	Ø6 × 7mm (0.2362 × 0.2756in.)
Rack mark injection volume	11.25cc/500st
Allowable error between cylinders	±0.25cc/500st
Nozzle	YDN-USDYD1
Injection pressure	160kg/cm² (2276 lb/in.²)

(3) Lock the control rack at the position at which the No. 2 cylinder pump injection conforms to the above table, and adjust to the prescribed volume by removing the control sleeve set screw and sliding the No. 1 cylinder pump control sleeve (B) and pinion. After adjustment, securely retighten the control sleeve set screw.

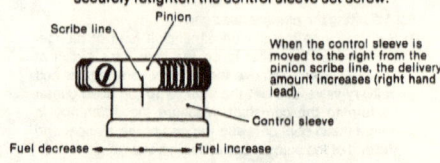

(4) The injection volumes of both cylinders must be adjusted to within 3% of each other.

Average injection volume =
$$\frac{\text{No. 1 cylinder injection volume + No. 2 cylinder injection volume}}{2}$$

$$\text{Difference} = \frac{\text{Maximum injection volume} - \text{average injection volume}}{\text{Average injection volume}} \times 100$$

When the difference exceeds 3%, the engine output position of the No. 1 cylinder pump control sleeve and pinion.
when the difference exceeds 3%, the engine output will drop and/or one cylinder will overheat.

3. Injection Nozzle

3-1 Construction
The injection nozzle atomizes the fuel sent from the injection pump and injects it into the precombustion chamber in the prescribed injection pattern to obtain good combustion through optimum fuel/air mixing.
The main parts of the injection nozzle are the nozzle holder and nozzle body. Since both these parts are exposed to hot combustion gas, they must be extremely durable.

Moreover, since they are operated sensitively and smoothly by the pressure of the fuel, high precision is required. Both are made of quality alloy steel that has been specially heat treated and lapped, so they must always be handled as a pair.

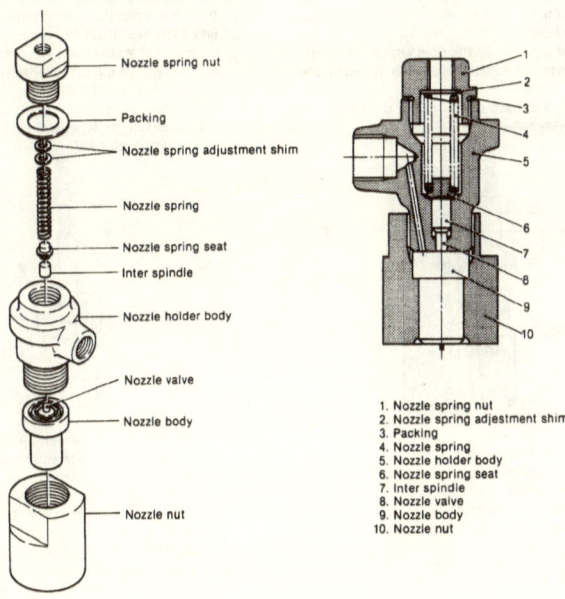

1. Nozzle spring nut
2. Nozzle spring adjestment shim
3. Packing
4. Nozzle spring
5. Nozzle holder body
6. Nozzle spring seat
7. Inter spindle
8. Nozzle valve
9. Nozzle body
10. Nozzle nut

3-2 Yanmar throttle nozzle
The semi-throttle nozzles used in this engine are designed and manufactured by Yanmar. A semi-throttle nozzle resembles a pintle nozzle, except that with the former the nozzle hole at the end of nozzle and nozzle body is longer and the end of the nozzle is tapered. This nozzle features a "throttling effect": relatively less fuel is injected into the precombustion chamber at the initial stage of injection, and the volume is increased as the nozzle rises. This type of throttle nozzle ideal for small, high-speed engines.

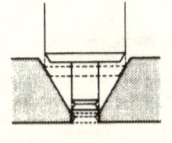

Pintle nozzle

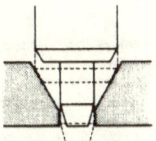

Yanmar semi-throttle nozzle

Chapter 3 Fuel System
3. Injection Nozzle

3-3 Nozzle operation
The nozzle is pushed down to its lowest position by the pressure-adjusting nozzle spring and contacts the valve seat of the nozzle body.
Under high pressure, fuel from the fuel pump passes through the hole drilled in the nozzle holder, enters the circular groove at the end of the nozzle body and then enters the pressure chamber at the bottom of the nozzle body.
When the force acting in the axial direction on the differential area of the nozzle at the pressure chamber overcomes the force of the spring, the nozzle is pushed up and the fuel is injected into the precombustion chamber through the throttle hole.
The nozzle is closed again when the pressure in the nozzle body's pressure chamber drops below the force of the spring.
This cycle is repeated at each opening and closing of the injection pump delivery valve.

3-4.2 Disassembly and reassembly precautions
(1) The disassembled parts must be washed in fuel oil, and carbon must be completely removed from the end of the nozzle body, the nozzle body and the nozzle mounting nut fitting section.
If reassembled with any carbon remaining, the nozle will not tighten evenly, causing faulty injection.
(2) Parts for, No. 1 cylinder and No. 2 cylinder must be kept separate.
The nozzle body and nozzle must always be handled as a pair.
(3) Precautions when using a new nozzle.
First immerse the new nozzle in rust-preventive oil, and then seal it on the outside with seal peel. After removing the seal peel, immerse the nozzle in diesel oil and remove the rust-preventive oil from both the inside and outside of the nozzle.
Stand the nozzle holder upright, lift the nozzle about 1/3 of its length: it should drop smoothly by it own weight when released.

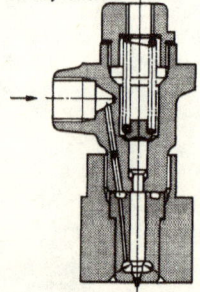

3-4 Disassembly and reassembly
3-4.1 Disassembly sequence
(1) Remove the carbon from the nozzle end.
(2) Loosen the nozzle spring holder.
(3) Remove the nozzle holder body from the nozzle mounting nut.

(4) The nozzle must be assembled to the nozzle holder with the nozzle spring retainer loosened.
If the nozzle is installed with the nozzle spring tightened, the nozzle mounting nut will be tightened unevenly and oil will leak from between the end of the nozzle holder body and the end of the nozzle mounting nut, causing faulty injection.
(5) When installing the injection nozzle on the cylinder head, tighten the nozzle holder nuts alternately, being careful to tighten them evenly. Tightening torque: 2 kg-m (14.5 ft-lb)
Moreover, the nozzle holder must be installed with the notch side on the nozzle side.

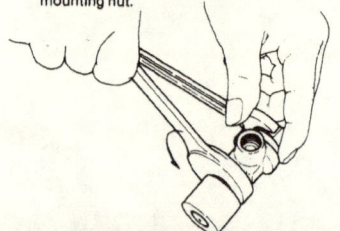

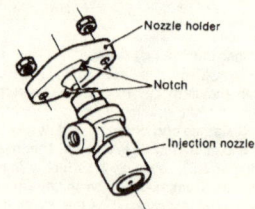

(4) Remove the nozzle body and nozzle ass'y from the nozzle mounting nut.
(5) Remove the nozzle spring retainer from the nozzle holder body, and remove the nozzle spring retainer, inter-spindle etc.
Reassemble in the reverse order of disassembly, paying special attention to the following items.

Chapter 3 Fuel System
3. Injection Nozzle

3-5 Injection nozzle inspection and adjustment
3-5.1 Carbon and corrosion on the nozzle body
Inspect the end and sides of the nozzle body for carbon build-up and corrosion. If there is considerable carbon build-up, check the properties of the fuel used, etc. Replace the body if heavily corroded.

3-5.2 Checking nozzle action
Wash the nozzle in clean fuel oil and hold the nozzle body upright, then lift the nozzle about 1/3 of its length with one hand. The nozzle is in good condition if it drops smoothly by its own weight when released. If the nozzle slides stiffly, repair or replace it.

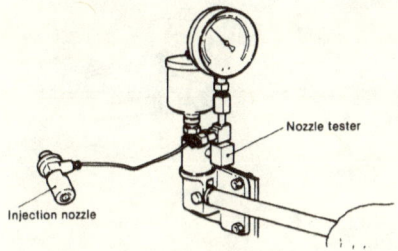

3-5.3 Adjusting the nozzle injection pressure
Install the injection nozzle to the high pressure pipe of a nozzle tester and slowly operate the lever of the tester. Read the pressure the instant injection from the nozzle begins.
If the injection pressure is lower than the prescribed pressure, remove the nozzle spring holder and adjust the pressure by adding nozzle spring shims.
The injection pressure increases about 10 kg/cm² (142.2 lb/in.²) when a 0.1 mm (0.004in.) shim is added.

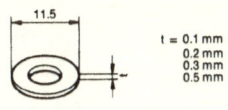

| Injection pressure | 160 ±10 kg/cm² (2134 ~ 2418 lb/in.²) |

3-5.4 Nozzle seat oil tightness check
After injecting fuel several times by operating the lever of the nozzle tester, wipe the oil off the injection port. Then raise the pressure to 20 kg/cm² (284.5 lb/in.²) (140kg/cm² (1991 lb/in.²)) lower than the prescribed injection pressure. The nozzle is faulty if oil drips from the nozzle. In this case, clean, repair or replace the nozzle.

3-5.5 Checking the spray conditon
Adjust the nozzle injection pressure to the prescribed value and check the condition of the spray while operating the tester at 4—6 times/sec. Judge the condition of the spray by referring to the below figure.

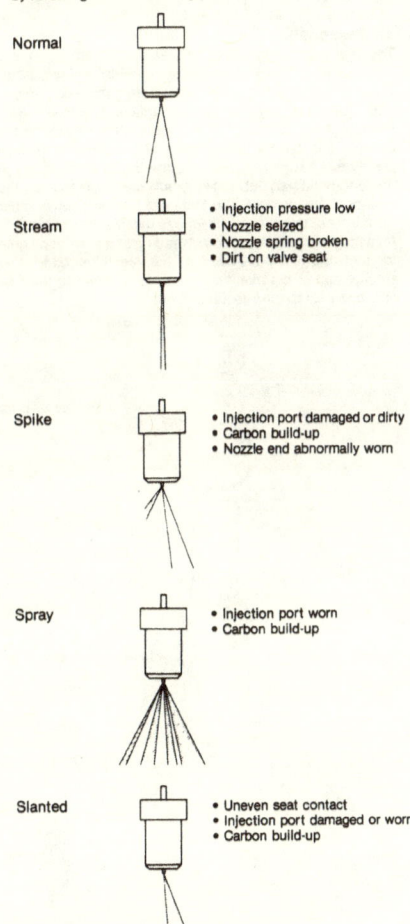

Normal

Stream
- Injection pressure low
- Nozzle seized
- Nozzle spring broken
- Dirt on valve seat

Spike
- Injection port damaged or dirty
- Carbon build-up
- Nozzle end abnormally worn

Spray
- Injection port worn
- Carbon build-up

Slanted
- Uneven seat contact
- Injection port damaged or worn
- Carbon build-up

3-5.6 Inspecting the nozzle spring
Inspect the nozzle spring for fractured coils, corrosion, and permanent strain, and replace the spring when faulty.

3-5.7 Inspecting the nozzle spring retainer and inter-spindle
Inspect the nozzle spring retainer and inter-spindle for wear and peeling of the contact face, and repair or replace the spring if faulty.

4. Fuel Filter

4-1 Construction

The fuel filter is installed between the feed pump and injection pump, and serves to remove dirt and impurities from the oil fed from the fuel tank through the feed pump.

The fuel filter incorporates a replaceable filter paper element. Fuel from the fuel tank enters the outside of the element and passes through the element under its own pressure. As it passes through, the dirt and impurities in the fuel are filtered out, allowing only clean fuel to enter the interior of the element. The fuel exits from the outlet at the top center of the filter and is sent to the injection pump.

An hexagonal head bolt for air bleeding and a threaded hole for fuel return are provided in the fuel filter body. The surplus fuel at the injection nozzle is returned to the fuel filter and then to the injection pump.

4-2 Inspection

The fuel filter must be periodically inspected. if there is water and sediment in the filter, remove all dirt, rust, etc. by washing the filter with clean fuel.

The normal replacement interval for the element is 100 hours, but the element should be replaced whenever it is dirty or damaged, even if the 100-hour replacement period has not elapsed.

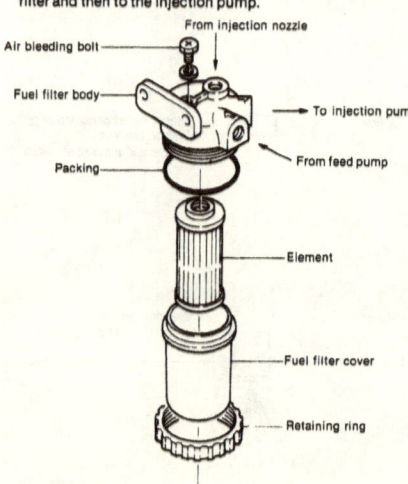

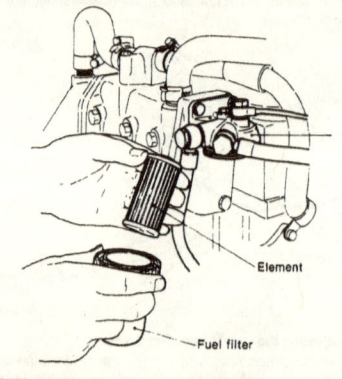

Filter cleaning	Every 50 hours
Filter element replacement	Every 100 hours

Chapter 3 Fuel System
5. Fuel Feed Pump   SM/2QM15

5. Fuel Feed Pump

5-1 Construction
The fuel pump feeds the fuel from the fuel tank to the injection pump through the fuel filter. When the fuel tank is installed at a higher position than the fuel filter and injection pump, the fuel will be fed by its head pressure, but if the fuel tank is lower than the filter and injection pump, a fuel pump is required.
The fuel pump of this engine is a diaphragm type and is installed on the exhaust side of the cylinder body. The diaphragm is operated by the movement of a lever by the fuel pump cam at the center of the No. 2 cylinder intake and exhaust cam.

5-2 Inspection
Disassemble the fuel pump body and cover and inspect the diaphragm for damage.
When replacement is necessary, replace the fuel pump ass'y.

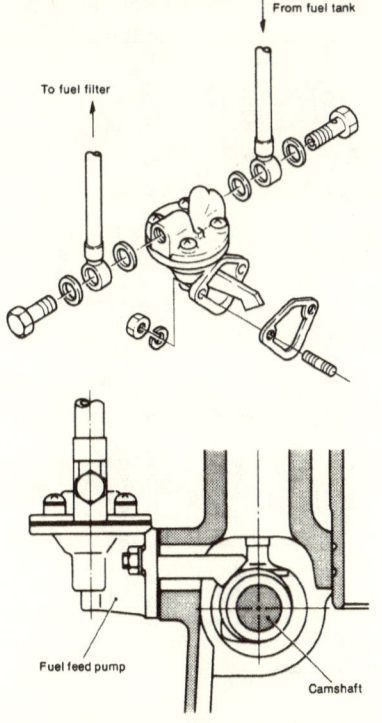

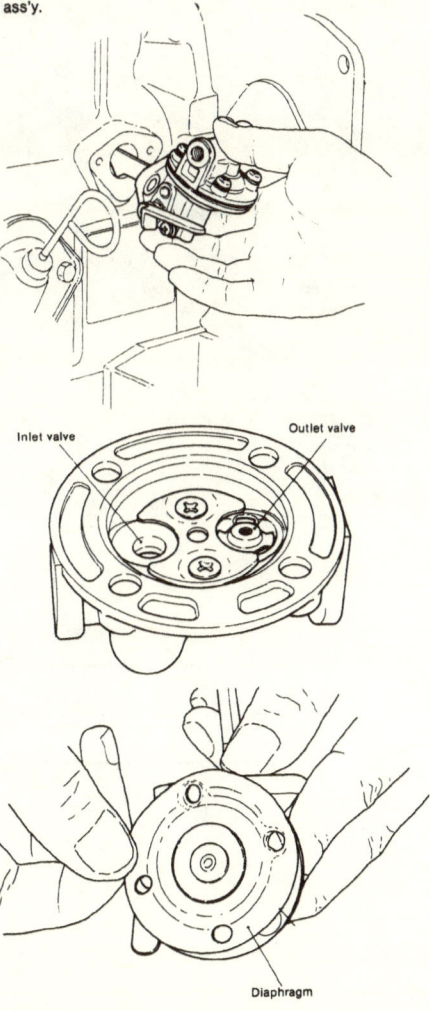

Suction head	Max. 0.8m
Capacity	0.3 ℓ/min. at 1000 rpm
Feed pressure	0.1kg/cm² (1.422 lb/in.²) at 600 ~ 1800 rpm

Printed in Japan
2F015A

3-15

Chapter 3 Fuel System
6. Fuel Tank

SM/2QM15

6. Fuel Tank (Option)

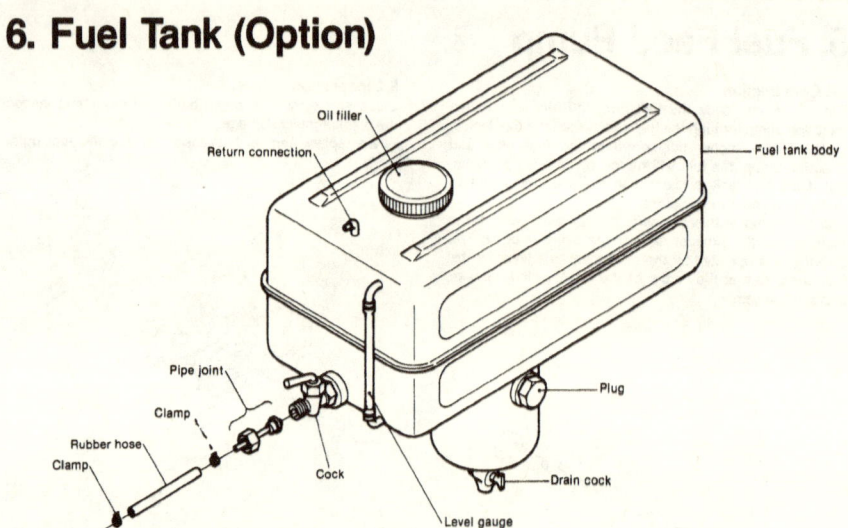

Material	Steel plate
Capacity	20*l*
Thread of outlet cock	PF 1/2
Size of rubber hose	ø7/ø13 × 2000 mm (0.2756/0.5118 × 78.74in.)

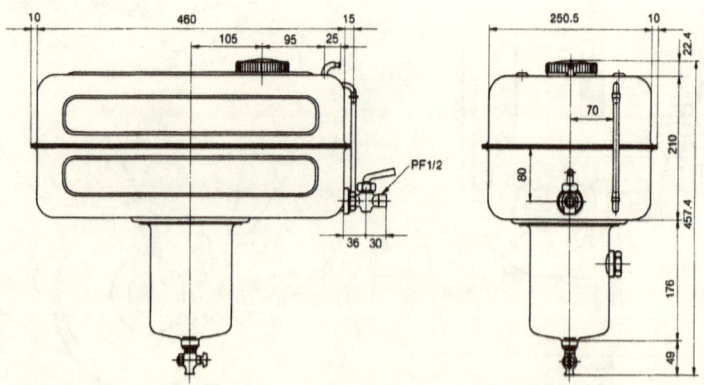

CHAPTER 4
GOVERNOR

1. Governor 4-1
2. Injection Limiter 4-6
3. No-Load Maximum Speed Limiter 4-7
4. Engine Stop Spring 4-8

Chapter 4 Governor
1. Governor

1. Governor

The governor serves to keep engine speed constant by automatically adjusting the amount of fuel supplied to the engine according to changes in the load. This protects the engine against sudden changes in the load, such as sudden disengagement of the clutch, the propeller leaving the water in rough weather, or other cases where the engine is suddenly accelerated.

This engine employs an all-speed governor in which the centrifugal force of the governor weight, produced by rotation of the governor shaft, and the load of the regulator spring are balanced.
The governor is remotely controlled by a wire. Refer to the "Control System" chapter for details.

1-1 Construction

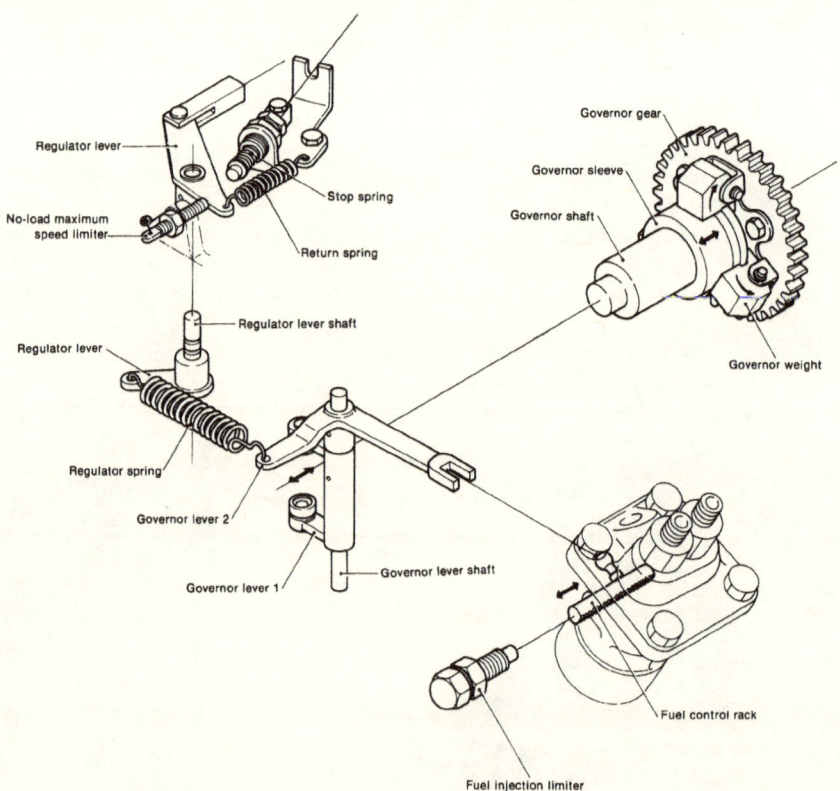

Chapter 4 Governor
1. Governor

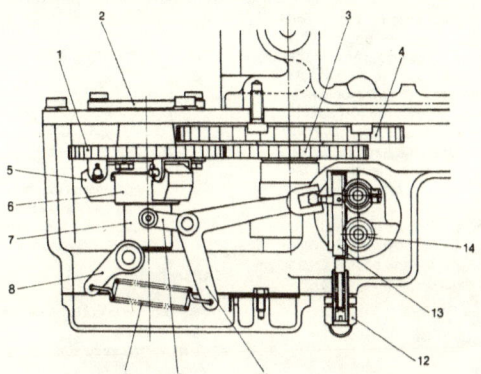

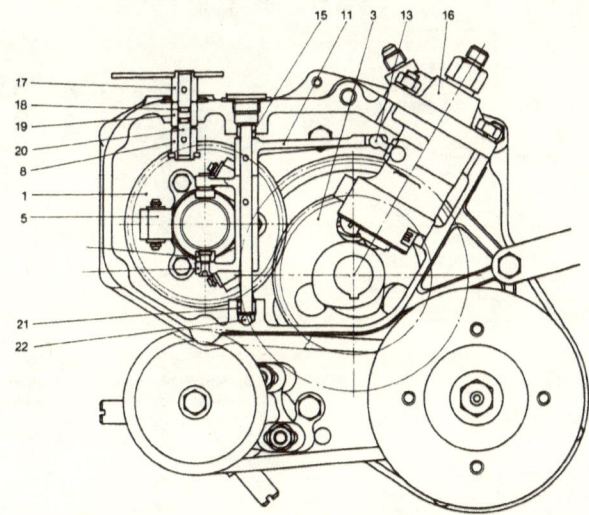

1 Governor gear
2 Governor shaft blind cover
3 Governor gear drive intermediate gear
4 Camshaft gear
5 Governor weight
6 Governor sleeve
7 Governor shaft
8 Regulator lever (B)
9 Regulator spring
10 Governor lever 1
11 Governor lever 2
12 Fuel injection limiter
13 Fuel control rack
14 Fuel control pinion
15 Needle bearing
16 Fuel injection pump
17 Regulator lever (A)
18 O-ring
19 Sleeve
20 Regulator lever shaft
21 Needle bearing
22 Steel ball

Chapter 4 Governor
1. Governor

1-2 Operation
The position of the three governor weights (open and closed) is regulated by the speed of the engine. The centrifugal force of the governor weights pivots around the governor weight pin and is changed to axial force that acts on the sleeve. This force is transmitted to governor lever 2 through governor lever 1, and lever 1 shifts the fuel control rack to increase or decrease the fuel supply. The governor lever is stabilized at the point at which the force produced by the governor weight is balanced with the load of the regulator spring connecting the regulator lever and governor lever 2.

When the speed is reduced by application of a load, the force of the regulator spring pushes the governor sleeve in the "fuel increase" direction, stabilizing the engine speed by changing the position of the regulator lever.

(When load is suddenly changed from rated load to low load)

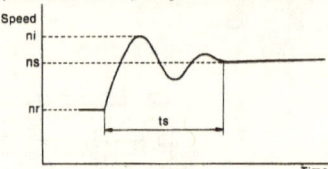

- ni: Instant maximum speed (rpm)
- ns: Stabilized speed (rpm)
- nr: Rated speed (rpm)
- ts: Stabilization time (sec.)

1-4 Disassembly
1-4.1 Disassembly
(1) Remove the injection limiter and governor cover from the gear case.
(2) Remove the regulator spring and then the injection pump.
(3) Remove the governor shaft; remove the gear case from the cylinder body while tapping the governor shaft lightly.

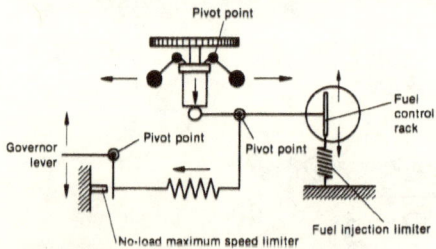

1-3 Performance

No-load maximum speed		$3250 ^{+50}_{0}$ rpm
No-load minimum speed		$600 ^{+50}_{0}$ rpm
Instant speed regulation	di	10% or less
Stabilization time	ts	10 sec. or less
Stabilized speed regulation	ds	5% or less

$$\text{Instant speed regulation} \quad di = \left|\frac{ni - nr}{nr}\right| \times 100$$

$$\text{Stabilized speed regulation} \quad ds = \left|\frac{ns - nr}{nr}\right| \times 100$$

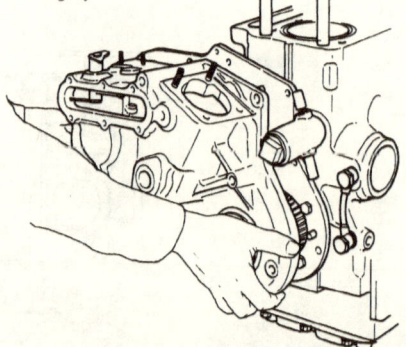

ni: Instant maximum (minimum) speed:
The maximum or minimum engine speed which is momentarily reached immediately after the load has been suddenly changed from the rated load to another load or from an arbitrary load to the rated load.

ns: Stabilized speed:
The speed which is set according to the lapse of time after the load has been changed from a rated load to another load or from an arbitrary load to the rated load.

nr: Rated speed

ts: Stabilization time:
The time it takes for engine to return to the set speed after a change.

(4) Remove the governor ass'y from the gear case and disassemble the bearing, sleeve, and gear from the shaft.

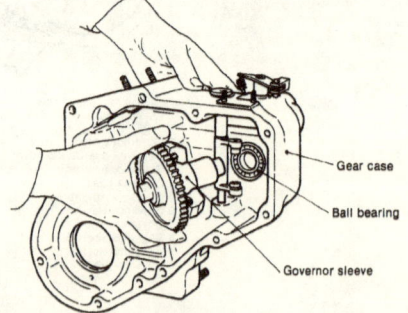

Chapter 4 Governor
1. Governor

SM/2QM15

(5) Pull the taper pins of governor lever 1 and governor lever 2, remove the governor lever shaft blind cover, and pull the governor lever shaft.
(6) Pull the needle bearing, using the special tool, and remove the steel ball.
(7) Pull the regulator lever and regulator handle taper pin.
(8) Pull the regulator lever shaft, and remove the bushing.

1-4.2 Disassembly and reassembly precautions
(1) Since a common taper pin hole is drilled in the governor lever shaft and governor levers 1 and 2, they must be replaced as an ass'y.
(2) Since a common taper pin hole is drilled in the regulator handle shaft, regulator handle and regulator lever, they must be replaced as an ass'y.
(3) Since the movement and play of the governor lever have a direct effect on the governors performance, they must be carefully checked.

1-5 Parts Inspection and repacement
1-5.1 Regulator spring
(1) Inspect the spring for coil damage, corrosion and hook deformation, and replace if faulty.
(2) Measure the spring's dimensions and spring constant. Since the spring constant determines the governor's performance, it must be carefully checked.

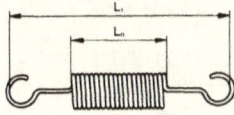

Spring specifications.

Wire diameter	1.4 mm (0.55in.)
Coil outside diameter	12.4 mm (0.488in.)
Number of coils	15
Spring constant	0.192 kg/mm (10.75 lb/in.)
Free length L_0	26 mm (1.024in.)
Free length L_1	49 mm (1.929in.)

1-5.2 Sleeve
(1) Slide the sleeve on the governor shaft to check that it slides smoothly.
(2) Measure the clearance between the governor shaft and the inside of the sleeve, check the contact between the governor lever 2 roller and governor weight, and inspect the roller for wear.

mm (in.)

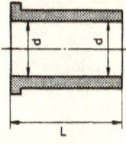

	Maintenance standard	Clearance when assembled	Maximum allowable clearance	Wear limit
Governor shaft outside diameter	$30_{-0.028}^{-0.007}$ (1.180 ~ 1.181)	0.08 ±0.02 (0.002 ~ 0.004)	0.2 (0.0079)	—
Governor sleeve inside diameter	$30_{+0.053}^{+0.074}$ (1.183 ~ 1.184)			—
Governor sleeve overall length	20 ±0.1 (0.738 ~ 0.791)	—	—	19.8 (0.7795)

1-5.3 Governor weight
(1) Check contact with the sleeve and for wear.

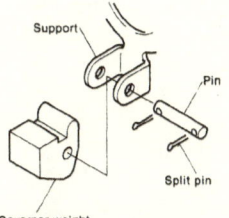

Governor weight

(2) Check governor weight and governor pin clearance.

mm (in.)

	Maintenance standard	Clearance at assembly	Maximum allowable clearance
Governor weight pin hole diameter	$5_{+0.20}^{+0.25}$ (0.2047 ~ 0.2067)	0.2 ±0.05 (0.0059 ~ 0.0098)	0.5 (0.0197)
Governor weight pin outside diameter	$5_{0}^{+0.05}$ (0.1969 ~ 0.1988)		

Chapter 4 Governor
1. Governor

1-5.4 Governor lever shaft
(1) Replace the governor lever shaft if there is play between the shaft and needle bearing, play when the lever is moved, or if the shaft does not move smoothly.
(2) Repair or replace the shaft if there is play between lever 1 or lever 2 and the shaft, or if the taper pin is loose.
(3) Inspect the contact and wear of the roller at the end of lever 1 and replace if the roller pin caulking is loose.
(4) Check the contact of the steel ball.

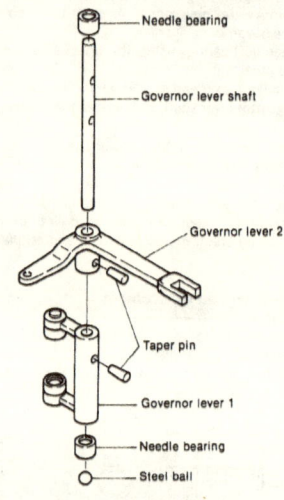

1-5.5 Regulator lever shaft
(1) Shaft and bushing clearance measurement.

mm (in.)

	Maintenance standard	Clearance at assembly	Maximum allowable clearance
Regulator lever shaft outside diameter	$8 \genfrac{}{}{0pt}{}{-0.020}{-0.050}$ (0.3130 ~ 0.3142)	0.035 ~ 0.08 (0.0014 ~ 0.0031)	0.25 (0.0098)
Bushing inside diameter	$8 \genfrac{}{}{0pt}{}{+0.030}{+0.015}$ (0.3156 ~ 0.3161)		

(2) Check for looseness between the gear case and bushing.
(3) Check for O-ring damage.
(4) Check for play in the regulator handle, regulator lever and shaft and for looseness in the taper pin.

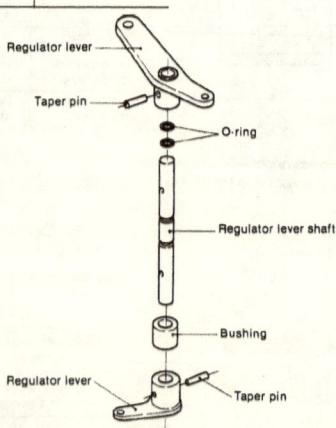

2. Injection Limiter

2·1 Construction
Since surplus power is required from the standpoints of sudden overloads and durability, the engine is equipped with an injection control shaft that limits the amount of fuel injected into the precombustion chamber to a fixed amount. Moreover, since the injection control spring (torque spring) affects engine performance by adjusting engine torque, care must be exercised in its handling and adjustment, and governor adjustment must be performed accurately.

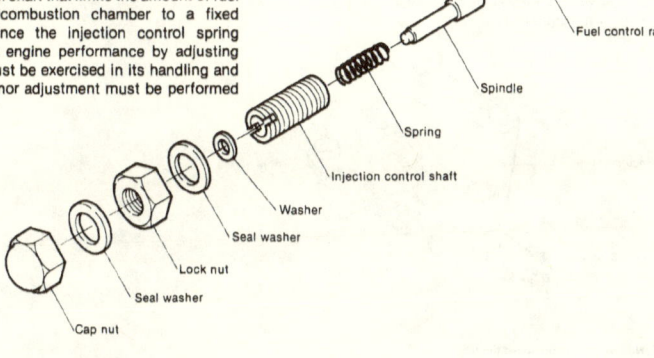

2·2 Inspection
(1) Hold the end of the spindle, and check it for smooth movement.
(2) Replace the spring if it is damaged, corroded or permanently strained.

2·3 Adjustment
1. Set the governor lever to the free position and remove the injection pump adjustment cover.
2. Remove the injection control shaft cap nut, loosen the hexagonal lock nut, and loosen the injection control shaft (so that the spring inside the injection control shaft is disabled).
3. Move governor lever 2 slowly to the left until the rack and injection control shaft contact lightly.
4. Set the governor lever to the free position and push the rack by slowly turning the injection control shaft clockwise.
5. Align the center mark of the rack with the reference face.
6. Lock the injection control shaft with the hexagonal nut and cap nut.

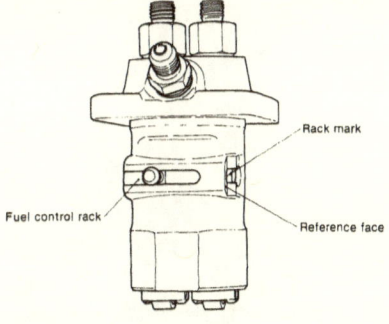
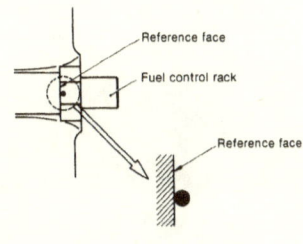

3. No-Load Maximum Speed Limiter

3-1 Construction
A stopper is installed on the regulator lever so that the engine speed at no-load does not exceed a fixed speed. The fuel control rack is stopped when the regulator lever contacts the stopper.

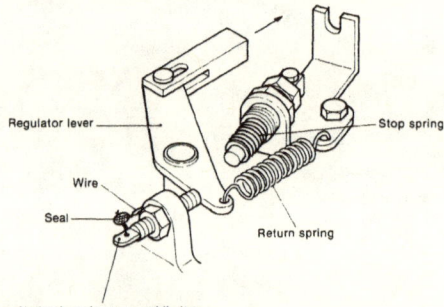

No-load maximum speed limiter

3-2 Handling precautions
The no-load maximum speed is adjusted during bench testing at the factory, and is locked with wire and sealed with lead. Care must be taken to keep the seal from being accidentally broken.

4. Engine Stop Spring

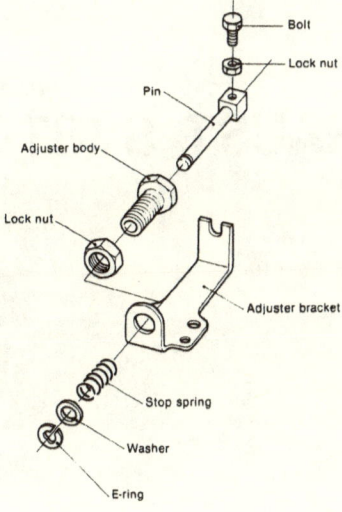

CHAPTER 5
INTAKE AND EXHAUST SYSTEM

1. Intake And Exhaust System 5-1
2. Intake Silencer 5-2
3. Exhaust System 5-3
4. Breather Pipe 5-4

Chapter 5 Intake and Exhaust System
1. Intake and Exhaust System

1. Intake and Exhaust System

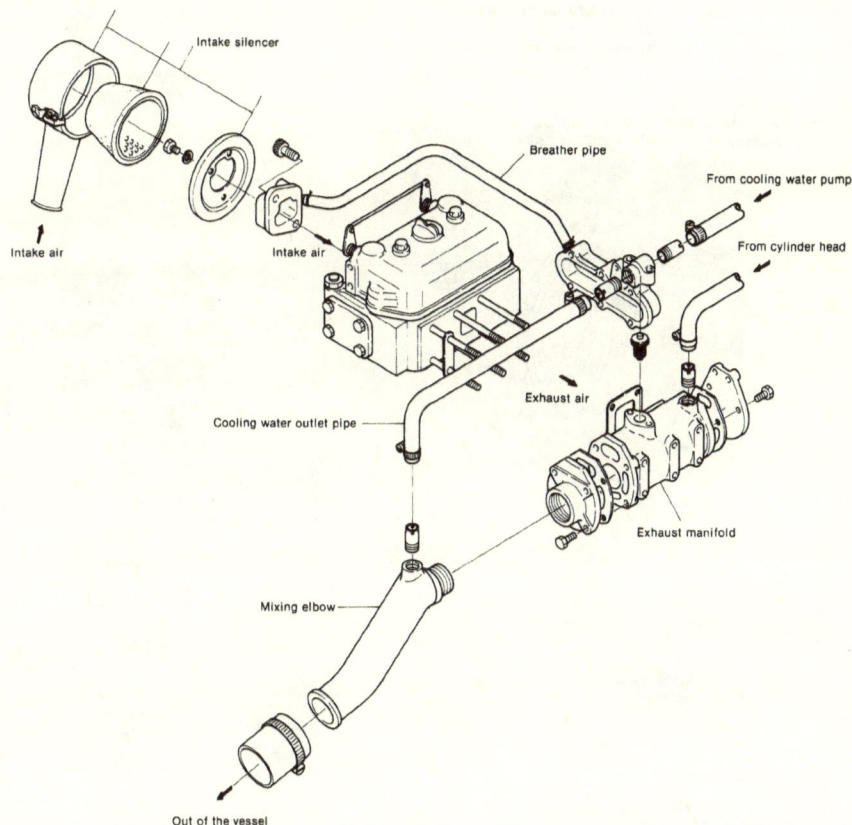

2. Intake Silencer

2-1 Construction
A round polyurethane sound absorbing type intake silencer is employed to silence the intake air sucked into the cylinder head from the intake port.
Besides providing a silencing effect, the silencer also acts as an air cleaner.

2-2 Inspection
When the intake silencer is disassembled, remove the internal polyurethane element and inspect it for clogging.

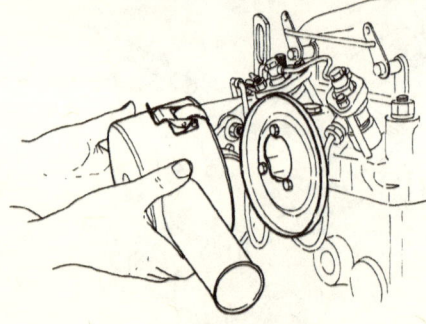

3. Exhaust System

3-1 Exhaust manifold and mixing elbow
The high temperature, high pressure exhaust gas emitted intermittently from the cylinders at the speed of sound enters the exhaust manifold where it is muffled by expansion and water cooling. It is then mixed with the cooling water at the mixing elbow to lower its temperature and muffle it further, and is discharged.
A water-cooled exhaust manifold is employed for a high muffling effect.

3-2 Exhaust manifold inspection

3-3 Mixing elbow inspection
Check for carbon build-up and for corrosion inside the pipe, and repair or replace the pipe if faulty.
Moreover, inspect the mixing elbow mounting threads for cracking and corrosion.
This section is affected by exhaust gas and vibration.

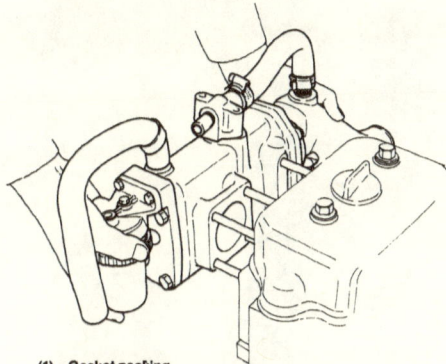

(1) **Gasket packing**
Inspect the gasket packing and replace if damaged.
(2) **Carbon build-up in the exhaust passage**
Remove the exhaust manifold elbow and cover and check carbon build-up in the exhaust passage. Remove any carbon in the passage. If carbon build-up becomes, heavy, the exhaust pressure will rise, causing overheating of the cylinders and difficult starting.
(3) **Corrosion and scale at the cooling water jacket**
Inspect the water passage for the build-up of scale and foreign matter and remove if existent. Also check for corrosion of the anticorrosion zinc installed on the cylinder head and the cylinder head water jacket and replace if corrosion is severe. Moreover, replace the cylinder head if it has been cracked by local overheating.
(4) **Drain cock**
Inspect the drain cock for clogging and check its action. Repair or replace if faulty.

4. Breather Pipe

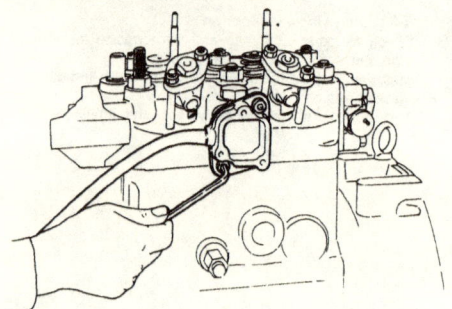

Engine blow-by gas is sent by hose from the injection pump adjusting cover to the intake port where it is sucked into the precombustion chamber with the intake air.
Since this blow-by gas is not exhausted, the engine room remains clean.

CHAPTER 6
LUBRICATION SYSTEM

1. Lubrication System 6-1
2. Oil Pump 6-3
3. Oil Filter 6-5
4. Oil Pressure Regulator Valve 6-6
5. Oil Pressure Measurement 6-7

Chapter 6 Lubrication System
1. Lubrication System

SM/2QM15

1. Lubrication System

Engine parts are lubricated by a trochoid pump forced lubrication system. To keep the engine exterior uncluttered and to eliminate vibration damage to piping, exterior piping has been minimized by transporting the lubricating oil through passages drilled in the cylinders and cylinder head.

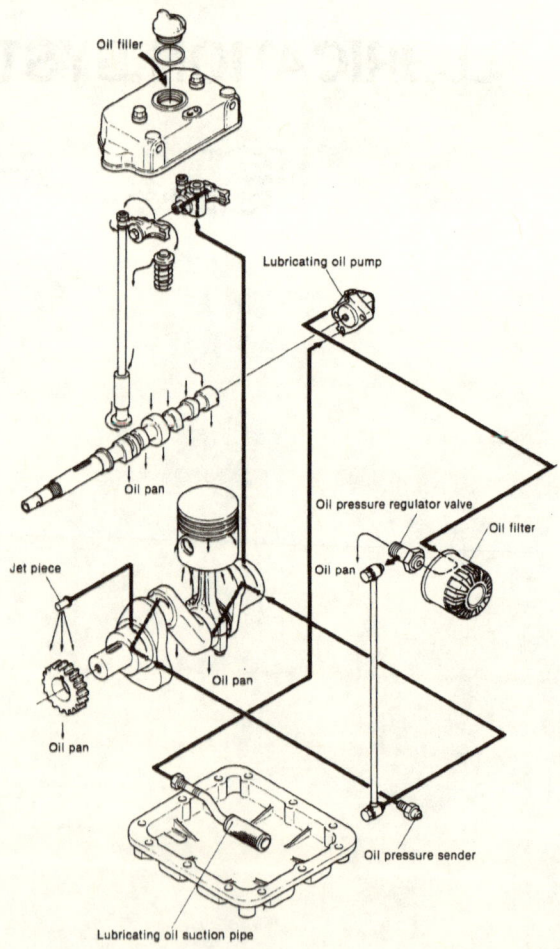

Chapter 6 Lubrication System
1. Lubrication System

The lubricating oil supplied from the oil filler in the rocker arm cover is collected in the oil pan at the bottom of the cylinder block thru the tappet holes.

The lubricating oil is drawn back up through the lubricating oil suction pipe by the trochoid pump and fed to the oil filter, where impurities are filtered out. Then it is adjusted to the prescribed pressure by the oil pressure regulating valve and sent to the main bearing through an oil pipe. The lubricating oil sent to the gear side main bearing flows in two paths: one from the main bearing to lubricate the crank pin through the hole drilled thru the crankshaft, and the other to the jet piece to lubricate the gears.

The lubricating oil sent to the flywheel side main bearing also flows in two paths: one from the main bearing to lubricate the crank pin through the hole drilled through the crankshaft, and the other to the rocker arm shaft through the hole drilled through the cylinders and cylinder head. From the rocker arm shaft, the lubricating oil flows through the small hole in the rocker arm to lubricate the push rods and part of the valve head.

The oil that has dropped to the push rod chamber from the rocker arm chamber lubricates the tappets, cam and cam bearing, and returns to the oil pan.

The pistons, piston pins and contact faces of the cylinder liners are splash lubricated by the oil that has lubricated the crank pin. Moreover, an oil pressure switch is provided in the lubricating system to monitor normal circulation and pressure of the lubricating oil. When the lubricating oil pressure drops $0.1 \, \text{kg/cm}^2$ (1.428 lb/in.²), the oil pressure switch illuminates the oil pressure lamp on the instrument panel to notify the operator.

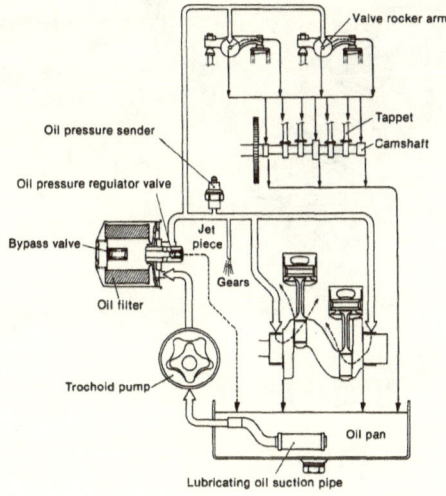

Chapter 6 Lubrication System
1. Lubrication System _____ SM/2QM15

2. Oil Pump

2-1 Construction

The oil pump is a compact, low pressure variation trochoid pump comprising a trochoid curve inner rotor and outer rotor. Pumping pressure is provided by the change in volume between the two rotors caused by rotation of the rotor shaft.
The oil pump is installed on the flywheel side of the camshaft end and is driven by a rotor shaft fitted to the slit in the end of the camshaft.

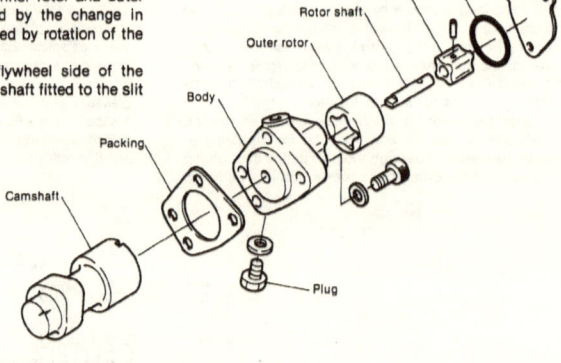

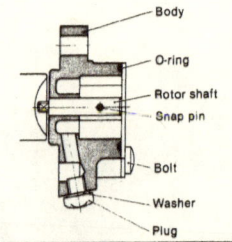

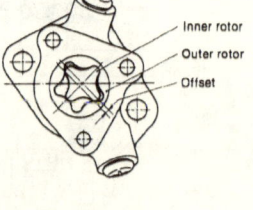

Lubricating oil feed volume (at 3,000 rpm)	260 l/hr.
Lubricating oil pressure (at 3,000 rpm)	2.5 kg/cm² ~ 3.5 kg/cm² (35.56~49.78 lb/in.²)

2-2 Disassembly

(1) Remove the reduction reversing gear ass'y.
(2) Remove the flywheel.
(3) Remove the oil pump ass'y.
(4) Remove the oil pump cover.
(5) Remove the inner rotor and rotor shaft ass'y.
(6) Remove the outer rotor.

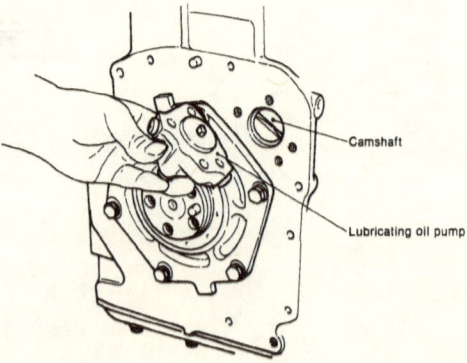

Printed in Japan
2F015A

6-3

Chapter 6 Lubrication System
2. Oil Pump

2-3 Inspection
When the discharge pressure of the oil pump is extremely low, check the oil level. If it is within the prescribed range, the oil pump must be inspected.

(1) Outer rotor and pump body clearance
Measure the clearance by inserting a feeler gauge between the outside of the outer rotor and the pump body casing. If the clearance exceeds the wear limit, replace the outer rotor and pump body as a set.

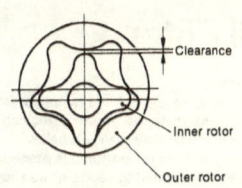

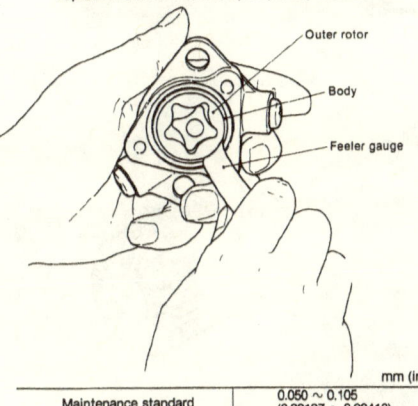

	mm (in.)
Maintenance standard	0.050 ~ 0.105 (0.00197 ~ 0.00413)
Wear limit	0.15 (0.00591)

(2) Outer rotor and inner rotor clearance
Fit one of the teeth of the inner rotor to one of the grooves of the outer rotor and measure the clearance at the point where the teeth of both rotors are aligned. Replace the inner rotor and outer rotor ass'y if the wear limit is exceeded.

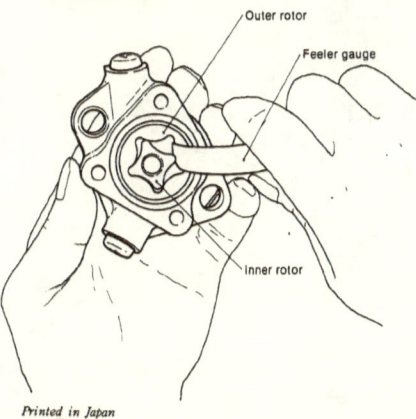

	mm (in.)
Maintenance standard	0.050 ~ 0.105 (0.00197 ~ 0.00413)
Wear limit	0.15 (0.00591)

(3) Pump body and inner rotor, outer rotor side clearance
Install the inner rotor and outer rotor into the pump body casing so that they fit snugly.
Check the clearance by placing a ruler against the end of the body and inserting a feeler gauge between the ruler and the end of the rotor. Replace as a set if the wear limit is exceeded.

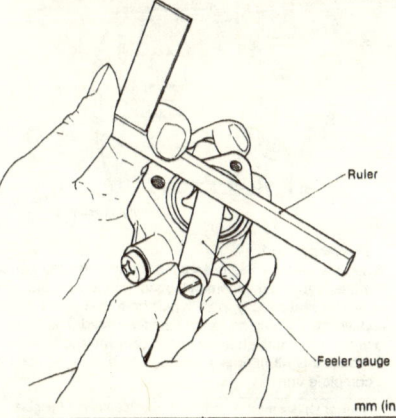

	mm (in.)
Maintenance standard	0.06 ~ 0.10 (0.00236 ~ 0.00393)
Wear limit	0.13 (0.00511)

(4) Rotor shaft and body clearance
Measure the outside diameter of the rotor shaft and the inside diameter of the body shaft hole, and replace the rotor shaft and body as an ass'y if the clearance exceeds the wear limit.

mm (in.)

	Maintenance standard	Clearance when assembled	Maximum allowable clearance
Rotor shaft outside diameter	29 $^{-0.020}_{-0.040}$ (1.14016 ~ 1.14094)	0.12 ~ 0.161 (0.0047 ~ 0.0063)	0.35 (0.0138)
Rotor shaft hole inside diameter	29.1 $^{+0.021}_{0}$ (1.14566 ~ 1.14649)		

3. Oil Filter

3-1 Construction

The oil filter removes the dirt and metal particles from the lubricating oil to minimize wear of moving parts. The construction of the oil filter is shown below.
The lubricating oil from the oil pump is passed through the filter paper and distributed to each part as shown by arrow A in the figure.
After extended use, the filter paper will become clogged and its filter performance will drop. When the pressure loss caused by the filter paper exceeds 1 kg/cm² (14.22 lb/in.²), the bypass valve inside the filter opens and the lubricating oil is sent to each part automatically as an emergency measure, without passing through the filter, as shown by arrow B.

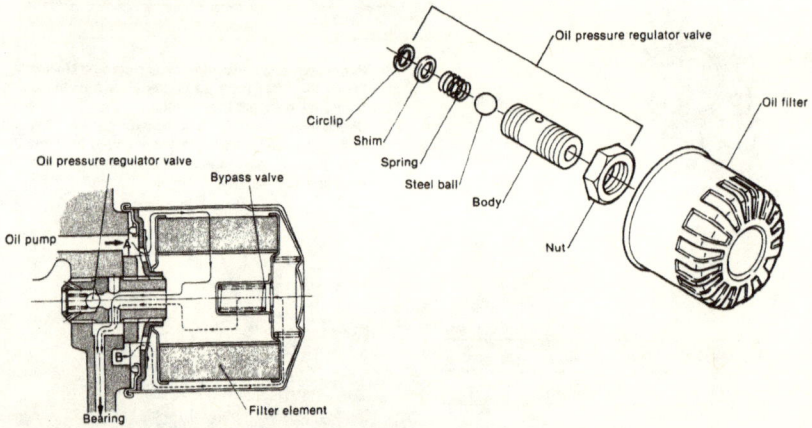

3-2 Replacement

When the oil filter has been used for an extended period, the filter paper will become clogged, unfiltered lubricating oil will be sent directly to each part from the bypass circuit, and wear of moving parts will be accelerated. Therefore, it is important that the filter be periodically replaced.
Because this oil filter is a cartridge type, it is replaced as a complete unit.

Oil filter replacement period	Every 300 hours of engine operation

3-2.1 Replacing the oil filter

(1) Clean the oil filter mounting face on the cylinder block.
(2) Before installing the new filter, coat the rubber packing with a thin coat of lubricating oil.
(3) Turn the filter gently until it contacts the rubber packing of the seal surface, then tighten another 2/3 turn.
(4) After installation, run the engine and check the packing face for oil leakage.

3-2.2 In case of oil leakage

If there is oil leakage, remove the oil filter and replace the packing. At the same time, inspect the cylinder block mounting face and repair the face with an oil stone if it is scored.

4. Oil Pressure Regulator Valve

4-1 Construction

The oil pressure regulator valve, located at the oil filter mounting, serves to adjust the pressure of the lubricating oil to the prescribed pressure during operation. When the pressure of the lubricating oil from the oil filter exceeds the force of the spring, the metal ball is pushed away from the valve seat and the lubricating oil flows to the oil pan through the gap between the ball and seat. The spring's force is adjusted with a shim.

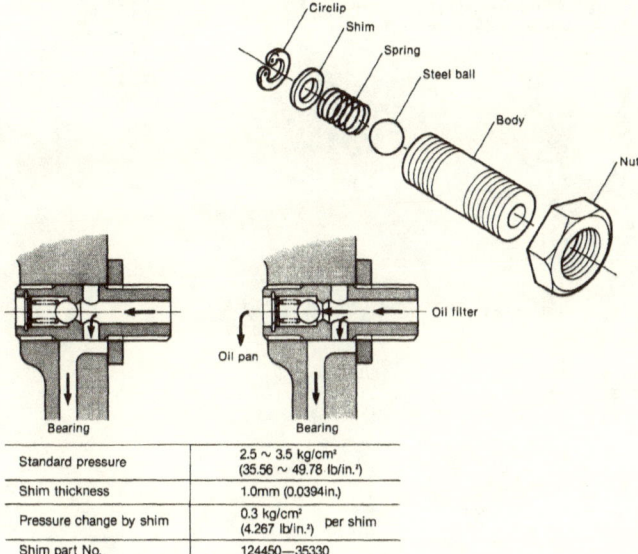

Standard pressure	2.5 ~ 3.5 kg/cm² (35.56 ~ 49.78 lb/in.²)
Shim thickness	1.0mm (0.0394in.)
Pressure change by shim	0.3 kg/cm² (4.267 lb/in.²) per shim
Shim part No.	124450—35330

4-2 Disassembly

(1) Remove the oil filter.
(2) Loosen the oil pressure regulator valve mounting nut and unscrew the adjustment valve.
(3) Remove the circlip and remove the shim, spring, and steel ball.

4-3 Inspection

(1) Check the steel ball and valve seat for contact and wear.
(2) Check the valve spring for damaged coils and permanent strain.

mm (in.)

	Maintenance standard	Wear limit
Valve spring free length	23 (0.9055)	—

5. Oil Pressure Measurement

The lubricating oil pressure is monitored by a pilot lamp, but it must also be measured using a pressure gauge. Connect the oil pressure gauge to the pilot lamp unit for the primary pressure and to the lubricating oil pipe connector for the secondary pressure, as shown in figure. The secondary oil pressure is especially important. Idle the engine at medium speed when measuring the oil pressure. Also check whether the oil pressure rises smoothly and to the standard value.

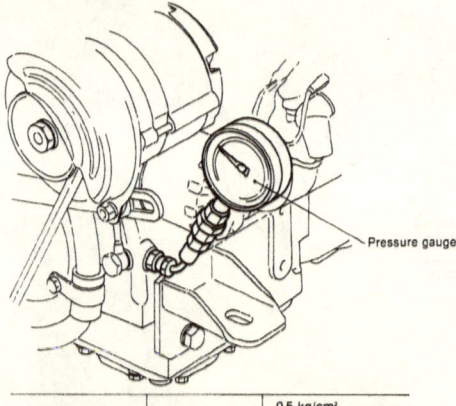
Pressure gauge

Secondary pressure standard value	Idling	0.5 kg/cm² (7.112 lb/in.²)
	3,000 rpm	2.5 ~ 3.5 kg/cm² (35.56 ~ 49.78 lb/in.²)

If the oil pressure is lower than the standard value, probable causes are:
(1) clearance of lubricated bearings in the lubricating oil circuit is too large (shaft or bearing is worn).
(2) excessive oil escaping from rocker arm support.
Therefore, inspection and repair of the bearings and rocker arm support are required.

CHAPTER 7
COOLING SYSTEM

1. Cooling System. 7-1
2. Water Pump 7-3
3. Thermostat 7-7
4. Anticorrosion Zinc. 7-8
5. Kingston Cock 7-9
6. Bilge Strainer. 7-10

Chapter 7 Cooling System
1. Cooling System

1. Cooling System

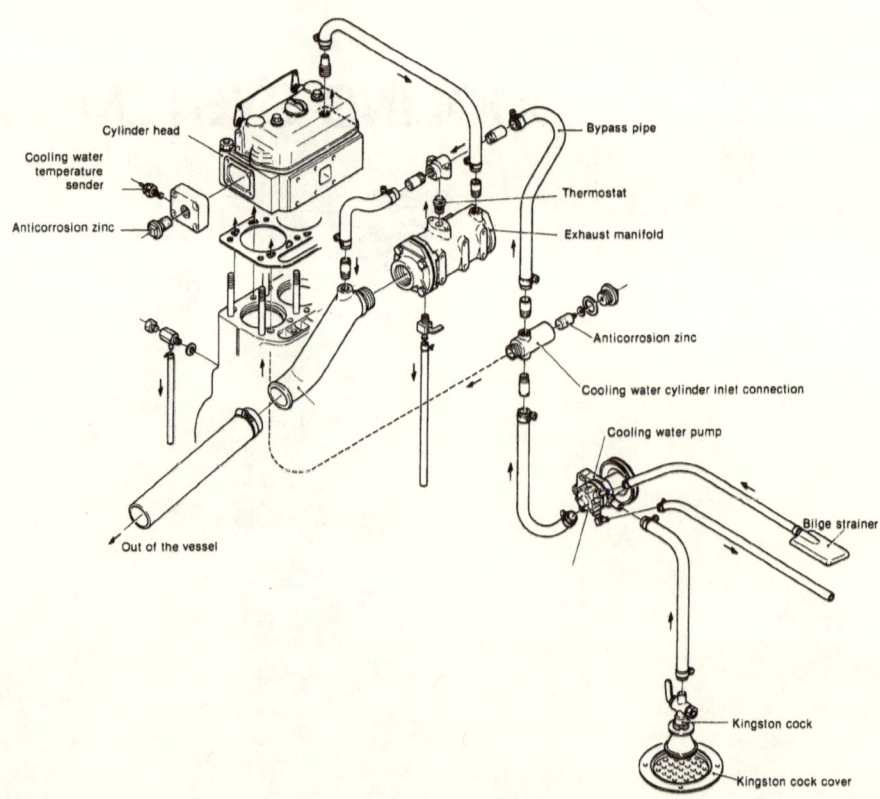

Chapter 7 Cooling System
1. Cooling System

1-1 Composition
(1) A sea water direct cooling system incorporating a rubber impeller pump is employed.
(2) A thermostat is installed on the water-cooled exhaust manifold and a bypass circuit is provided to keep the cooling water temperature constant at all times. This not only prevents overcooling at initial operation, but also improves the combustion performance and increases the durability of moving parts by keeping the temperature constant.
(3) Anticorrosion zinc is provided at the inlet coupling of the cylinder for the cooling water side cover of the cylinder head to prevent electrolytic corrosion of the cylinder jacket and cylinder head by the sea water.
(4) A cooling water temperature sender is installed so that an abnormal rise in the cooling water temperature is indicated at the lamp on the instrument panel.
(5) A tandem type bilge pump for bilge pumping is also available.
(6) A scoop strainer is provided at the water intake Kingston cock to remove dirt and vinyl from the water.
(7) Rubber hoses are used for all interior piping. This eliminates pipe brazing damage due to engine vibration and simplifies the engine's vibration mounting.

1-2 Cooling water route
The cooling water is sucked up by the water pump through a kingston cock installed on the hull. The water delivered from the water pump is branched in two directions at the cylinder intake coupling: one part of the water enters the cylinder jacket and the other bypasses the cylinder jacket and enters the mixing elbow.
The water that enters the cylinder jacket cools the cylinders and then rises to the cylinder head through the passage between the cylinder and cylinder head and cools the cylinder head. From the cylinder head, the water enters the water jacket of the exhaust manifold to reduce the exhaust heat, and enters the mixing elbow through the thermostat mounting. At the mixing elbow, this water is mixed with the exhaust gas and is discharged out of the vessel.
The thermostat is closed until the cooling water temperature reaches a fixed temperature (42°C), making the flow to the cylinder head and then through the bypass circuit.
When the cooling water temperature exceeds 42°C, the thermostat opens, and the cooling water begins to flow through the entire system. At 52°C, the thermostat valve is opened fully and the cooling water temperature is maintained at that level.

1-3 Piping
To simplify the cooling system piping and eliminate cracking of the brazed parts by vibration, rubber or vinyl hoses connected with hose clips are adapted for this engine.
Therefore, the following items must be checked when inspecting the cooling system:
(1) There must be no extreme bends in the piping.
(2) The cross section of the piping must not be changed by heavy objects on the piping.
(3) There must be no fractures or cracks which allow water leakage.
(4) Piping must not touch high temperature parts, and piping must be securely clamped.
(5) Hose clips must be securely tightened and there must be no leakage from the insertion sections.

2. Water Pump

2-1 Construction and operation

The water pump is a rubber impeller type pump driven from the crankshaft by a V-belt.
The rubber impeller, which has ample elasticity, is deformed by the offset plate inside the casing, causing the water to be discharged. This pump is ideal for small, high-speed engines.

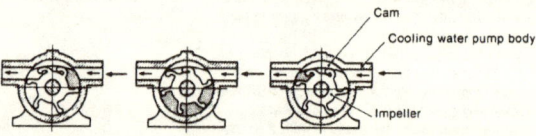

2-1.1 Cooling water pump (without bilge pump)

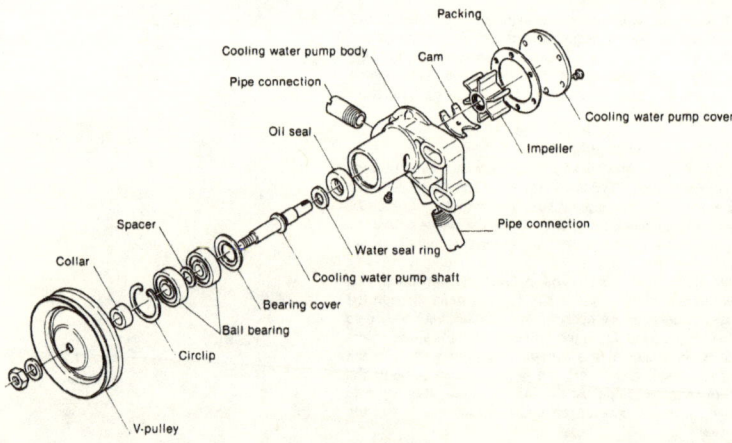

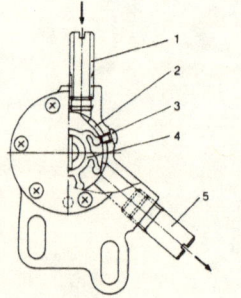
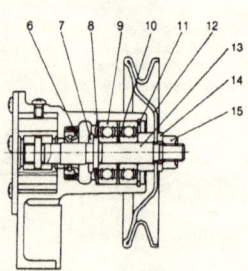

1. Pipe connection (inlet)
2. Cam
3. Set screw
4. Impeller
5. Pipe connection (outlet)
6. Oil seal
7. Water seal ring
8. Bearing cover
9. Ball bearing
10. Spacer
11. Circlip
12. V-pulley
13. Cooling water pump shaft
14. Washer
15. Nut

Chapter 7 Cooling System
2. Water Pump

2-1.2 Cooling water pump (with bilge pump)

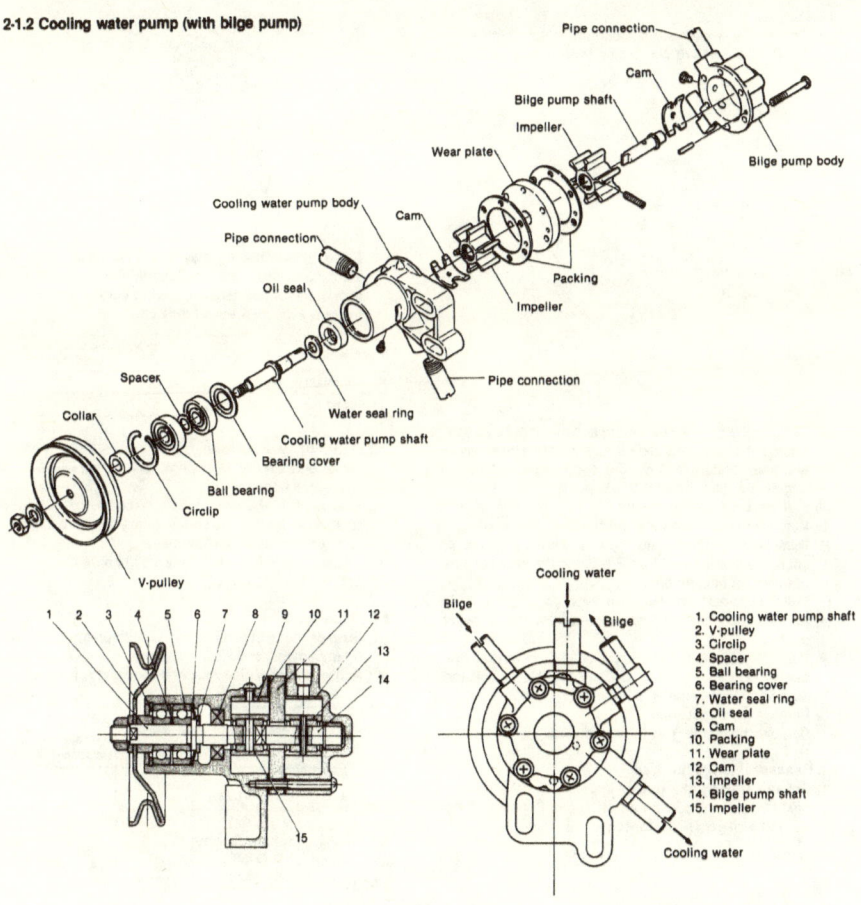

2-1.3 Specifications

m (in.)

	Water pump	Bilge pump
Rated speed	2000rpm	
Suction head	1 (39.37)	1 (39.37)
Total head	3 (118.11)	2 (78.74)
Delivery capacity	400 ℓ/hr.	150 ℓ/hr.

Chapter 7 Cooling System
2. Water Pump

2-2 Disassembly
(1) Loosen the water pump mounting bolts, remove the V-belt and remove the water pump ass'y from the cylinder.

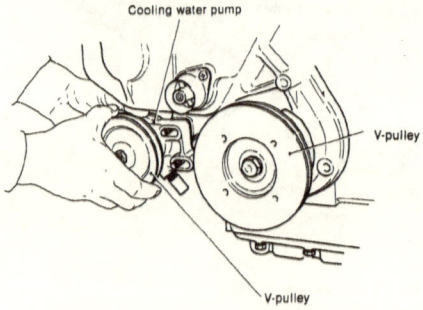

Cooling water pump
V-pulley
V-pulley

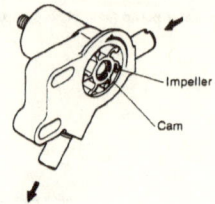

Impeller
Cam

(2) Remove the V-pulley mounting bolt and V-pulley.
(3) Loosen the set screw and remove the bilge pump ass'y and wear plate. (Remove the pump cover when the engine is not equipped with a bilge pump.)
(4) Pull the water pump impeller.
(5) Remove the set screw and remove the offset plate.
(6) Remove the bearing snap ring and remove the impeller shaft and bearing ass'y while tapping the impeller side of the impeller shaft lightly.
(7) Pull the oil seal from the pump body.
(8) Pull the ball bearing and spacer from the impeller shaft.
(9) Remove the impeller and impeller shaft from the bilge pump body as an ass'y. Loosen the set screw and disassemble the shaft and impeller.
(10) Remove the offset plate.
(11) Remove the bushing as far as required.

2-3 Reassembly precautions
(1) Before inserting the rubber impeller into the casing, coat the sliding face, pump shaft and impeller fitting section with grease or Monton X.

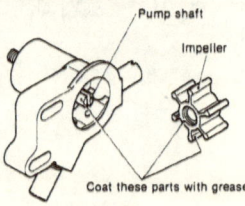

Pump shaft
Impeller
Coat these parts with grease

(2) Be sure that the direction of curving of the impeller is correct.
The impeller is curved in the direction opposite the direction of rotation.

(3) Adjust the V-belt tension.
Since pump bearing play and wear plate wear will increase rapidly if the V-belt is too tight, adjust the belt to the prescribed tension, paying careful attention to the operating direction of the belt.

V-belt tension	10 ~ 15mm (0.3937 ~ 0.5906 in.) deflection when pushed with finger	
Type of V-belt	HM23	
V-belt part No.	104514—77350	

2-4 Handling precautions
(1) Never operate the water pump dry as this will damage the rubber impeller.
(2) Always turn the engine in the correct direction of rotation as turning the engine in the opposite direction will damage the rubber impeller.
(3) Inspect the pump after every 1,500 hours of operation and replace if faulty.

2-5 Inspection
(1) Inspect the rubber impeller for fractures, cracks and other damage, and replace if faulty.
(2) Rubber impeller side wear and wear plate clearance.

mm(in.)

		Maintenance standard	Clearance at assembly	Maximum allowable clearance	Wear limit
Water pump	Impeller width	19±0.1 (0.744 ~ 0.752)			
	Housing width	18.9 (0.7441) (without packing) 19.2 (0.7559) (with packing)	0.2 (0.0079)	0.4 (0.0157)	
	Wear plate wear				0.2 (0.0079)
Bilge pump	Impeller width	19 ±0.1 (0.744 ~ 0.752)			
	Housing width	18.9 (0.7441) (without packing) 19.2 (0.7559) (with packing)	0.2 (0.0079)	0.4 (0.0157)	
	Wear plate wear				0.2 (0.0079)

Chapter 7 Cooling System
2. Water Pump

(3) Water pump impeller shaft oil seal section wear.

mm(in.)

	Maintenance standard	Wear limit
Oil seal section shaft diameter	10.0 (0.3937)	9.9 (0.3898)

(4) Inspect the bearing for play and check for seizing at the impeller shaft fitting section. Replace the bearing if there is any play.

(5) Bilge pump impeller shaft and bushing clearance measurement.

mm(in.)

		Maintenance standard	Clearance at assembly	Maximum allowable clearance
Wear plate	Impeller shaft outside diameter	9.5 (0.3740)	0.005 ~ 0.045 (0.0002 ~ 0.0018)	0.2 (0.0079)
	Bushing inside diameter	9.5 (0.3740)		
Bilge pump body	Impeller shaft outside diameter	9.5 (0.3740)	0.005 ~ 0.045 (0.002 ~ 0.0018)	0.2 (0.0079)
	Bushing inside diameter	9.5 (0.3740)		

3. Thermostat

3-1 Construction and operation
The thermostat remains closed until the cooling water temperature reaches a fixed temperature. When the cooling water reaches this fixed temperature, it collects at the cylinder head and the water flowing from the water pump is discharged through the bypass circuit. When the cooling water temperature exceeds a fixed temperature, the thermostat opens and the cooling water flows through the main circuit of the cylinder and cylinder head. The thermostat serves to prevent overcooling and improve combustion performance by maintaining the cooling water temperature at a specified level. The thermostat of this engine is installed at the exhaust manifold cooling water outlet.

(2) In general, inspect the thermostat after every 250 hours of operation. However, always inspect it when the cooling water temperature has risen abnormally and when white smoke is emitted for a long period of time after the engine starts.

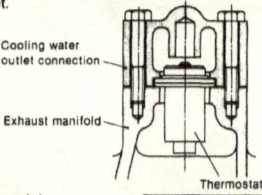

Thermostat operating temperature	Opening temperature	42±2°C
	Full open temperature	52±2°C

The cylinder → cylinder head → exhaust manifold cooling water is blocked by this thermostat and is not discharged from the exhaust manifold until it reaches 42 ±2°C. Therefore, the water sucked up by the water pump is discharged from the bypass circuit.
When the cooling water temperature exceeds 42° ±2°C, the thermostat opens and the cooling water begins to flow. At 52 ±2°C, the thermostat is fully opened and the cooling water system works at full capacity.

3-2 Inspection
(1) Remove the thermostat cover at the top of the exhaust manifold to remove and inspect the thermostat. Remove any dirt or foreign matter that has built up in the thermostat, and check the spring, etc. for damage and corrosion.

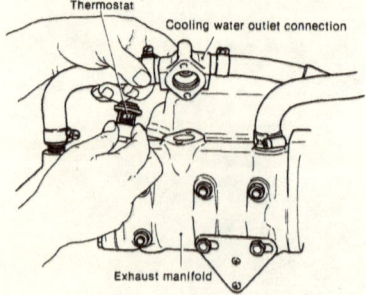

Chapter 7 Cooling System
4. Anticorrosion Zinc

4. Anticorrosion Zinc

4-1 Principles
Anticorrosion zinc is installed to prevent electrolytic corrosion by sea water.
When different metals, i.e., iron and copper, are placed in an highly conductive liquid, such as sea water, the iron gradually rusts. The anticorrosion zinc provides protection against corrosion by corroding in place of the cylinder, cylinder liners and other iron parts.
Anticorrosion zinc is provided at the cooling water cylinder inlet three-way coupling and at the cylinder head cover.

4-2 Inspection
Generally, replace the anticorrosion zinc after every 500 hours of operation. However, since this period depends on the properties of the sea water and operating conditions, periodically inspect the anticorrosion zinc and remove the oxidized film on its surface.
Replace the anticorrosion zinc after 50% corrosion.

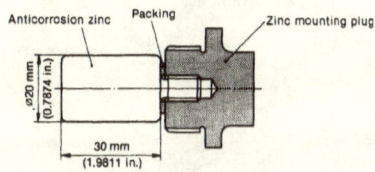

Replace the anticorrosion zinc by pulling the old zinc from the zinc mounting plug and screwing in the new zinc.

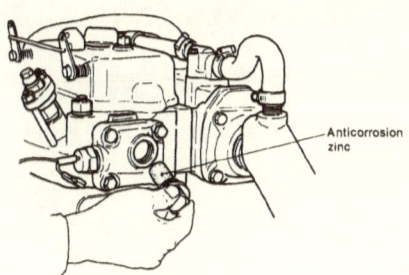

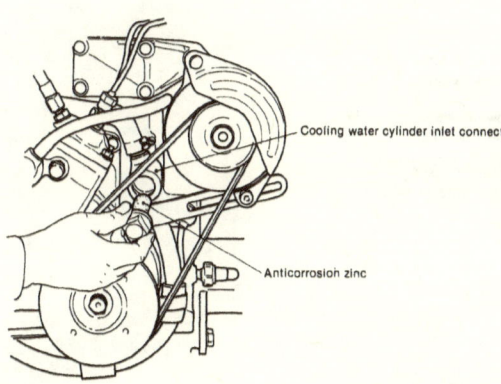

5. Kingston Cock

5-1 Construction
The Kingston cock, installed on the bottom of the hull, controls the intake of cooling water into the boat. The Kingston cock serves to filter the raw water so that mud, sand, and other foreign matter in the water does not enter the water pump.
Numerous holes are drilled in the raw water side of the Kingston cock, and a scoop strainer is installed to prevent sucking in of vinyl, etc.

5-3 Inspection
When the cooling water volume has dropped and the pump is normal, remove the vessel from the water and check for clogging of the Kingston cock.
Moreover, when water leaks from the cock, disassemble the cock and inspect it for wear, and repair or replace it.

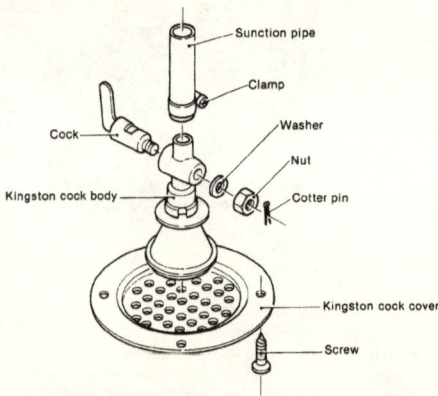

5-2 Handling precautions
Caution the user to always close the Kingston cock after each day of use and to confirm that it is open before beginning operation.
If the Kingston cock is left open, water will flow in reverse and the vessel will sink if trouble occurs with the water pump.
Moreover, if the engine is operated with the Kingston cock closed, the cooling water will not be able to come in, resulting in engine and pump trouble.

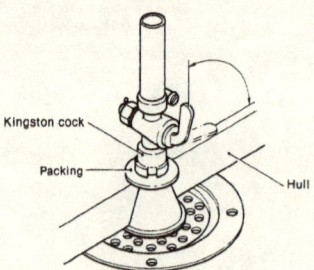

6. Bilge Strainer

6-1 Construction
Water collected in the bilge is sucked up and discharged to the outside of the vessel by the bilge pump. The bilge strainer serves to filter slagged oil, iron particles and other dirt mixed in the bilge. If the bilge strainer becomes clogged, the bilge pump will operate dry, reducing the durability of the impeller.

6-2 Inspection
Since the bilge strainer moves around the bilge and frequently becomes clogged with dirt and other foreign matter, periodically pull it from the bilge and wash it with clean water.

CHAPTER 8
REDUCTION AND REVERSING GEAR

1. Construction 8-1
2. Installation 8-5
3. Operation and Maintenance 8-6
4. Inspection and Servicing 8-7
5. Disassembly 8-12
6. Reassembly 8-16

1. Construction

1-1 Construction

The Kanzaki-Carl Hurth KBW10 reduction reversing gear was developed jointly by Kanzaki Precision Machine Co., Ltd., a subsidiary of Yanmar and one of Japan's leading gear manufacturers, and Carl Hurth Co.
The KBW10 consists of a multi-disc clutch and reduction gear housed in a single case. It is small, light, simply constructed and extremely reliable.
*The force required to shift between forward and reverse can be controlled by a cable type remote control system much smaller and simpler than other types of reduction reversing gears.
*The friction discs are durable sinter plates, and the surface of the steel plates are corrugated in a sine curve shape to ensure positive engagement and disengagement and minimum loss of transmission force.
*Because of the special construction of this gear, the optimum pressure is automatically applied to the clutch plate in direct proportion to the input shaft torque.

1-2 Specifications

Nomenclature			KBW10
Reduction system			One-stage reduction, helical gear
Reversing system			Constant mesh gear
Clutch			Wet type multi-disc, mechanically operated
Reduction ratio		Forward	2.14, 2.83
		Reverse	2.50, 2.50
Direction of rotation	Input shaft		Counterclockwise as viewed from stern
	Output shaft	Forward	Clockwise as viewed from stern
		Reverse	Counterclockwise as viewed from stern
Lubricating oil			ATF-A
Lubricating oil capacity			0.7ℓ
Dry weight			19kg (41.9lb.) (17kg (37.5lb.) without mounting feet)

8-1

Chapter 8 Reduction and Reversing Gear
1. Construction
_____SM/2QM15

1-3 Power transmission system

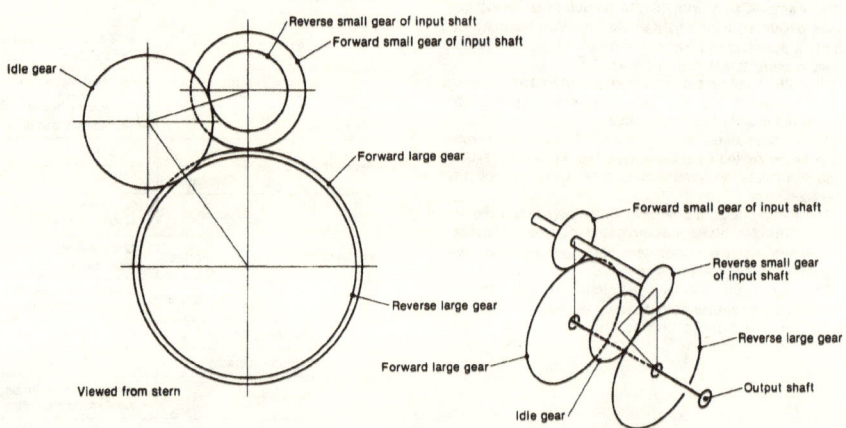

			(Reduction ratio)
Forward	Forward small gear of input shaft →	Forward large gear	
	Z = 22	Z = 47	i = 47/22 = 2.14
	Z = 18	Z = 51	i = 51/18 = 2.83
Reverse	Reverse small gear of input shaft →	Idle gear → Reverse large gear	
	Z = 18	Z = 25 Z = 45	i = 45/18 = 2.50

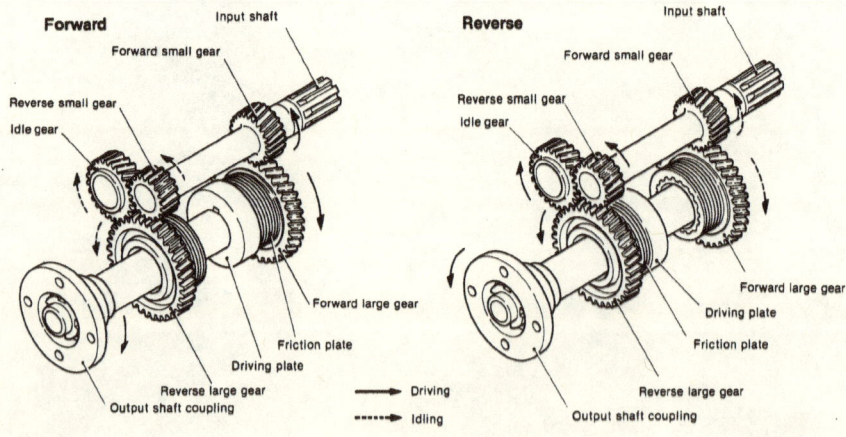

→ Driving
------> Idling

Chapter 8 Reduction and Reversing Gear
1. Construction

SM/2QM15

1-4 Drawing

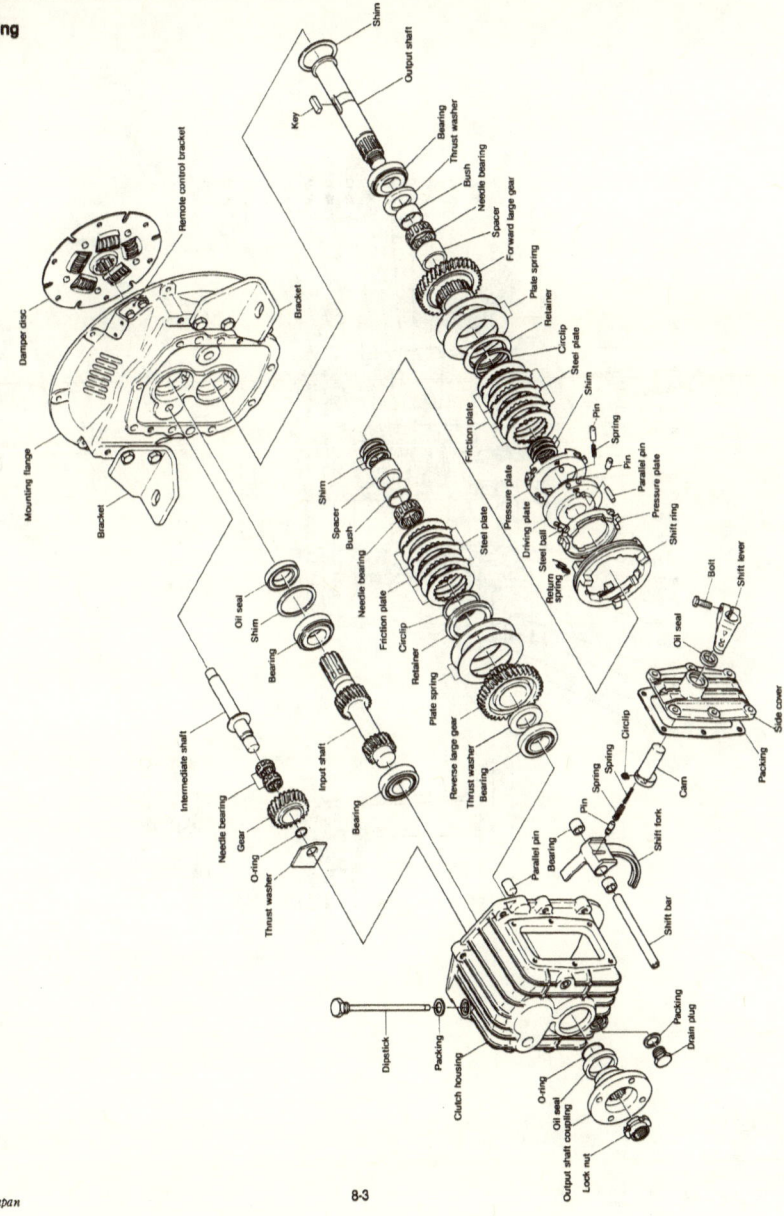

Chapter 8 Reduction and Reversing Gear
1. Construction

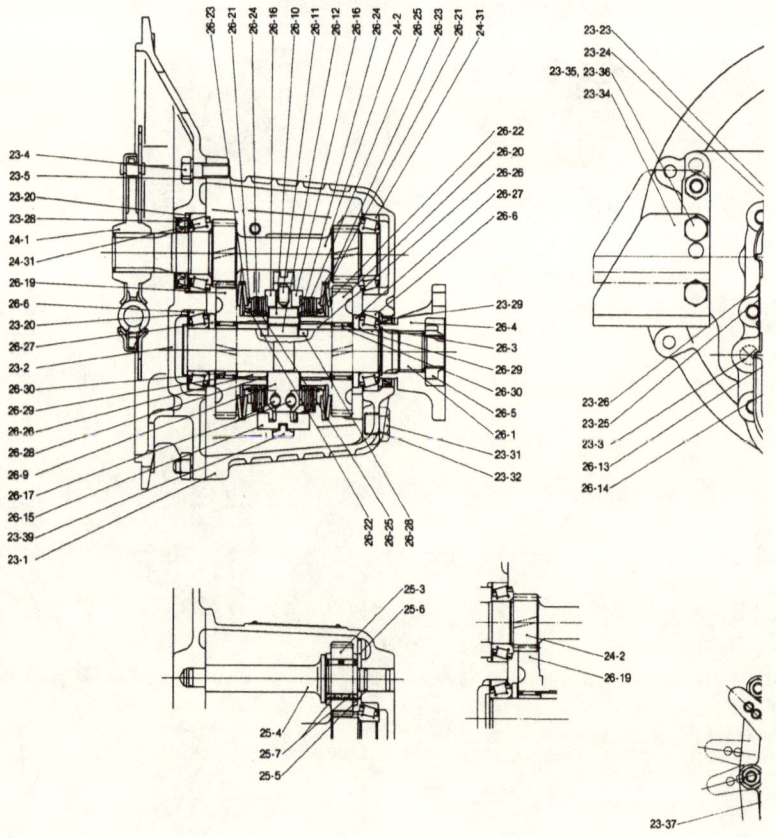

SM/2QM1

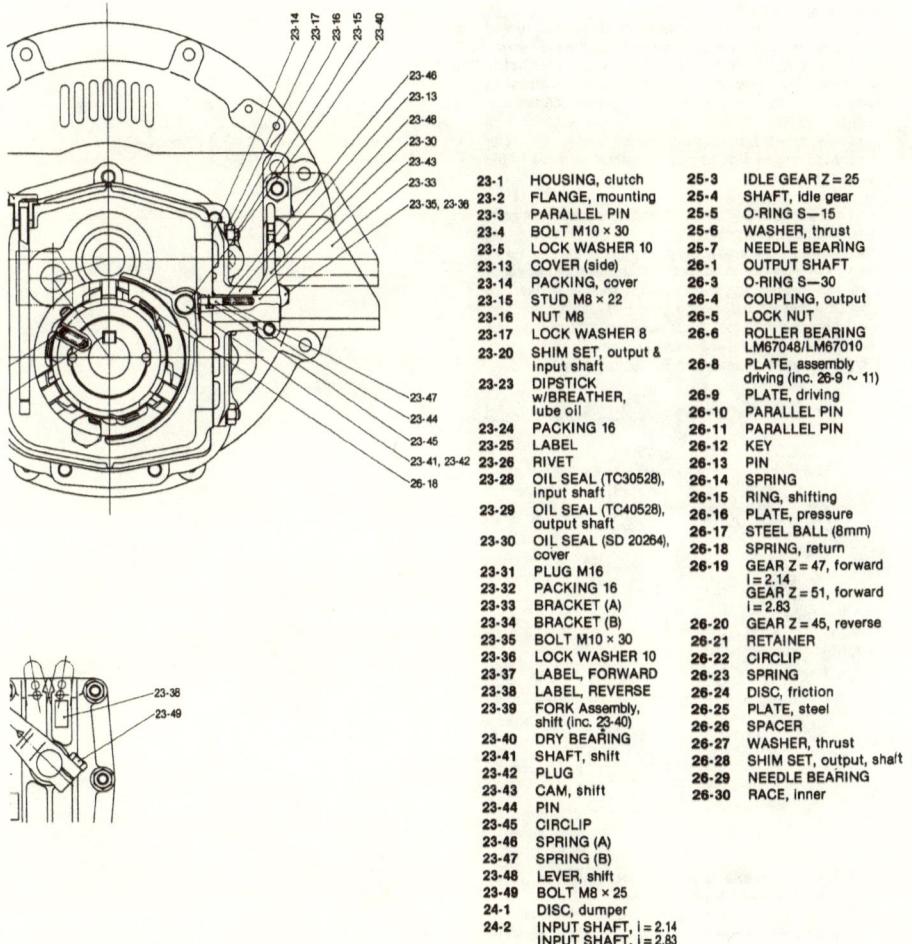

23-1	HOUSING, clutch	25-3	IDLE GEAR Z = 25
23-2	FLANGE, mounting	25-4	SHAFT, idle gear
23-3	PARALLEL PIN	25-5	O-RING S—15
23-4	BOLT M10 × 30	25-6	WASHER, thrust
23-5	LOCK WASHER 10	25-7	NEEDLE BEARING
23-13	COVER (side)	26-1	OUTPUT SHAFT
23-14	PACKING, cover	26-3	O-RING S—30
23-15	STUD M8 × 22	26-4	COUPLING, output
23-16	NUT M8	26-5	LOCK NUT
23-17	LOCK WASHER 8	26-6	ROLLER BEARING LM67048/LM67010
23-20	SHIM SET, output & input shaft	26-8	PLATE, assembly driving (inc. 26-9 ~ 11)
23-23	DIPSTICK w/BREATHER, lube oil	26-9	PLATE, driving
23-24	PACKING 16	26-10	PARALLEL PIN
23-25	LABEL	26-11	PARALLEL PIN
23-26	RIVET	26-12	KEY
23-28	OIL SEAL (TC30528), input shaft	26-13	PIN
		26-14	SPRING
23-29	OIL SEAL (TC40528), output shaft	26-15	RING, shifting
		26-16	PLATE, pressure
23-30	OIL SEAL (SD 20264), cover	26-17	STEEL BALL (8mm)
		26-18	SPRING, return
23-31	PLUG M16	26-19	GEAR Z = 47, forward i = 2.14
23-32	PACKING 16		GEAR Z = 51, forward i = 2.83
23-33	BRACKET (A)		
23-34	BRACKET (B)	26-20	GEAR Z = 45, reverse
23-35	BOLT M10 × 30	26-21	RETAINER
23-36	LOCK WASHER 10	26-22	CIRCLIP
23-37	LABEL, FORWARD	26-23	SPRING
23-38	LABEL, REVERSE	26-24	DISC, friction
23-39	FORK Assembly, shift (inc. 23-40)	26-25	PLATE, steel
		26-26	SPACER
23-40	DRY BEARING	26-27	WASHER, thrust
23-41	SHAFT, shift	26-28	SHIM SET, output, shaft
23-42	PLUG	26-29	NEEDLE BEARING
23-43	CAM, shift	26-30	RACE, inner
23-44	PIN		
23-45	CIRCLIP		
23-46	SPRING (A)		
23-47	SPRING (B)		
23-48	LEVER, shift		
23-49	BOLT M8 × 25		
24-1	DISC, dumper		
24-2	INPUT SHAFT, i = 2.14		
	INPUT SHAFT, i = 2.83		
24-31	ROLLER BEARING LM67048/LM67010		

Chapter 8 Reduction and Reversing Gear
2. Installation

2. Installation

2-1 Installation angle
During operation the angular inclination of the gearbox in the longitudinal direction must be less than 20° relative to the water line.

2-2 Remote control unit
This marine gearbox is designed for single lever control to permit reversing at full engine speed (e.g. to avoid danger, etc.). Normally, Morse or Teleflex single lever control is employed. During installation, make sure that the remote control lever and shift lever on the marine gearbox are coordinated. Shifting the lever toward the propeller side produces forward movement, while moving the lever toward the engine side causes the vessel to move in the reverse direction.
To connect the linkage, the operating cable must be positioned at right angles to the shift lever when the shift lever is in the neutral position.
The shift play, measured at the pivot point of the shift lever, must be at least 35mm to each side (reverse and forward) from the neutral position. Greater shift play has no adverse effect on the marine gearbox. After connecting the linkage, confirm that the remote control and the shift lever on the marine gearbox work properly.
A typical linkage arrangement is illustrated in the figure below.

When the cable is attached to the hole 52mm (2.0472in.) from the center of the rotation of the shift lever, these strokes must be 30mm (1.1811in.).

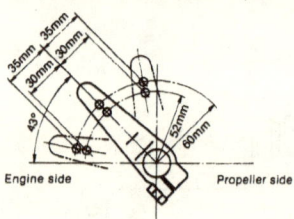

Engine side   Propeller side

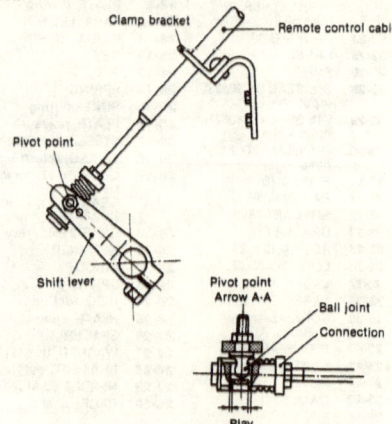

NOTE: Since the cable stroke may be insufficient, two holes are drilled in the shift lever.
When the cable is attached to the hole 60mm (2.3622in.) from the center of the rotation of the shift lever, the strokes from the center to the forward and reverse sides must both be 35mm (1.3780in.).

Chapter 8 Reduction and Reversing Gear
3. Operation and Maintenance

3. Operation and Maintenance

3-1 Lube oil

1) Oil level
The oil level should be checked each month and must be maintained between the groove and the end of the dipstick. The groove indicates the maximum oil level and the end of the dipstick is the minimum oil level. When checking the oil level with the dipstick, do not screw in the oil filler screw; it should rest on top of the oil filler hole.

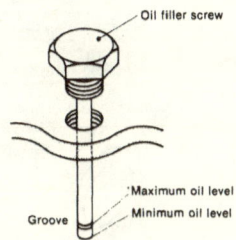

2) Oil change
Change the oil after the first 100 hours of operation, and every 300 hours of operation thereafter. When adding oil between oil changes, always use the same type of oil that is in the marine gearbox.

3) Recommended brands of lube oil

Supplier	Brand name
SHELL	SHELL DEXRON
CALTEX	TEXAMATIC FLUID (DEXRON)
ESSO	ESSO ATF
MOBIL	MOBIL ATF220
B.P. (British Petroleum)	B.P. AUTRAN DX

3-2 Precautions

Do not stop the shift lever halfway between the neutral and forward or reverse positions. The lever must be set to the neutral position or shifted into forward or reverse in a single motion.

3-3 Side cover

The internal shifting mechanism has been carefully aligned at the factory. Improper removal of the side cover can cause misalignment. If the side cover must be removed, proceed as follows:
—Before removing the cover, scribe alignment marks on the side cover and the case to facilitate accurate installation.
—When installing the side cover, put the shift lever in neutral so that the cam lobe on the shift lever engages the groove on the internal shift mechanism. When the cam lobe and groove are engaged properly there will be no clearance between the body and the side cover. Do not use packing or gaskets when installing the side cover.

—After making sure that the cam lobe and notches are aligned properly, securely tighten all the bolts. After tightening the bolts, move the lever back and forth. Positive contact should be felt and a click should be clearly audible as the gears shift; otherwise, the cam and notch are not properly engaged, and the cover must be loosened and readjusted until proper engagement is achieved.

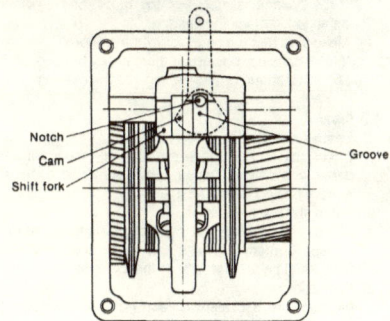

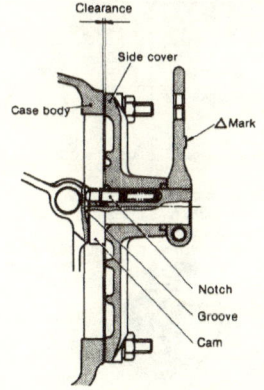

4. Inspection and Servicing

4-1 Clutch case
1) Check the clutch case with a test hammer for cracking. Perform a color check when required. If the case is cracked, replace it.
2) Check for staining on the inside surface of the bearing section.
   Also, measure the inside diameter of the case. Replace the case if it is worn beyond the wear limit.

4-2 Bearing
1) Rusting and damage
   If the bearing is rusted or the taper roller retainer is damaged, replace the bearing.
2) Make sure that the bearings rotate smoothly.
   If rotation is not smooth, if there is any binding, or if an abnormal sound is evident, replace the bearing.

4-3 Gear
1) Tooth surface wear
   Check the tooth surface for pitching, abnormal wear, dents, and cracks. Repair lightly damaged gears and replace heavily damaged gears.
2) Tooth surface contact
   Check the tooth surface contact. The amount of tooth surface contact between the tooth crest and tooth flank must be at least 70% of the tooth width.
3) Backlash
   Measure the backlash of each gear, and replace the gear when it is worn beyond the wear limit.

mm (in.)

	Maintenance standard	Wear limit
Input shaft forward gear and output shaft forward gear	0.1 ~ 0.2 (0.0040 ~ 0.0079)	0.3 (0.0118)
Input shaft reverse gear and intermediate gear	0.1 ~ 0.2 (0.0040 ~ 0.0079)	0.3 (0.0118)
Intermediate gear and output shaft reverse gear	0.1 ~ 0.2 (0.0040 ~ 0.0079)	0.3 (0.0118)

4) Forward/reverse gear spline
   (1) Check the spline for damage and cracking.
   (2) Step wear of spline
      Step wear depth limit: 0.1mm (0.0040in.)

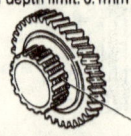
Step wear of spline

5) Forward/reverse gear needle bearing
   When an abnormal sound is produced at the needle bearing, visually inspect the rollers; replace the bearing if the rollers are faulty.

Rollers

4-4 Steel plate
1) Burning, scratching, cracking
   Replace any steel plates that are discolored or cracked.
2) Measurement of warping

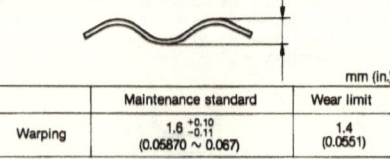

mm (in.)

	Maintenance standard	Wear limit
Warping	1.6 +0.10 −0.11 (0.05870 ~ 0.067)	1.4 (0.0551)

3) Steel plate pawl width measurement

Pawl

Measure the width of the steel plate pawl and the width of the pressure plate; replace the plate when the clearance exceeds the wear limit.

Steel plate width
Wear must be under 0.2mm (0.0079 in.)

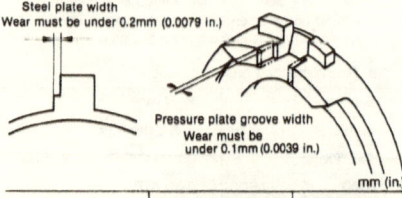

Pressure plate groove width
Wear must be under 0.1mm (0.0039 in.)

mm (in.)

	Maintenance standard	Wear limit
Steel plate width	12 0 −0.2 (0.4646 ~ 0.4724)	Worn 0.2 (0.0079)
Pressure plate groove	12 +0.1 0 (0.4724 ~ 0.4764)	Worn 0.1 (0.0039)
Clearance	0 ~ 0.3 (0 ~ 0.0118)	0.3 ~ 0.6 (0.0118 ~ 0.0236)

4-5 Friction plate

1) Check the friction plate for burning, scoring, or cracking.
   Repair the plate when the damage is light and replace the plate if the damage is heavy.
2) Friction surface wear
   Measure the thickness of the friction plate, and replace the plate when it is worn beyond the wear limit.

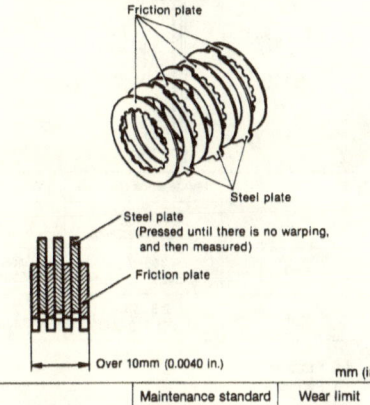

	Maintenance standard	Wear limit
Friction plate thickness	$1.7 ^{\ 0}_{-0.05}$ (0.0650 ~ 0.0670)	1.5 (0.0591)

mm (in.)

The assembled friction plate and steel plate dimensions must be over 10mm (0.0040in.).

Both sides of the friction plate have a 0.35mm copper sintered layer. Replace the friction plate when this layer is worn more than 0.2mm on one side (standard thickness $1.7 ^{\ 0}_{-0.05}$ mm). However, the sum of the wear of the four friction plates must not exceed 0.8mm. When this value is exceeded, replace all friction plates. In unavoidable circumstances, it is permissible to replace only the friction plate with the greatest amount of wear.

3) Friction plate and gear spline back clearance
   Measure the clearance between the friction plate spline collar and the output shaft gear spline, and replace the plate or spline when they are worn beyond the wear limit.

mm (in.)

	Maintenance standard	Wear limit
Standard backlash	0.20 ~ 0.61 (0.0079 ~ 0.0240)	0.9 (0.0354)

4-6 Pressure plate

1) Steel ball groove
   Check the steel ball groove for stains and wear.
   Replace the pressure plate if the groove is noticeably worn.
2) Friction plate contact surface
   Check the contact face for stains and damage.
3) Shifting plate contact surface
4) Parts wear measurement

mm (in.)

	Maintenance standard	Wear limit
Thickness: t	$6.6 ^{\ 0}_{-0.2}$ (0.2520 ~ 0.2598)	6.3 (0.2480)

6) Return spring permanent strain.
   Make sure the length (free length) is within the values specified in the figure.

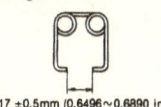

17 ±0.5mm (0.6496~0.6890 in.)

Chapter 8 Reduction and Reversing Gear
4. Inspection and Servicing
_____ SM/2QM15

4-7 Driving plate

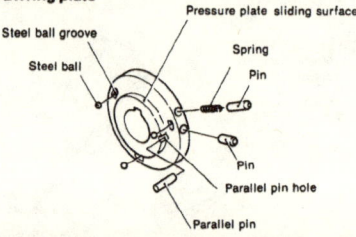

1) Check the key groove for scoring and cracking, and the output shaft fitting section for burning. Repair if the damage is light and replace the driving plate if the damage is heavy.
2) Outside diameter of pressure plate sliding part; others

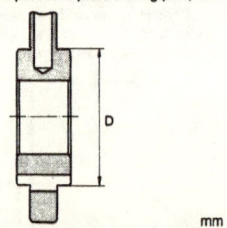

mm (in.)

	Maintenance standard	Wear limit
Outside diameter: D	⌀59 $^{-0.060}_{-0.134}$ (2.3176 ~ 2.3205)	⌀58.8 (2.3150)

3) Steel ball groove wear and stains.
4) Determine the amount of wear and play of both the axial and circumferential direction pins.
5) Spring permanent strain.

mm (in.)

	Maintenance standard	Wear limit
Spring free length	32.85 (1.2933)	32 (1.2598)

6) Pin end wear.

4-8 Retainer

1) Check for stains and damage on the friction plate contact surface.
2) Check for wear and cracking on the plate spring contact surface.
3) Measurement of dimensions

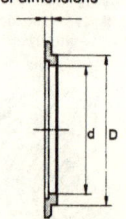

mm (in.)

	Maintenance standard	Wear limit
d	⌀57.5 $^{+0.106}_{+0.060}$ (2.2661 ~ 2.2680)	⌀57.8 (2.2756)
D	⌀66 $^{0}_{-0.1}$ (2.5945 ~ 2.5984)	⌀65.7 (2.5866)
t	2.8 $^{0}_{-0.08}$ (0.1071 ~ 0.1102)	2.6 (0.1024)

4-9 Plate spring
1) Permanent strain

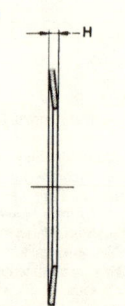

mm (in.)

	Maintenance standard	Wear limit
H: when plate spring is free	6.25 ±0.1 (0.2421 ~ 0.2500)	6.0 (0.2362)

4-10 Thrust collar
The gear side of the thrust washer has a 0.3mm copper sintered layer. Replace the thrust collar when the thickness is less than 4.75mm (standard thickness: 5 $^{0}_{-0.1}$ mm).

Chapter 8 Reduction and Reversing Gear
4. Inspection and Servicing
SM/2QM15

4-11 Shift ring

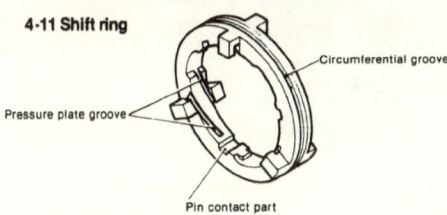

1) Circumferential groove wear.

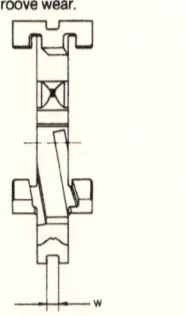

	Maintenance standard	Wear limit
Shifting groove: w	$6^{+0.1}_{0}$ (0.2362 ~ 0.2402)	6.3 (0.2480)

mm (in.)

2) Pressure plate groove wear.
   Whenever uneven wear and/or scratches are found, replace with a new part.
3) Parallel pin contact part wear.
   Whenever uneven wear and/or scratches are found, replace with a new part.

4-12 Shift fork and shift lever

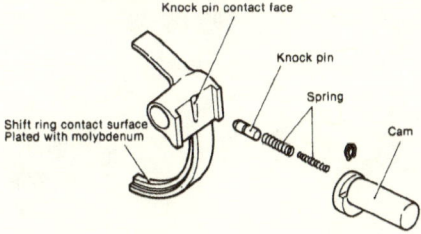

1) End wear.
   The shift ring contact surface of the shift fork is plated with molybdenum (thickness: 0.04—0.05mm). If this plating is peeled or worn to such an extent that the base metal of the shift fork is exposed, replace the shift fork.
2) Cam surface wear and stains.
   Whenever uneven wear and/or scratches are found, replace with a new part.
3) Pin part play.
   Whenever uneven wear and/or scratches are found, replace with a new part.
4) Notch end wear.
   Whenever uneven wear and/or scratches are found, replace with a new part.

4-13 Output shaft

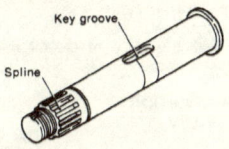

1) Key groove.
   Whenever uneven cracks and/or stains are found, replace with a new part.

4-14 Damper disc

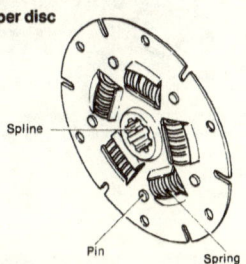

1) Spline part
   Whenever uneven wear and/or scratches are found, replace with a new part.
2) Spring.
   Whenever uneven wear and/or scratches are found, replace with a new part.
3) Pin wear.
   Whenever uneven wear and/or scratches are found, replace with a new part.

4-15 Input shaft

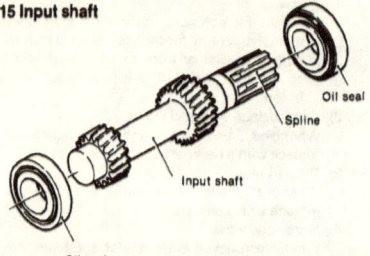

1) Spline part
   Whenever uneven wear and/or scratches are found, replace with a new part.
2) Surface of oil seal.
   If the sealing surface of the oil seal is worn or scratched, replace.

4-16 Intermediate shaft

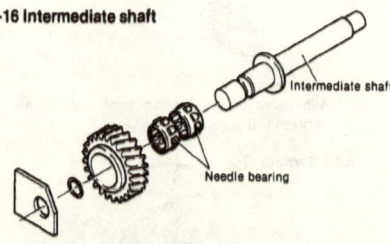

1) Needle bearing dimensions, staining.
   Check the surface of the roller to see whether the needle bearing sticks or is damaged. Replace if necessary.

5. Disassembly

5-1 Disassembling the clutch and accessories
1) Remove the drain plug and packing, and drain the oil from the clutch.
2) Uncaulk the output shaft lock nut, and remove the nut using a disassembly tool.

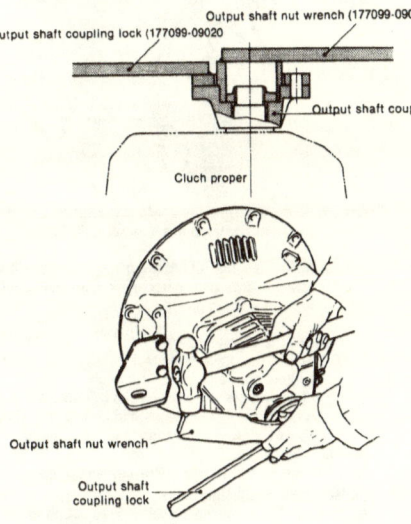

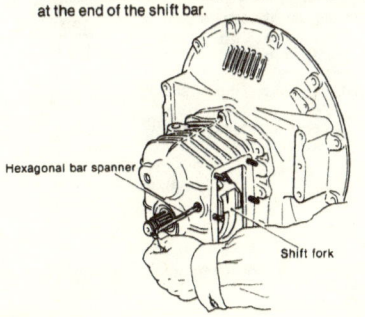

3) Remove the output coupling.
4) Remove the dipstick and packing.
5) Remove the case cover M8 nut super lock washer; remove the case cover, with the operating lever, shift cam, etc. in position.
6) Remove the shift bar plug with a hexagonal bar spanner (width across flats: 8mm (0.0394in.), and pull the shift bar from the case, using the M10 pulling bolt at the end of the shift bar.

7) Remove the shift fork.

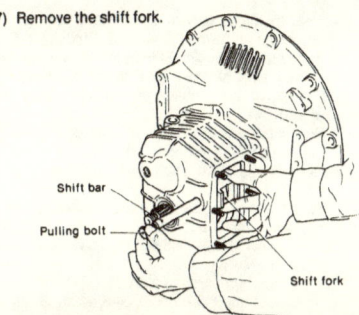

8) Remove the M10 bolt and super lock washer on the mounting flange.
9) Screw the M10 bolt into the M10 pulling bolt hole of the mounting flange, and remove the mounting flange. Do not remove the parallel pin.

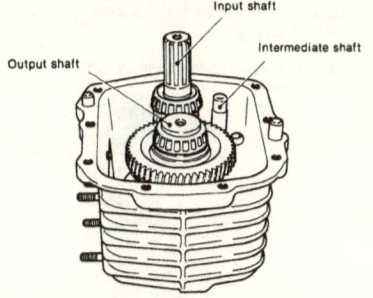

10) Remove the output shaft, intermediate shaft, and input shaft from the case, in that order.

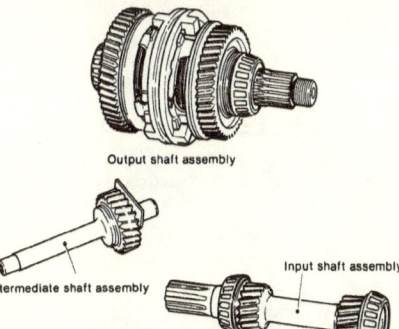

Chapter 8 Reduction and Reversing Gear
5. Disassembly
SM/2QM15

11) Heat the case body to about 100°C and remove the outer race of the input shaft and output shaft bearings. If the outer races are difficult to remove, tap them out with a plastic hammer from the rear of the case, or pull them by using the pulling groove in the case at the rear of the races.
12) Remove the outer race of the bearing from the mounting flange as described in step (11) above.
13) Remove the input shaft and output shaft adjusting plates.
NOTE: If the following parts are not replaced, the adjusting plates may be reused without readjustment. However, if even one part is replaced, readjustment is necessary.
  Input shaft part : 24-2, 24-31
  Output shaft part : 26-6, 26-9, 26-26, 26-27, 26-28, 26-30
14) Pull the oil seal from the case.
15) Pull the oil seal from the mounting flange.

5-2 Disassembling the input shaft
1) Pull the bearing from the input shaft.
NOTE: Do not disassemble unless the input shaft parts are damaged.

5-3 Disassembling the output shaft
1) Remove the O-ring.

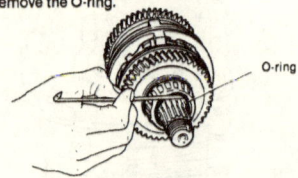
O-ring

2) Remove the output shaft by pressing the threaded end of the output shaft with a press, or tapping it with a hammer.

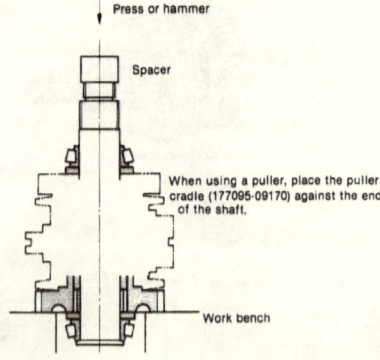
Press or hammer
Spacer
When using a puller, place the puller cradle (177095-09170) against the end of the shaft.
Work bench

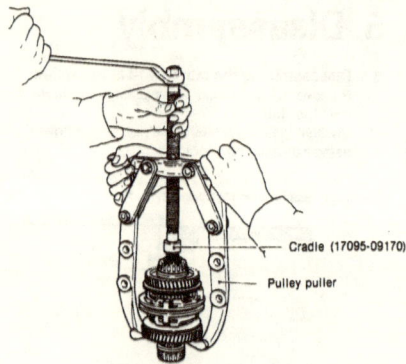
Cradle (17095-09170)
Pulley puller

NOTE 1: When removing the shaft, place spacers between the shaft and the press to prevent damage.

NOTE 2: Make sure that the forward large gear parts and reverse large gear parts are not mixed together once they are removed.

3) Remove the adjusting plate.
NOTE: Record the thickness of the adjusting plate to facilitate reassembly.
If the parts are not replaced, the adjusting plate may be reused without readjustment. However, if even one part is replaced, readjustment is required.
4) Remove the key.
To facilitate removal, clamp the key with a vice.
5) Remove the adjusting plate.
NOTE: Record the thickness of the adjusting plate to facilitate reassembly.
If the parts are not replaced, the adjusting plate may be reused without adjustment. However, if even one part is replaced, readjustment is required.
6) Remove the spacer and needle bearing.
7) Cover the outer race of the forward bearing, and pull out the output shaft about 10mm (0.3937in.) by pressing the threaded end of the output shaft with a press, or tapping it with a hammer.
NOTE: Do not pull it out more than 10mm (0.3937in.); otherwise damage may result.

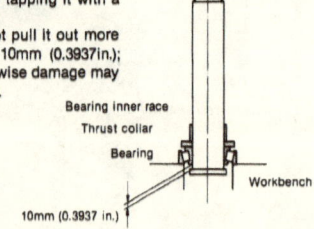
Press or hammer
Spacer
Bearing inner race
Thrust collar
Bearing
Workbench
10mm (0.3937 in.)

Chapter 8 Reduction and Reversing Gear
5. Disassembly

8) Insert the disassembly tool between the collar of the output shaft and the bearing; next remove the bearing inner race, thrust collar, and bearing from the output shaft with a press or hammer.

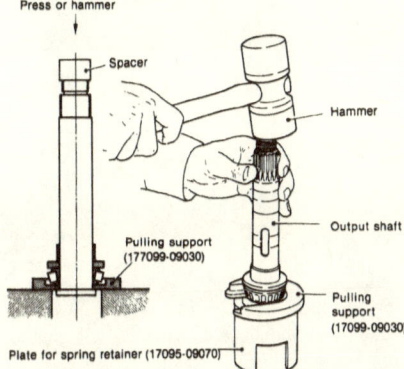

9) Remove the friction plates and steel plates from the forward large gear.
10) Using a disassembly tool, compress the plate spring and remove the circlip from the forward large gear.

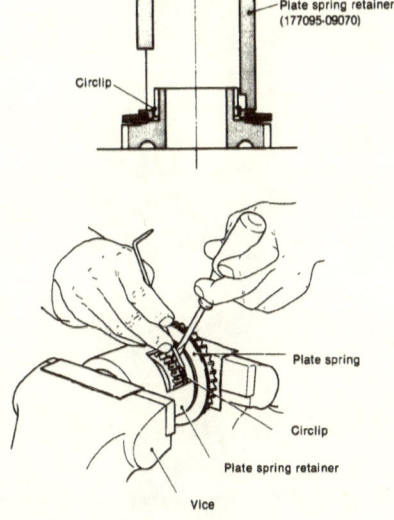

11) Remove the retainer and plate spring.
12) Remove the parts from the reverse large gear as described in steps (9)—(11) above.
13) Remove the pressure plate return spring; remove the pressure plate and steel ball.

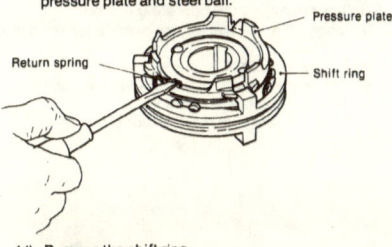

14) Remove the shift ring.
To disassemble, remove the three knock pins. When disassembling the shift ring, cover it with a cloth to prevent missing.
15) Remove the knock pin and spring from the driving plate.

5-4 Disassembling the intermediate shaft
1) Place a spacer against the case side end of the intermediate shaft and remove the shaft from the case by tapping the spacer with a hammer.

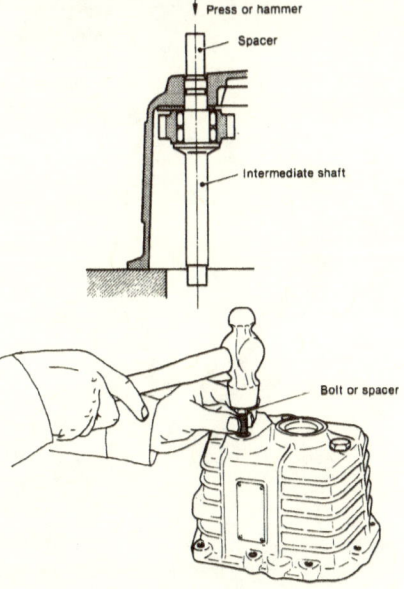

Chapter 8 Reduction and Reversing Gear
5. Disassembly
_____ SM/2QM15

2) Remove the O-ring.
3) Remove the idle gear, needle bearing, and thrust washer.

5-5 Disassembling the operating system
1) Loosen the M8 bolt of the shift lever; remove the shift lever.
2) Pull the shift cam.
3) Push in the knock pin and remove the circlip.
4) Remove the knock pin and spring.
5) Pull the oil seal from the case side cover.

Chapter 8 Reduction and Reversing Gear
6. Reassembly
_____SM/2QM15

6. Reassembly

6-1 Reassembly precautions
1) Before reassembling, clean all parts in washing oil, and replace any damaged or worn parts.
   Remove non-dry packing agent from the mating surface with a blunt knife.
2) Pack the oil seal and O-ring parts with grease.
3) Coat the mating surfaces of the case with wet packing.

6-2 Reassembling the output shaft
1) Reassembling forward large gear and plate spring
   (1) Insert the two plate springs of the forward large gear so that their large diameter sides are opposite each other.
   (2) Insert the retainer and install the circlip.
   (3) Compress the plate spring, using the disassembly tool, and snap the circlip into the groove on the outside of the spline of the forward large gear.

Press [approx. 1 metric ton (2200 lb)]

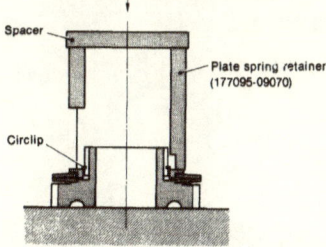

2) Reassemble the reverse large gear and plate spring, retainer, and circlip as described in step (1) above.
3) Determining the forward adjusting plate thickness

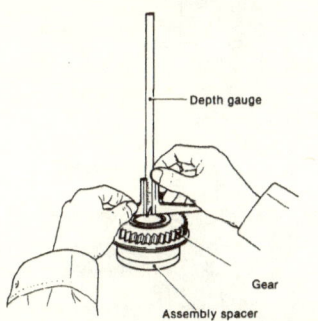

NOTE: As mentioned in section 5-3 (5) if no parts need to be replaced, the adjusting plate can be reused without adjustment.

(1) Position the assembled large gear on the assembly tool so that the spline part is on the bottom; insert the spacer and bearing inner race into the gear.

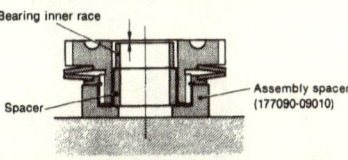

(2) Adjust the thickness of the adjusting plate until it conforms with the dimension shown in the figure.
(3) Two adjustment plates of 0.5mm (0.0197in.) and 0.3mm (0.0118in.) are available.
   Combine these plates to obtain the "t" dimension.
4) Determine the thickness of the reverse adjusting plate by following the procedure described in step(3)above.
5) First, insert a friction plate into the spline part of the forward large gear; next insert steel plates and friction plates alternately. Finally, insert a friction plate (four friction plates and three steel plates).
6) Insert the friction plates and steel plates into the spline part of the reverse large gear in the same manner as described in step (5) above (four friction plates and three steel plates).
7) Press the inner race of the bearing onto the output shaft up to the collar, using an assembly tool.
   NOTE: The inner race can be installed easily by preheating it to approximately 100°C.

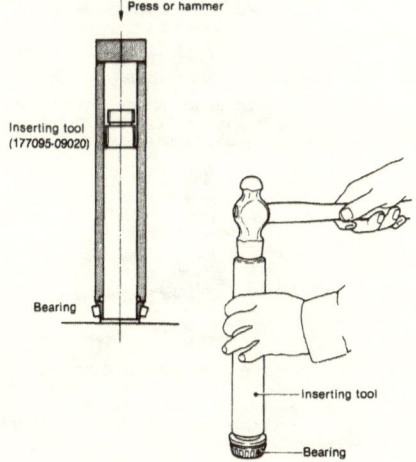

8-16

Chapter 8 Reduction and Reversing Gear
6. Reassembly

8) Insert the thrust collar, with the sintered surface (brown surface) facing the gear side.
9) Press the bearing inner race onto the output shaft, using an assembly tool.

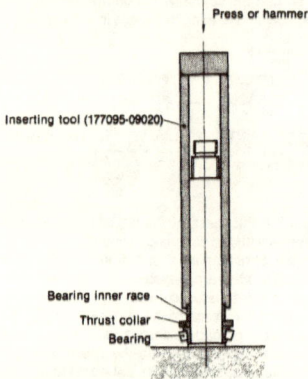

16) Insert the drive plate into the output shaft so that the side with the identification groove faces the forward large gear side.

   NOTE: Make sure that the three steel balls are in the three grooves of the driving plate.
   At the same time, make sure that the pin for the driving plate fits into the groove of the torque limiter for the pressure plate.

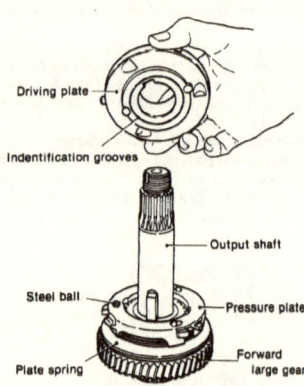

10) Insert the needle bearing.
11) Insert the spacer and adjusting plate.
12) Fit the key so that the fillet side is facing the threaded part of the output shaft.

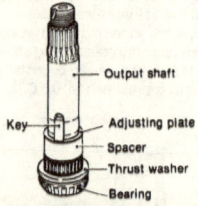

13) Insert the forward large gear, together with the friction plates and steel plates. At this time, align the three pawls on the outside of the steel plates.

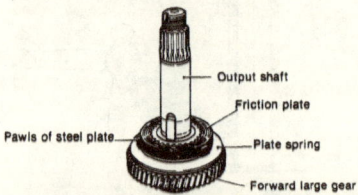

14) Cover the friction plates and steel plates with the pressure plate so that the pawls of the steel plate fit into the three notches on the pressure plate.
15) Insert the three steel balls into the three grooves in the pressure plate.

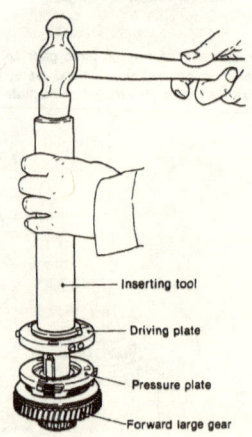

Chapter 8 Reduction and Reversing Gear
6. Reassembly
_____SM/2QM15

17) Insert the adjusting plate and spacer.
18) Press the bearing inner race, using an assembly tool.

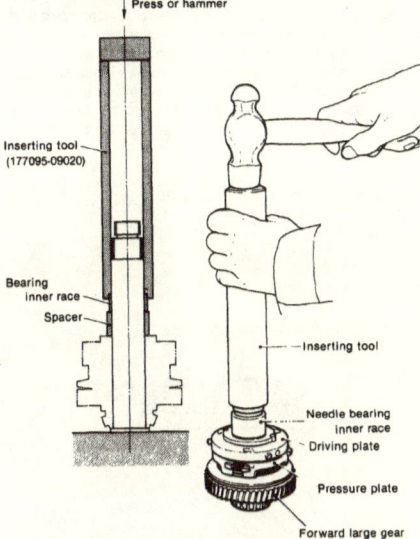

21) Insert the three steel balls into the three grooves in the driving plate.
22) Place the pressure plate onto the driving plate so that the steel balls enter the three grooves of the pressure plate.
23) Insert the three pressure plate return springs between the shift ring and the driving plate, and attach them to the small holes in the side of the pressure plate.
24) Insert the reverse large gear [see step (6)] so that the three pawls of the steel plates enter the notches around the circumference of the pressure plate.
25) Insert the needle bearing.
26) Insert the thrust washer so that the sintered side (brown side) faces the gear side.
27) Press the inner race of the bearing, using an assembly tool. At this time, make sure that the direction of the bearing is correct.

NOTE: The bearing inner race can be installed easily by preheating it to approximately 100°C.

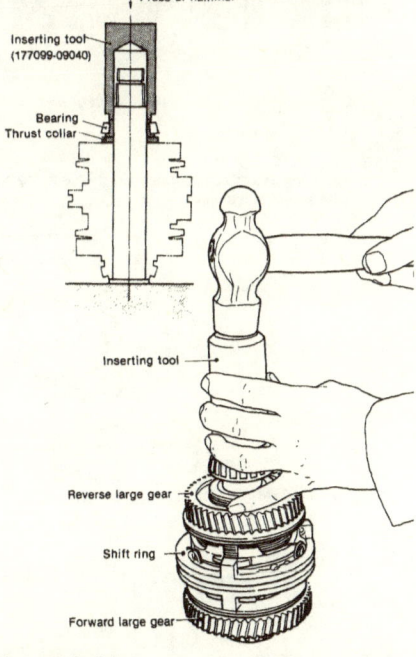

19) Insert the knock pins and springs into the three holes around the circumference of the driving plate.
20) Cover the driving plate with the shift ring so that the side with the identification groove faces the forward large gear side; install the ring so that the knock pins are pushed in.

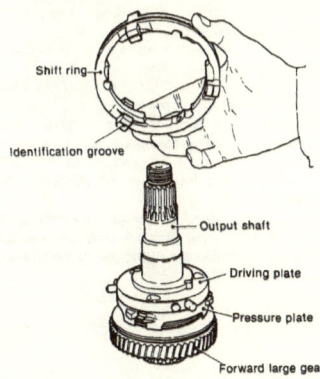

28) Insert the O-ring.
29) With the shift ring in the reverse position, check the forward large gear to make sure it rotates smoothly. Next, with the shift ring in the forward position, check the reverse large gear to make sure it rotates smoothly.

8-18

Printed in Japan
2F015A

Chapter 8 Reduction and Reversing Gear
6. Reassembly

6-3 Reassembling the input shaft
1) Press the inner race of the bearing onto the input shaft. At this time, make sure that the direction of the bearing is correct.

NOTE: The bearing inner race can be easily installed by preheating it to approximately 100°C.

6-4 Reassembling the intermediate shaft
NOTE: Assemble the intermediate shaft as described in section 6-5 (5).

1) Insert the needle bearing and idle gear on the intermediate shaft. Then insert the thrust washer.

NOTE: Pay careful attention to the assembly direction of the thrust washer.

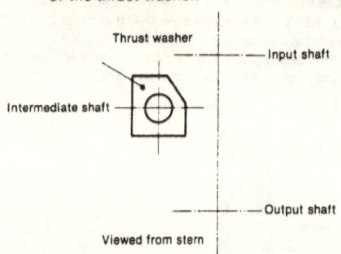

2) Insert the O-ring.
3) Press the assembled intermediate shaft into the case with a press or hammer.

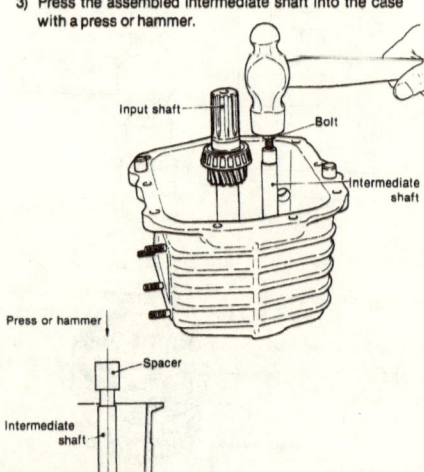

4) Make sure that the idle gear rotates smoothly.

6-5 Installing the input shaft and output shaft
1) Determining the thickness of the input shaft adjusting plate and output shaft adjusting plate

NOTE: As mentioned in section 5-1 (13), when none of the parts are replaced, the adjusting plate can be reused without readjustment.

(1) Measure length "A" "D" between the cases of each shaft of the case body and mounting flange.
(2) Cover each bearing with the bearing outer race, and measure length "B" "C" between the bearings.

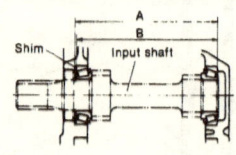

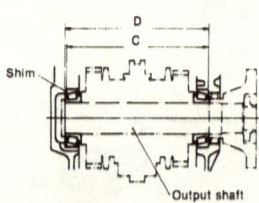

(3) Adjust the input shaft adjusting plate thickness so that the clearance or tightening allowance is less than 0.05mm (0.0020in.).
(4) Adjust the output shaft adjusting plate thickness so that the tightening allowance is within 0 ~ 0.1mm (0~0.0040in.).
(5) Four adjusting plates of 1mm (0.0394in.), 0.5mm (0.0197in.), 0.3mm (0.0118in.) and 0.1mm (0.0040in.) are available.
Combine these plates to obtain the desired adjusting plate measurement.

2) Insert the adjusting plate into the mounting flange, and press the outer race of the bearing.
Also, press the outer race of the bearing into the case.

NOTE: The outer race can be installed easily by heating the mounting flange and case to approximately 100°C, or by cooling the bearing outer race with liquid nitrogen, etc.

3) Coat the circumference of the oil seal with a non-dry packing agent, and press it onto the mounting flange and case so that the spring part of the oil seal is inside the case.

Chapter 8 Reduction and Reversing Gear
6. Reassembly

4) Coat the mating surfaces of the mounting flange and case with a non-dry packing agent.
Wipe off oil and dirt on the mating surface of the case and coat with a thin film of non-dry packing agent.

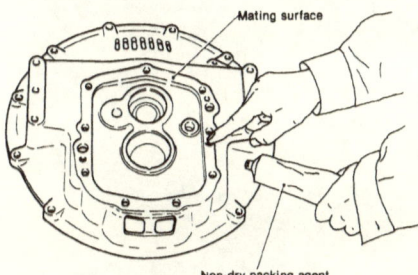

Mating surface

Non-dry packing agent

5) Insert the input shaft into the case, assemble the intermediate shaft as described in section 6-4 and then insert the output shaft into the case.
6) Align the mounting flange with the case, and insert the parallel pin by tapping the mounting flange with a plastic hammer.
7) Insert the super lock washer and tighten the M10 bolt.
8) Install the dipstick and packing.
9) Install the drain plug and packing.

6-6 Reassembling and installing the operating system

1) Insert the shift fork into the case from the side, insert the shift bar.

NOTE: Insert the shift bar with the threaded end towards the outside (output shaft coupling side).

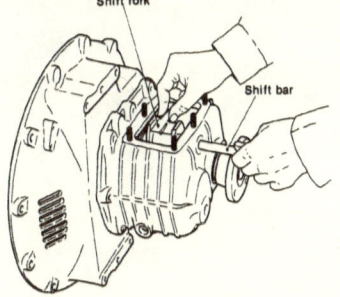

Shift fork

Shift bar

2) Coat the threaded part of the shift bar plug with a non-dry packing agent and secure it to the case with a hexagonal bar spanner (width across flats: 8mm (0.3150in.).

NOTE: Put the shift fork into neutral before installing.

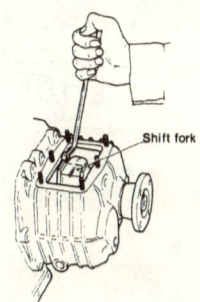

Shift fork

3) Coat the circumference of the oil seal with a non-dry packing agent and press the seal to the case cover.
4) Insert the spring into the shift cam.
5) Insert the knock pin into the shift cam from the front end, and lock with the circlip.
6) Insert the assembled shift cam into the case cover.
7) Fit the shift lever to the shift cam, and tighten the M8 bolt.

NOTE: The shift cam must rotate smoothly.

8) Replace the packing if it is damaged.
9) Attach the case side cover together with the operating system to the case body.
At this time, make sure that the shift cam is fitted to the shift fork, and that the shift lever is in neutral.

NOTE: Put the shift fork into neutral before installing.

10) Insert the super lock washer, and tighten the M8 nut.
11) Shift the shift lever to forward and reverse to make sure that the lever operates normally.
If the lever does not operate normally, loosen the M8 nut, slide the case side cover forward, backward, and to the left and right, then re-tighten with the M8 nut in the position at which the lever operates normally.

NOTE: If the lever operates normally a click will be heard when it is put into forward and reverse.

Chapter 8 Reduction and Reversing Gear
6. Reassembly

6-7 Installing the output shaft coupling
1) Install the output shaft coupling to the output shaft.
2) Tighten and caulk the output shaft lock nut, using the assembly tool.
   Tightening torque......... 9.5kg-m (687.1ft-lb)

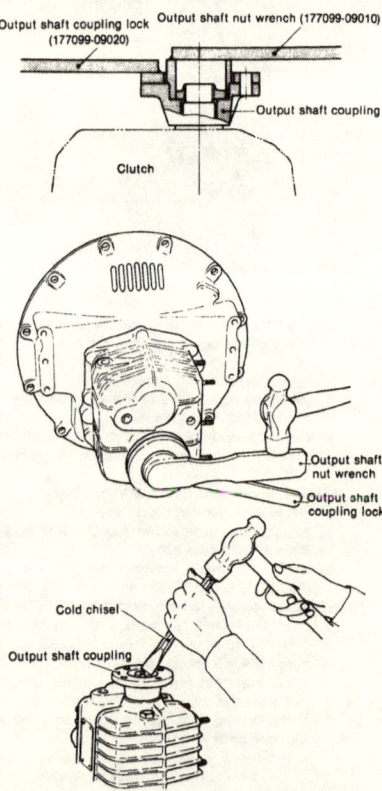

3) Shift the shift lever to the neutral position and make sure the clutch engages when the shift lever is put into forward and reverse.
   The input/output shafts will not rotate smoothly if the side gap of the bearing is too small in relation to the thickness of the adjusting plate.

CHAPTER 9
REMOTE CONTROL SYSTEM

1. Construction... 9-1
2. Clutch Regulator One-Handle Remote Control... 9-2
3. Decompression Remote Control... 9-4
4. Engine Stop Remote Control... 9-5

Chapter 9 Remote Control System
1. Construction

SM/2QM15

1. Construction

This engine is designed primarily for remote control operation. A remote control cable bracket can be installed by merely adding a remote control lever and link to the engine. Engine stop control and decompression remote control may also be installed, in addition to one-handle remote control, which permits engine speed adjustment and one-handle forward-astern switching.
For this engine, two-handle control cannot be used to replace one-handle control.

Clutch regulator remote control stand
Morse one-handle MT2

Decompression remote control cable

Engine stop remote control cable

Chapter 9 Remote Control System
2. Clutch Regulator One-Handle Remote Control _____ SM/2QM15

2. Clutch Regulator One-Handle Remote Control

2-1 Construction

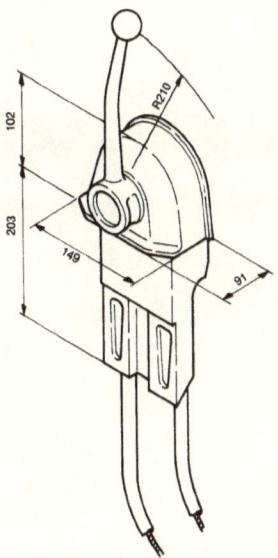

head and engine connection kits ensures dependable, smooth operation with an absolute minimum of backlash. The thread size on cable ends is 10-32. Travel is up to 3". The core is a solid wire, with a 3/32" diameter.

(2) Ball joints
Quick-release

A31126-Quick-release type, the stud is 9/16" long with 1/4" 28 UNF threads. 15/16" from center of stud to end of barrel. Complete with nut and lock washer.

(3) Clamps and fasteners
A31804: Clamp A31509 and Shim A31538.

A31509-Cable clamp 7/32" diameter holes on 1" centers.
A31538-Shim, for use with clamp A31509. 7/32" diameter holes on 1" centers.

2-3 Engine side installation

1) Action of the lever on the engine side

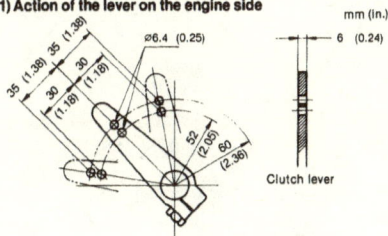

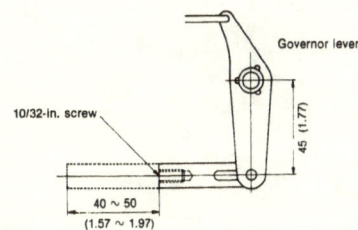

2-2 One-handle remote control composition

Speed control	Remote control cable	33-C
	Clamp	A31804
Clutch control	Remote control cable	33-C
	Clamp	A31804
	Ball joint	A31126

(1) Control Cable
Morse Type "33-C" push-pull control cables, P/N D032377003 (to length).

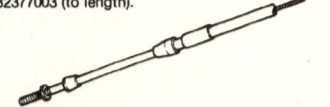

Use only Super-Responsive Morse Control Cables. They are designed specifically for use with Morse control heads. This engineered system of Morse cables, control

9-2

Chapter 9 Remote Control System
2. Clutch Regulator One-Handle Remote Control

SM/2QM15

2) Cable connection

(1) Standard clutch cable (control from bow side)

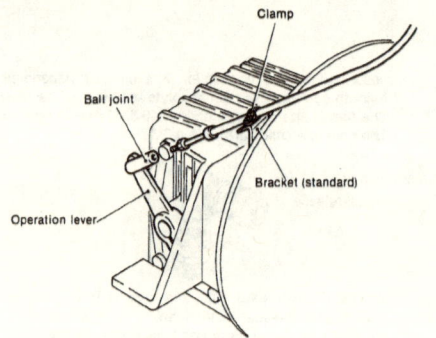

(2) Option (control from stern side)

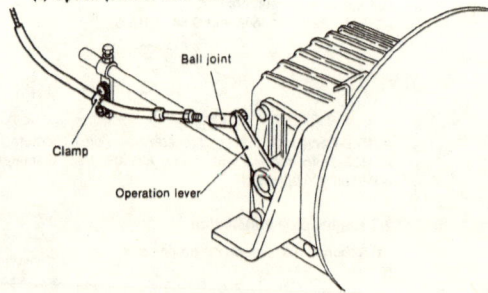

(3) Speed cable

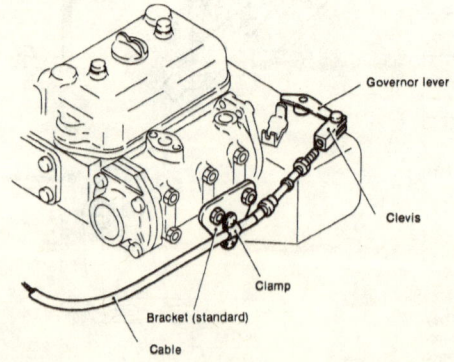

9-3

Printed in Japan
2F015A

3. Decompression Remote Control

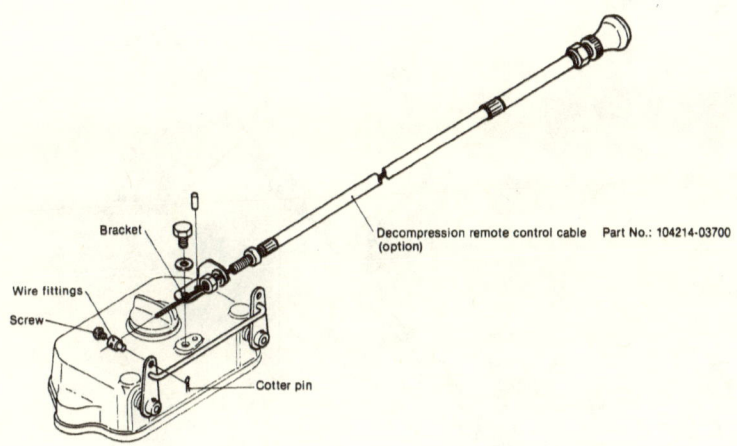

4. Engine Stop Remote Control

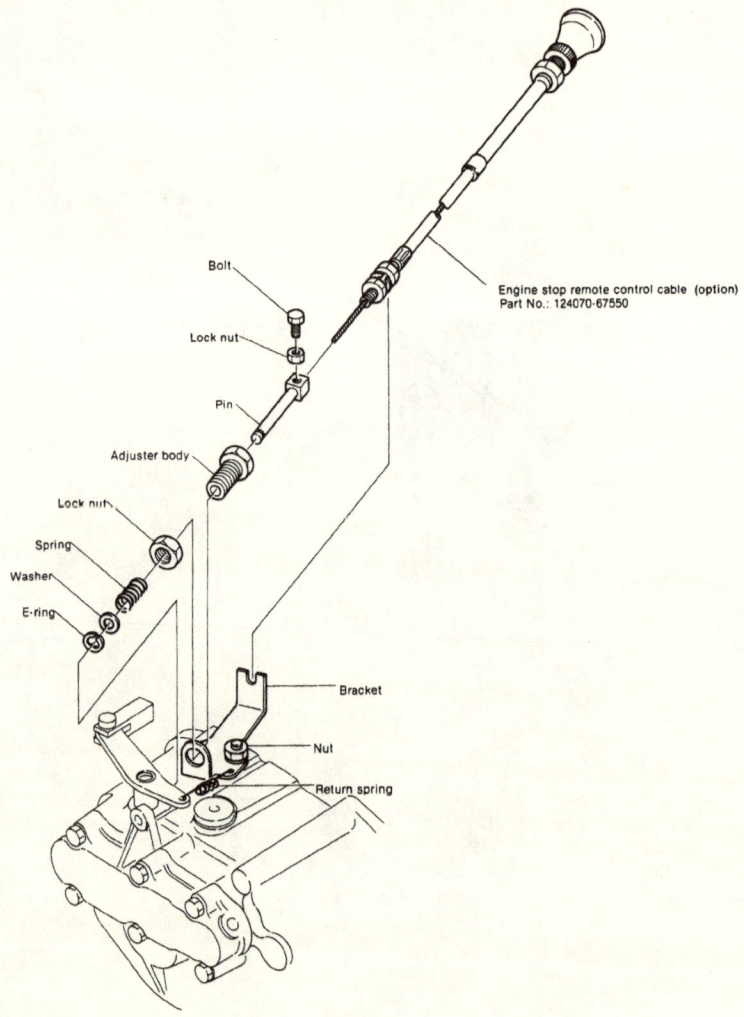

CHAPTER 10
ELECTRICAL SYSTEM

1. Composition 10-1
2. Battery. 10-3
3. Starter Motor. 10-6
4. Alternator 10-13
5. Alarm Circuit. 10-23

Chapter 10 Electrical System
1. Composition

1. Composition

1-1. Composition

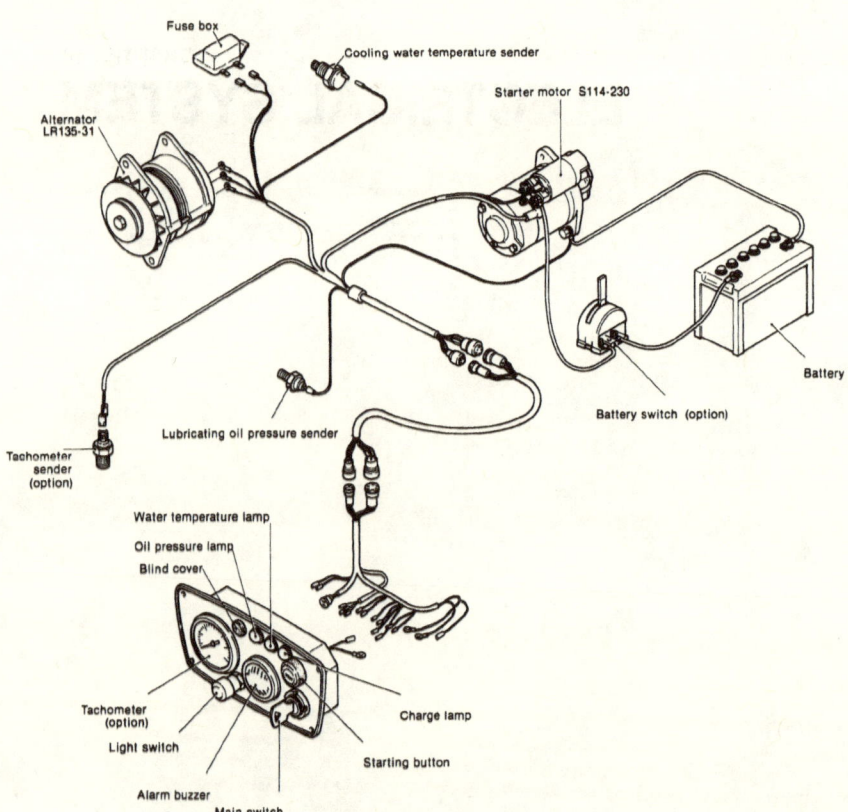

Chapter 10 Electrical System
1. Composition

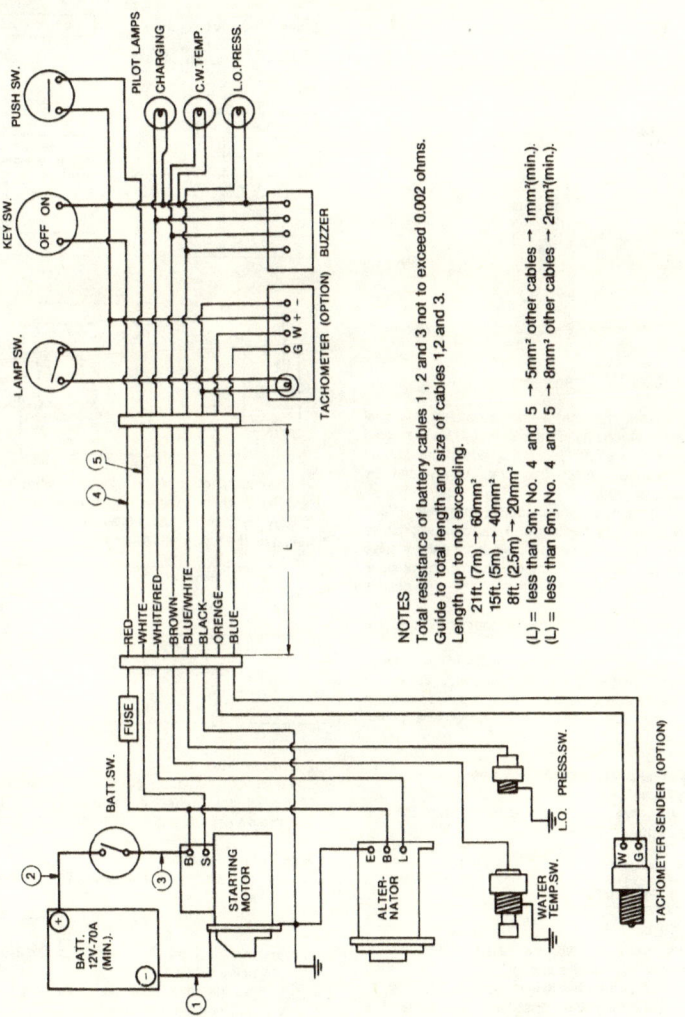

2. Battery

2-1 Construction

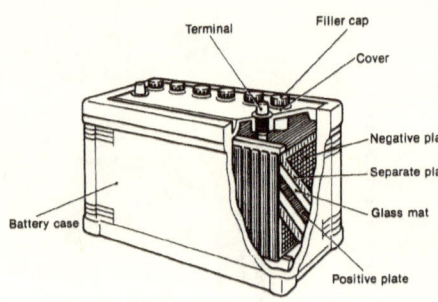

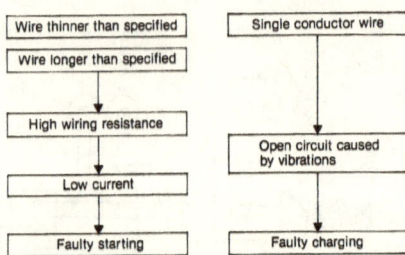

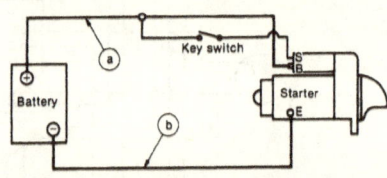

The battery utilizes chemical action to convert chemical energy to electrical energy. This engine uses a lead acid battery which stores a fixed amount of power that can be used when required. After use, the battery can be recharged and used again.
As shown in the figure, a nonconductive container is filled with dilute sulfuric acid electrolyte. Lead dioxide positive plates and lead dioxide negative plates separated by glass mats are stacked alternately in the electrolyte. The positive and negative plates are connected to their respective terminals.
Power is removed from the battery by connecting the load across these two terminals.
When the battery is discharging, an electric current flows from the positive plates to the negative plates. When the battery is being charged, electric current is passed through the battery in the opposite direction by an external power source.

The overall lengths of the wiring between the battery (+) terminal and the starter (B) terminal, and between the battery (−) terminal and the starter (E) terminal should be based on the following table.

Voltage system	Allowable wiring voltage drop	Conductor cross-section area	a + b allowable length
12V	0.2V or less/100A	15mm² (0.0233in.²)	Up to 1.5 m (59.06in.)
		20mm² (0.031in.²)	1.5 ~ 2.5 m (59.06 ~98.43in.)

2-2 Battery capacity and battery cables

2-2.1 Battery capacity

Since the battery has a minimum capacity of 12V, 70AH, it can be used for 100 ~ 150AH.

Minimum battery capacity	12V 70AH
Fully charged specific gravity	1.280

2-2.2 Battery cable

Wiring must be performed with the specified electric wire. Thick, short wiring should be used to connect the battery to the starter, (soft automotive low-voltage wire [AV wire]).
Using wire other than that specified may cause the following troubles:

- Wire thinner than specified
- Wire longer than specified
- High wiring resistance
- Low current
- Faulty starting

- Single conductor wire
- Open circuit caused by vibrations
- Faulty charging

2-3 Inspection

The quality of the battery governs the starting performance of the engine. Therefore the battery must be routinely inspected to assure that it functions perfectly at all times.

2-3.1 Visual inspection

(1) Inspect the case for cracks, damage and electrolyte leakage.
(2) Inspect the battery holder for tightness, corrosion, and damage.
(3) Inspect the terminals for rusting and corrosion, and check the cables for damage.
(4) Inspect the caps for cracking, electrolyte leakage and clogged vent holes.
Correct any abnormal conditions found. Clean off rusted terminals with a wire brush before reconnecting the battery cable.

Chapter 10 Electrical System
2. Battery

2-3.2 Checking the electrolyte
(1) Electrolyte level

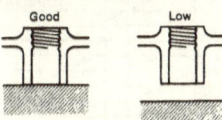
Good — Low — High

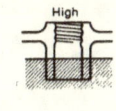

Check the electrolyte level every 7 to 10 days. The electrolyte must always be 10 ~ 20mm over the tops of the plates.

NOTES:
• The "LEVEL" line on a transparent plastic battery case indicates the height of the electrolyte.
• Always use distilled water to bring up the electrolyte level.
• When the electrolyte has leaked out, add dilute sulfuric acid with the same specific gravity as the electrolyte.

(2) Measuring the specific gravity of the electrolyte
1) Draw some of the electrolyte up into a hydrometer.

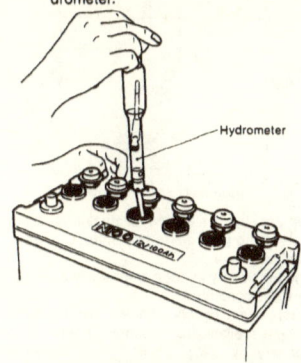
Hydrometer

2) Take the specific gravity reading at the top of the scale of the hydrometer.

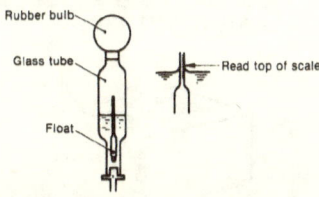
Rubber bulb
Glass tube — Read top of scale
Float

3) The battery is fully charged if the specific gravity is 1.260 at an electrolyte temperature of 20°C. The battery is discharged if the specific gravity is 1.200 (50%). If the specific gravity is below 1.200, recharge the battery.
4) If the difference in the specific gravity among the cells of the battery is ±0.01, the battery is OK.
5) Measure the temperature of the electrolyte.
Since the specific gravity changes with the temperature, 20°C is used as the reference temperature.
Reading the specific gravity at 20°C
S_{20} = St + 0.0007 (t − 20)
S_{20}: Specific gravity at the standard temperature of 20°C
St: Specific gravity of the electrolyte at t°C
0.0007: Specific gravity change per 1°C
t: Temperature of electrolyte

2-3.3 Voltage test
Using a battery tester, the amount of discharge can be determined by measuring the voltage drop which occurs while the battery is being discharged with a large current.

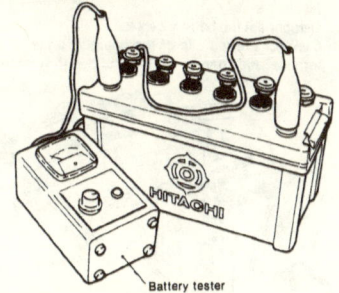
Battery tester

(1) Connect the tester to the battery.
12V battery tester
Adjust the current (A).
(2) Connect the (+) lead of the tester to the (+) battery terminal, and the (−) tester lead to the (−) battery terminal.
(3) Push the TEST button, wait 5 seconds, and then read the meter.
• Repeat the test twice to make sure that the meter indication remains the same.

2-3.4 Washing the battery
(1) Wash the outside of the battery with a brush while running cold or warm water over the battery. (Make sure that no water gets into the battery.)
(2) When the terminals or other metal parts are corroded due to exposure to electrolyte leakage, wash off all the acid.
(3) Check the vent holes of the caps and clean if clogged.
(4) After washing the battery, dry it with compressed air, connect the battery cable, and coat the terminals with grease. Since the grease acts as an insulator, do not coat the terminals before connecting the cables.

Chapter 10 Electrical System
2. Battery
SM/2QM15

2-4 Charging
2-4.1 Charging methods
There are two methods of charging a battery: normal and rapid.
Rapid charging should only be used in emergencies.
- Normal charging...Should be conducted at a current of 1/10 or less of the indicated battery capacity (10A or less for a 100AH battery).
- Rapid charging...Rapid charging is done over a short period of time at a current of 1/5 ~ 1/2 the indicated battery capacity (20A ~ 50A for a 100AH battery). However, since rapid charging causes the electrolyte temperature to rise too high, special care must be exercised.

2-4.2 Charging procedure
1. Check the specific gravity and adjust the electrolyte level.
2. Disconnect the battery cables.
3. Connect the red clip of the charger to the (+) battery terminal and connect the black clip to the (−) terminal.

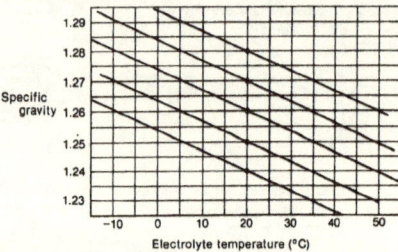

Electrolyte temperature and specific gravity

2-5 Battery storage precautions
The life of a battery depends considerably on how it is handled. Generally speaking, however, after about two years its performance will deteriorate, starting will become difficult, and the battery will not fully recover its original charge even after recharging. Then it must be replaced.

(1) Since the battery will self-discharge about 0.5%/day even when not in use, it must be charged 1 or 2 times a month when it is being stored.

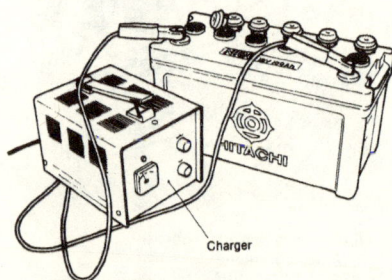
Charger

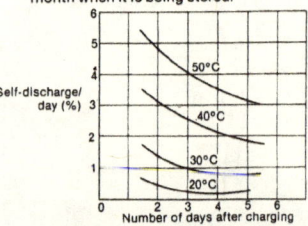

4. Set the current to 1/10 ~ 1/5 of the capacity indicated on the outside of the battery.
5. Periodically measure the specific gravity during charging to make sure that the specific gravity remains at a high fixed value. Also check whether gas is being generated.

2-4.3 Charging precautions
1. Remove the battery caps to vent the gas during charging.
2. While charging, ventilate the room and prohibit smoking, welding, etc.
3. The electrolyte temperature should not exceed 45°C during charging.
4. Since an alternator is used on this engine, when charging with a charger, always disconnect the battery (+) cable to prevent destruction of the diodes.
(Before disconnecting the (+) battery cable, disconnect the (−) battery cable [ground side].)

(2) If charging by the engine alternator is insufficient because of frequent starts and stops, the battery will rapidly lose power.
Charge the battery as soon as possible after it is used under these conditions.
(3) An easy-to-use battery charger that permits home charging is available from Yanmar. Take proper care of the battery by using the charger as a set with a hydrometer.
When the specific gravity has dropped to about 1.16 and the engine will not start, charge the battery up to a specific gravity of 1.26 (24 hours).

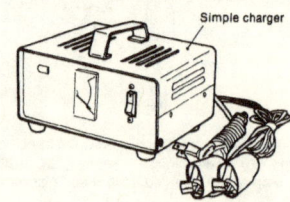
Simple charger

3. Starter Motor

The starter motor is installed on the flywheel housing. When the starting button is pushed, the starter motor pinion flies out and engages the ring gear of the flywheel. Then the main contact is closed, current flows, and the engine is started.
After the engine starts, the pinion automatically returns to its initial position when the starting button is released. Once the engine starts, the starting button should be released immediately. Otherwise, the starter motor may be damaged or burned out.

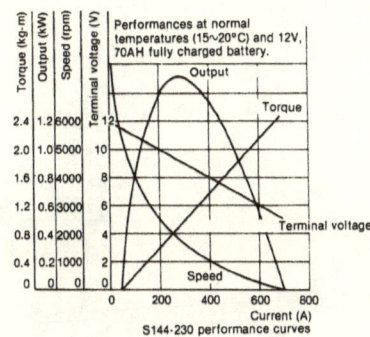

S144-230 performance curves

3-1 Specifications and Performance.

Model		S114-230
Rating (sec)		30
Output (kw)		1.3
Clutch system		Overrunning
Engagement system		Magnetic shift
Pinion flyout voltage (V)		8 or less
No-load	Terminal voltage (V)	12
	Current (A)	60 or less
	Speed (rpm)	6000 or greater

3-2 Construction

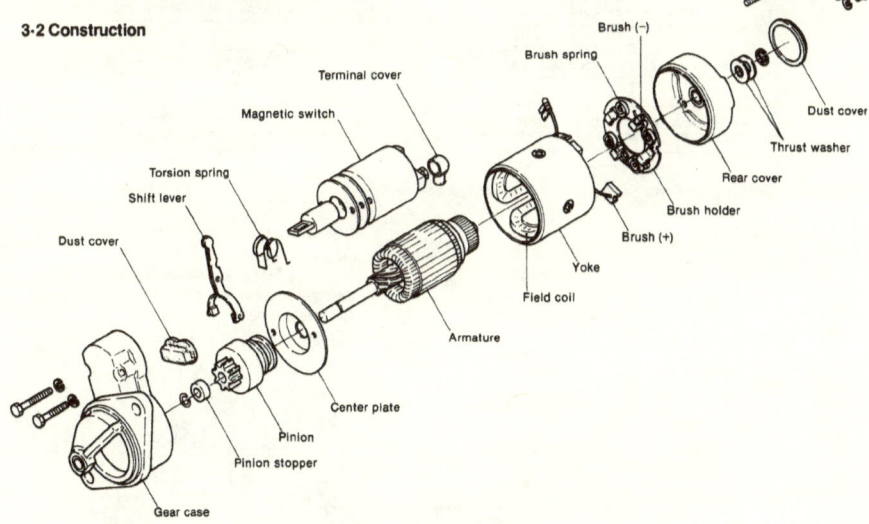

Chapter 10 Electrical System
3. Starter Motor — SM/2QM15

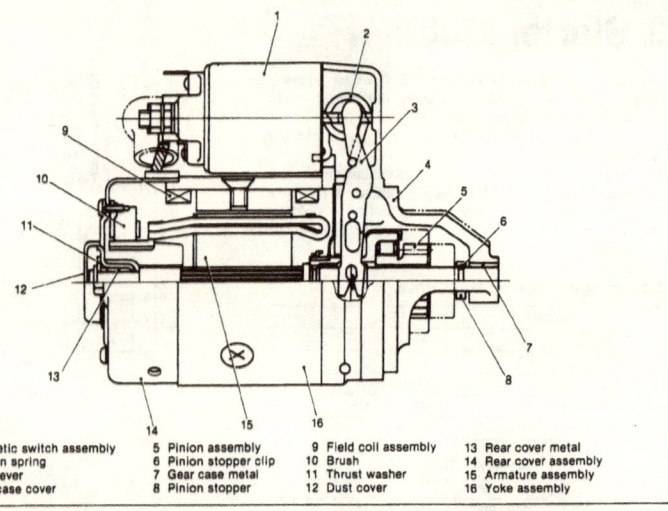

1 Magnetic switch assembly
2 Torsion spring
3 Shift lever
4 Gear case cover
5 Pinion assembly
6 Pinion stopper clip
7 Gear case metal
8 Pinion stopper
9 Field coil assembly
10 Brush
11 Thrust washer
12 Dust cover
13 Rear cover metal
14 Rear cover assembly
15 Armature assembly
16 Yoke assembly

3-3 Operation

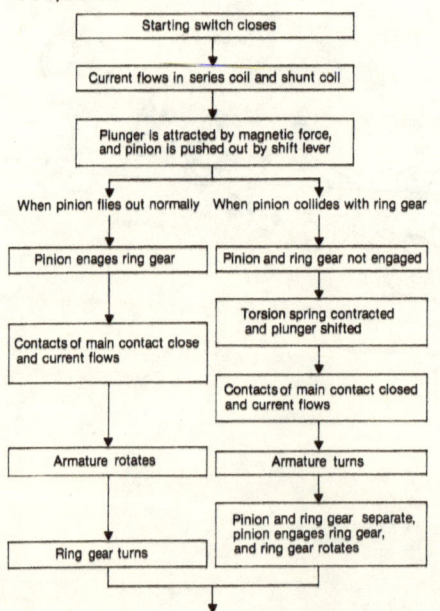

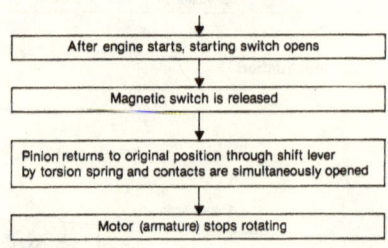

3-4 Disassembly

3-4.1 Magnetic switch

1. Disconnect magnetic switch wiring.
2. Remove through bolt mounting magnetic switch.
3. Remove magnetic switch.

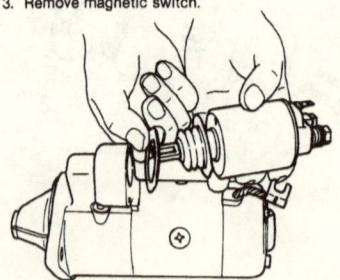

Printed in Japan
2F015A

3-4.2 Rear cover
1. Remove dust cover.

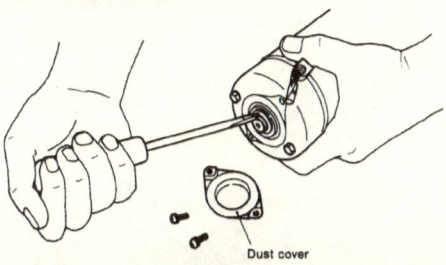

Dust cover

2. Remove E-ring, and remove thrust washer (be careful not to lose the washer and shim).
3. Remove the two through bolts holding the rear cover and the two screws holding the brush holder.
4. Remove rear cover.

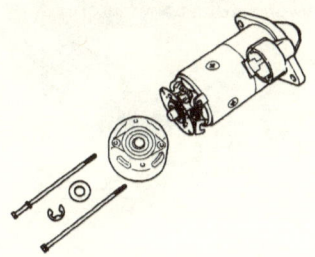

3-4.3 Brush holder
1. Float (−)brush from the commutator.
2. Remove (+)brush from the brush holder.
3. Remove brush holder.

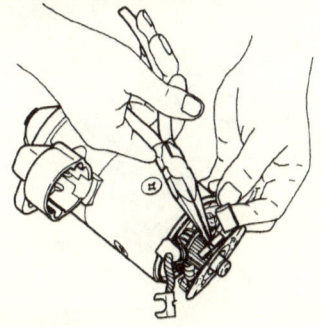

3-4.4 Yoke
1. Remove yoke. Pull it out slowly so that it does not strike against other parts.

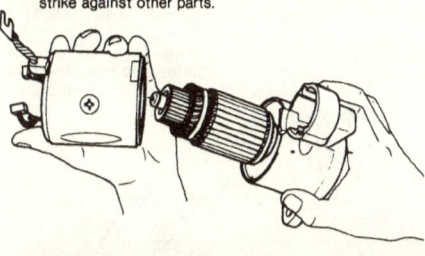

3-4.5 Armature
1. Slide pinion stopper to pinion side.

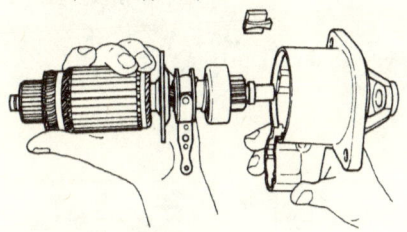

2. Remove the pinion stopper clip.

3-4.6 Pinion
1. Slide the pinion stopper to the pinion side.
2. Remove the pinion stopper clip.
3. Remove the pinion from the armature.

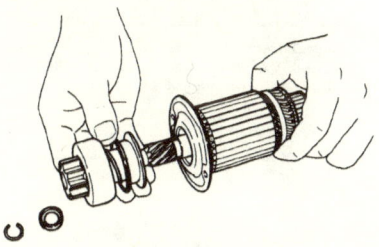

Chapter 10 Electrical System
3. Starter Motor

3-5 Inspection
3-5.1 Armature
(1) Commutator

Inspect the surface of the commutator. If corroded or pitted, sand with #500 ~ #600 sandpaper. If the commutator is severely pitted, grind it to within a surface roughness of at least 0.2 by turning it on a lathe. Replace the commutator if damage is irreparable.

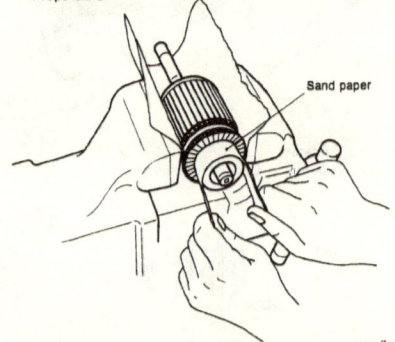

mm (in.)

	Maintenance standard	Wear limit
Commutator outside diameter	Ø43 (1.693)	Ø40 (1.575)
Commutator run-out	Within 0.03 (0.0012)	0.2 (0.0079)
Difference between maximum diameter and minimum diameter	Repair limit 0.4(0.0157)	Repair accuracy 0.05 (0.002)

(2) Mica undercut
Check the mica undercut, correct with a hacksaw blade when the undercut is too shallow.

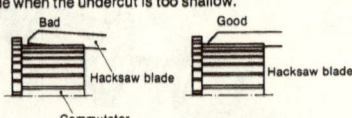

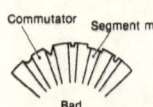 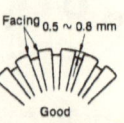

mm (in.)

	Maintenance standard	Repair limit
Mica undercut	0.2 (0.0079)	0.5 ~ 0.8 (0.0197 ~ 0.0315)

(3) Armature coil ground test
Using a tester, check for continuity between the commutator and the shaft (or armature core). Continuity indicates that these points are grounded and that the armature must be replaced.

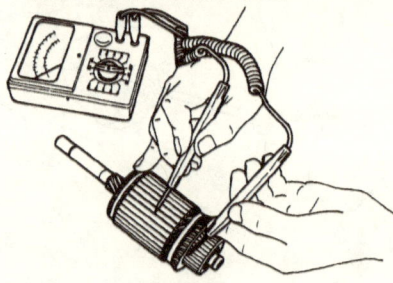

(4) Armature shaft outside diameter
Measure the outside diameter of the armature shaft at four locations: front, center, end, and pinion. Replace the armature if the shaft is excessively worn.
Check the bend of the shaft; replace the armature if the bend exceeds 0.08mm (0.0031in.).

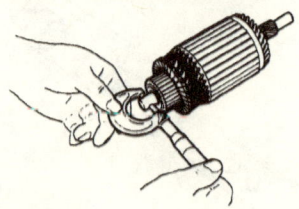

3-5.2 Field coil
(1) Open test
Check for continuity between the terminals connecting the field coil brushes. Continuity indicates that the coil is open and that the coil must be replaced.

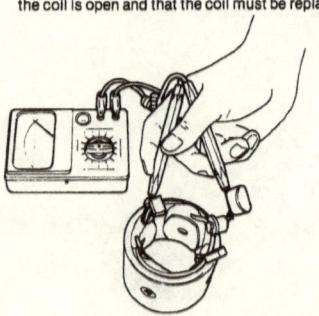

Chapter 10 Electrical System
3. Starter Motor

(2) Short test
Check for continuity between the yoke and any field coil terminal. Continuity indicates that the coil is shorted and that it must be replaced.

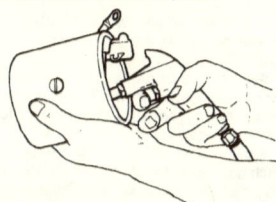

(3) Cleaning the inside of the yoke
If any carbon powder or rust has collected on the inside of the yoke, blow the yoke out with dry compressed air.
*Do not remove the field coil from the yoke.

3-5.3 Brush
The brushes are quickly worn down by the motor. When the brushes are defective, the output of the motor will drop.

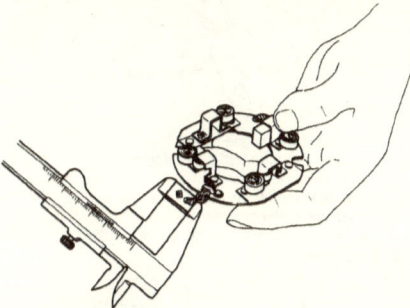

(1) Brush dimensions
Replace brushes which have been worn beyond the specified wear limit.

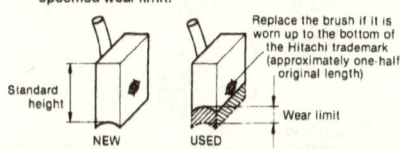

mm (in.)

	S114-230
Brush standard height	16 (0.6299)
Wear limit	4 (0.1575)

(2) Brush appearance and movement in brush holder
If the outside of the brush is damaged, replace it. If the movement of the brushes in the brush holder is hampered because the holder is rusted, repair or replace the holder.

(3) Brush spring
Since the brush spring pushes the brush against the commutator while the motor is running, a weak or defective spring will cause excessive brush wear, resulting in sparking between the brush and the commutator during operation. Measure the spring force with a spring balance; replace the spring when the difference between the standard value and the measured value exceeds ±0.2kg.

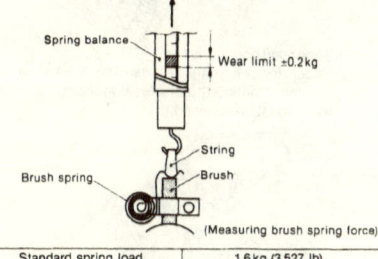

(Measuring brush spring force)

Standard spring load	1.6 kg (3.527 lb)

(4) Brush holder ground test
Check for continuity between the insulated brush holder and the base of the brush holder assembly. Continuity indicates that these two points are grounded and that the holder must be replaced.

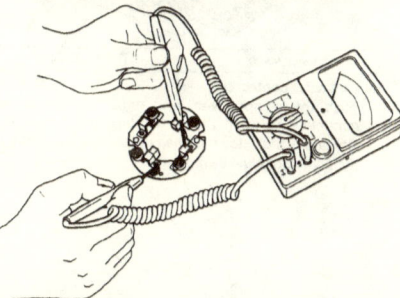

3-5.4 Magnetic switch
(1) Shunt coil continuity test
Check for continuity between the S terminal and the magnetic switch body (metal part). Continuity indicates that the coil is open and that the switch must be replaced.

Coil resistance	0.25Ω (at 20°C)

Chapter 10 Electrical System
3. Starter Motor

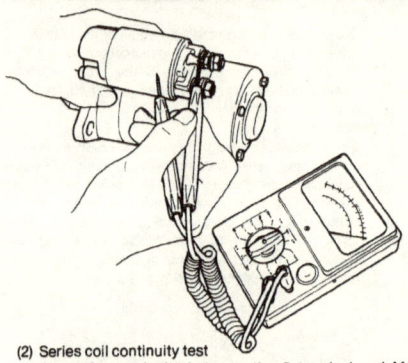

(2) Series coil continuity test
Check for continuity between the S terminal and M terminal. Continuity indicates that the coil is open and that it must be replaced.

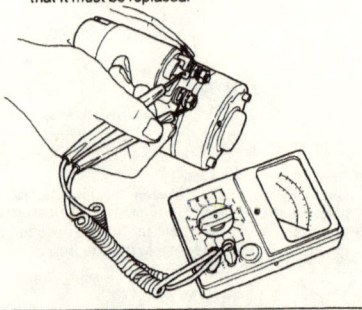

| Resistance value | 0.78Ω (at 20°C) |

(3) Contactor contact test
Push the plunger with your finger and check for continuity between the M terminal and B terminal. Continuity indicates that the contact is faulty and that the contactor must be replaced.

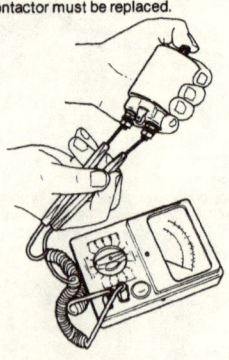

3-5.5 Pinion
(1) Inspect the pinion teeth and replace the pinion if the teeth are excessively worn or damaged.
(2) Check if the pinion slides smoothly; replace the pinion if faulty.
(3) Inspect the springs and replace if faulty.
(4) Replace the clutch if it slips or seizes.

3-6 Reassembly precautions
Reassemble the starter motor in the reverse order of disassembly, paying particular attention to the following:
(1) Torsion spring and shift lever
Hook the torsion spring into the hole in the magnetic switch and insert the shift lever into the notch in the plunger of the magnetic switch through the torsion spring.

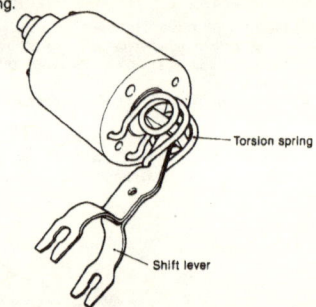

(2) Mounting the magnetic switch
Attach the shift lever to the pinion; assemble the gear case as shown below.
Do not forget to install the dust cover before assembling the gear case.
After reassembly, check by conducting no-load operation.

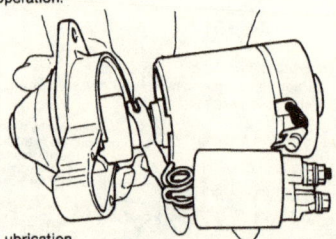

(3) Lubrication
Lubricate each bearing and spline (points indicated GREASE in the construction drawing) with high quality "Hitachi Electrical Equipment Grease A".
The following lubricants may be used in place of Hitachi Electrical Equipment Grease A.

| Magnetic switch plunger | Shell | Aeroshell No. 7 |
| Bearing and spline | Shell | Albania Grease No. 2 |

3-7 Testing
3-7.1 No load test
Test procedure
(1) Connect the positive side of the ammeter (A) to the positive terminal of the battery, and connect the negative side of the ammeter to the B terminal of the starter.

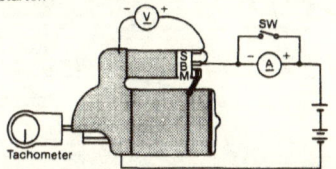
Tachometer

(2) Connect the negative terminal of the battery to the body of the starter.
(3) Connect the positive side of the voltmeter (V) to the B terminal of the starter, and connect the negative side of the voltmeter to the body of the starter.
(4) Attach the tachometer.
(5) Connect the B terminal of the starter to the S terminal of the magnetic switch.
- The magnetic switch should begin operating, and the speed, current, and voltage should be the prescribed values.
- A fully charged battery must be used.
- Since a large current flows when the starter is operated, close the protection circuit switch before initial operation, then open the switch and measure the current after the starter reaches a constant speed.

3-8 Various problems and their remedies

(1) Pinion fails to advance when the starting switch is closed

Problem	Cause	Corrective action
Wiring	Open or loose battery or switch terminal	Repair or retighten
Starting switch	Threaded part connected to pinion section of armature shaft is damaged, and the pinion does not move	Repair contacts, or replace switch
Starter motor	Threaded part connected to pinion section of armature shaft is damaged, and the pinion does not move	Replace
Magnetic switch	Plunger of magnetic switch malfunctioning or coil shorted	Repair or replace

(2) Pinion is engaged and motor rotates, but rotation is not transmitted to the engine

Problem	Cause	Corrective action
Starting motor	Overrunning clutch faulty	Replace

(3) Motor rotates at full power before pinion engages ring gear

Problem	Cause	Corrective action
Starter motor	Torsion spring permanently strained	Replace

(4) Pinion engages ring gear, but starter motor fails to rotate

Problem	Cause	Corrective action
Wiring	Wires connecting battery and magnetic switch open or wire connecting ground, magnetic switch and motor terminals loose	Repair, retighten, or replace wire
Starter motor	Pinion and ring gear engagement faulty Motor mounting faulty Brush worn or contacting brush spring faulty Commutator dirty Armature, field coil faulty Field coil and brush connection loose	Replace Remount Replace Repair Repair or replace Retighten
Magnetic switch	Contactor contact faulty Contactor contacts pitted	Replace Replace

(5) Motor fails to stop when starting switch is opened after engine starts

Problem	Cause	Corrective action
Starting switch	Switch faulty	Replace
Magnetic switch	Switch faulty	Replace

4. Alternator

The alternator serves to keep the battery constantly charged. It is installed on the cylinder block by a bracket, and is driven from the V-pulley at the end of the crankshaft by a V-belt.
The type of alternator used in this engine is ideal for high speed engines having a wide range of engine speeds. It contains diodes that convert AC to DC, and an IC regulator that keep the generated voltage constant even when the engine speed changes.

4-1 Specifications

Type		Standard	Option
	Alternator	LR135-31	LR155-04
	Regulator	TR1Z-28	TR1Z-28
Battery voltage		12 V	12 V
Output current		35A/5000 rpm	55A/5000 rpm
Polarity		2-wire system	2-wire system
Direction of rotation		CW/CCW	CW/CCW
Regulated voltage		14.3 ±0.3V	14.3 ±0.3V
Speed at 13V		1000 rmp or less	1000 rpm or less
Weight		3.8kg (8.3776lb)	5.5kg (12.125lb)

CW: Clockwise CCW: Counterclockwise

4-2 Characteristics

(1) LR135-31
Standard speed characteristic of 12V-35A Alternator with IC regulator.
—Cold
...Warm ("Warm" is the state of the engine reached after a temperature rise test is conducted at a constant 5000 rpm maximum output.)

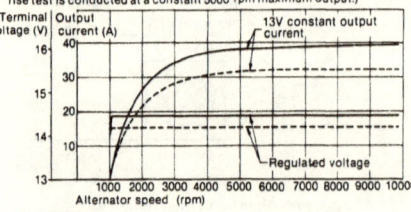

(2) LR155-04
Standard speed characteristic of 12V-55A alternator with IC regulator.
—Cold ...Warm (see above)

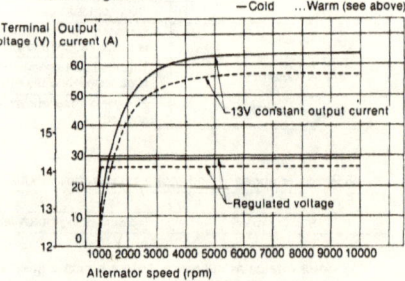

Chapter 10 Electrical System
4. Alternator

4-3 Construction

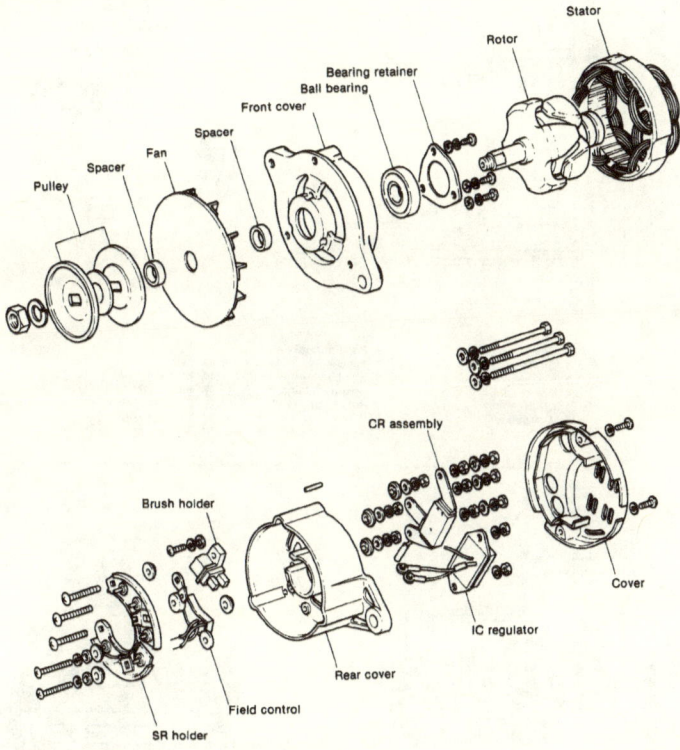

Chapter 10 Electrical System
4. Alternator

LR135-31

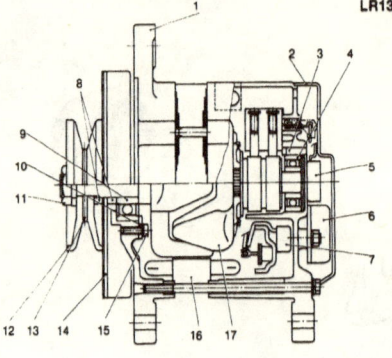

1 Front cover assembly	7 Field control unit	13 Pulley spacer
2 Cover	8 Spacer	14 Fan
3 Pin (nylon resin)	9 Ball bearing	15 Screw
4 Ball bearing	10 Bearing retainer	16 Stator assembly
5 CR assembly	11 Pulley nut	17 Rotor assembly
6 IC regulator	12 Pulley	18 Through bolt
		19 Screw

LR155-04

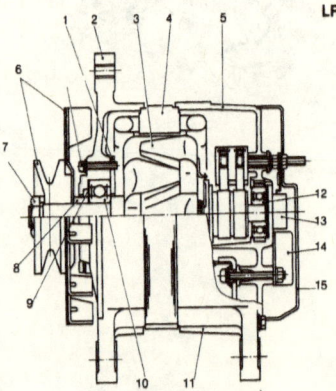 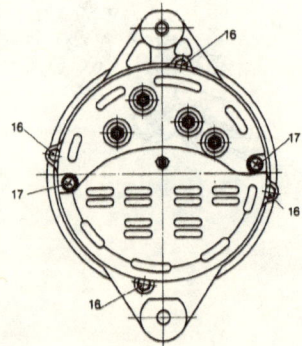

1 Bearing retainer	7 Pully nut	13 CR assembly
2 Front cover assembly	8 Spacer	14 IC regulator
3 Rotor assembly	9 Bearing stopper	15 Cover
4 Stator assembly	10 Ball bearing	16 Through bolt
5 Rear cover	11 Rear cover assembly	17 Screw
6 Pully asembly	12 Ball bearing	

4-4 Operation (LR135-31)
4-4.1 Circuit diagram

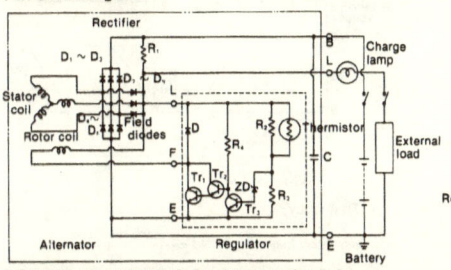

B: Generator output terminal   D: Transistor protection diode
L: Charge lamp terminal   ZD: Zener diode
E: Ground (battery (−)) terminal
$Tr_1 \sim Tr_3$: Transistor $D_1 \sim D_9$: Output rectification diodes
$R_1 \sim R_4$: Resistor
$D_7 \sim D_9$: ON/OFF operation of charge lamp and rotor coil current field supply diodes   C: Condenser

Basically, this circuit consists of an output Tr_1 transistor that turns the alternator rotor coil current on and off, a Tr_2 transistor that passes the base current to Tr_1, a Tr_3 control transistor that controls Tr_2, a zener diode ZD, and resistors R_1, R_2, R_3, and R_4, which pass on the current when the battery voltage reaches the regulated voltage, and a thermistor, as shown in the above figure.

4-4.2 Description of operation
(1) Initial excitation

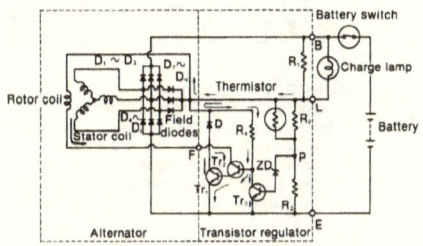

When the battery switch is closed, current flows into Tr_2 and Tr_1, and the charge lamp lights up. At this time, the voltage at point P is lower than the zener voltage and current does not flow through the ZD (zener diode). Therefore, the base current does not flow through Tr_3, and Tr_3 is turned OFF.
The resistor R_1 is inserted in series with the charge lamp to prevent interruption of the rotor coil current if the charge lamp blows out, and to reduce the rise in speed (speed automatically adjusted) caused by the increase in the initial exciting current.

(2) Initial rotation

The alternator consists of field diodes (D7 ~ D9).
When the alternator is operated, generation begins. When the speed of the alternator rises until its output voltage exceeds the battery terminal voltage, battery charging beings.

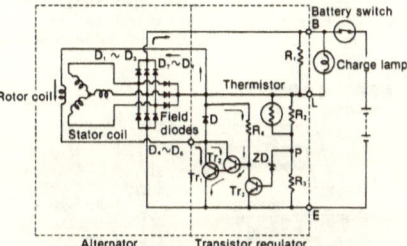

At this stage, the voltages at terminal B and terminal L are equal, and the charge lamp goes out to indicate that charging has begun. When charging begins, the Tr_2 base current, Tr_1 base current, and Tr_1 collector current (rotor coil current) are supplied from the alternator through D7 ~ D9 (field diodes). Since R_2 and R_3 are selected so that the voltage across P-E turns the ZD (zener diode) ON when the voltage across B-E exceeds the regulated voltage of the regulator, when the ZD (zener diode) is conducting, current flows through the path indicated above.

(3) Operation

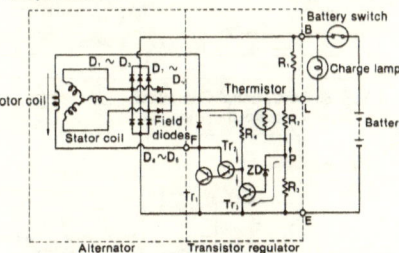

A Tr_3 collector-emitter voltage of at least 0.6V is necessary to allow the base current to flow through Tr_2 and Tr_1. But since the Tr_3 collector-emitter voltage is about 0.3V when Tr_3 is conducting, the Tr_2 and Tr_1 base current is interrupted, Tr_2 and Tr_1 are turned OFF, and current does not flow through the rotor coil.
When the rotor coil current is stopped, the alternator output voltage drops, the voltage across P-E applied to the ZD (zener diode) drops below the zener voltage, the zener diode is turned OFF, and the Tr_3 base current is interrupted.
As a result, Tr_3 is turned OFF, the base voltage of Tr_2 rises, and base current begins to flow through Tr_2.
This causes Tr_1 to conduct and the rotor coil current to

Chapter 10 Electrical System
4. Alternator

begins to flow again.
As can be seen from the above description, when the output voltage of the generator is lower than the regulated voltage the Tr_1 output transistor conducts and rotor coil current flows. When the alternator output voltage is higher than the regulated voltage, control transistor Tr_3 conducts, output transistor Tr_1 is turned OFF, and the rotor coil current is interrupted. The battery charging voltage is kept constant by turning the output transistor ON and OFF repeatedly in this manner.

4-5 Wiring (LR135-31)
(1) Wiring diagram

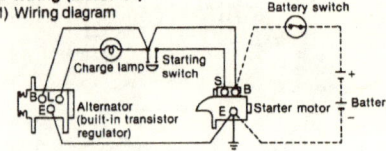

(2) Terminal connections
The alternator has the following terminals. Connect these terminals as indicated below.

Symbol	Terminal name	Connection to external wiring
B	Battery terminal	To battery (+) side
E	Ground terminal	To battery (−) side
L	Lamp (charge) terminal	To charge lamp terminal

The IC regulator terminals are as follows:

Symbol	Lead color
B	W (white)
E	B (black)
L	L (red)

4-6 LR155-04 (Optional) R terminal
(1) Characteristics of the R terminal

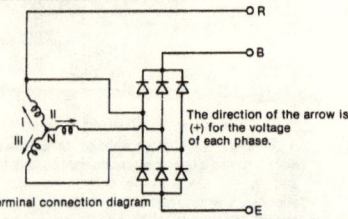

On the Y-connection (star connection) type alternator, these terminals are known as the N and R terminals, respectively. Since a large-ripple, half-wave, rectified wave form appears at this terminal, and the frequency is proportional to the speed of the alternator, this terminal is used to detect engine speed. In this case a pulse type tachometer is required.

(2) Output wave form and voltage

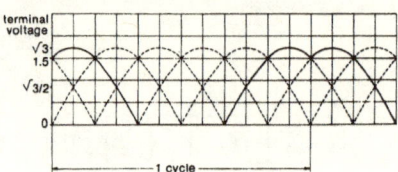

(3) Frequency

$$\text{Generation frequency Rf (Hz)} = \frac{\text{Alternator speed}}{10}$$

The generation frequency when the altenator pully ratio is i = 2.1 and the engine speed is 1000 rpm is,

$$Rf = \frac{1000 \times 2.1}{10} = 210 Hz$$

The tachometer should be adjusted to conform to the above ratio.

(4) R terminal wiring
(1) Incorrect wiring of the R terminal will cause various troubles. When wiring the R terminal, check carefully by observing the charge lamp; make sure that the wiring has been done correctly.

• Wiring example

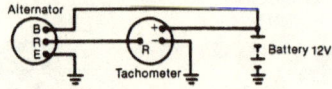

(2) The R terminal voltage is a large-ripple, half-wave, rectified wave form. Its frequency is equal to the frequency of each phase. Consequently, the same tachometer cannot be used if the number of poles of the alternator is different. When a tachometer is used to detect frequency, careful attention must be given to the number of poles.

4-7 Alternator handling precautions
(1) Pay attention to the polarity of the battery; be careful not to connect it in reverse polarity. If the battery is connected in reverse polarity, the battery will be shorted by the diode of the alternator, an overcurrent will result, the diodes and transistor regulator will be destroyed, and the wiring harness will be burned.
(2) Connect the terminals correctly.
(3) When charging the battery from outside, such as during rapid charging, disconnect the alternator B terminal or the battery terminals.
(4) Do not short the terminals.
(5) Never test the alternator with a high voltage megger.

4-8 Alternator disassembly

Disassemble the alternator as follows.
The major points of disassembly are the removal of the cover, the separation of the front and rear sides, and detailed disassembly.

(1) Remove the cover attached to the rear cover, remove the through bolts, and disassemble into front and rear sides.

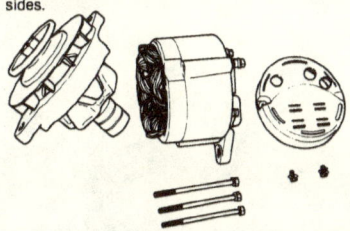

(2) Then when disassembling the front side pulley and fan, front cover and rotor, clamp the rotor in a vice through the copper plates and loosen the pulley nut, as shown in the figure.

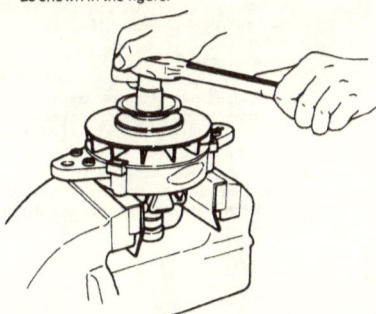

(3) When the fan and pulley have been removed, the rotor can be pulled from the front cover by hand.

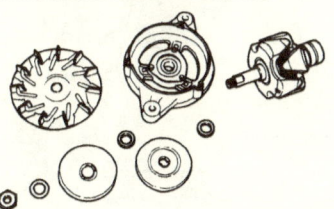

(4) Next, remove the bearing attached to the front cover. Loosen the bearing protector mounting bolts and pull the bearing by applying pressure to the bearing from the front cover.

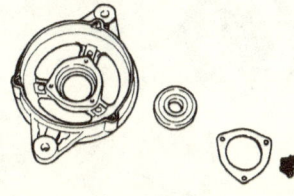

(5) Disassemble the rear side.
First, disconnect the resistor and IC regulator from the terminals.

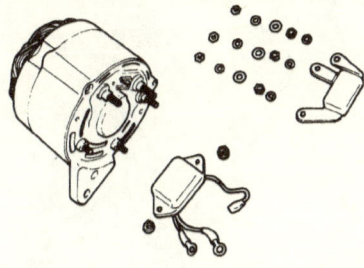

(6) Remove the bolts holding the SR holder and brush holder, remove the B.E.L. terminal nuts, and disassemble into the rear cover and stator (with SR holder).

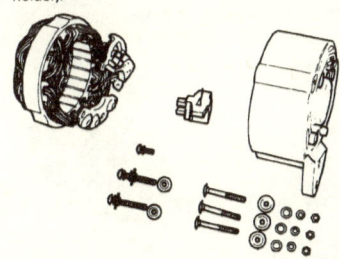

Chapter 10 Electrical System
4. Alternator
SM/2QM15

(7) Melt the solder connecting the stator and the diode, and break it down to the stator, SR holder and auxiliary diode.

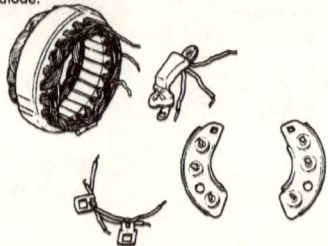

(8) Pull out the pin (nylon resin) inserted into the brush cover mounting section of the rear cover, and disassemble the rear cover.

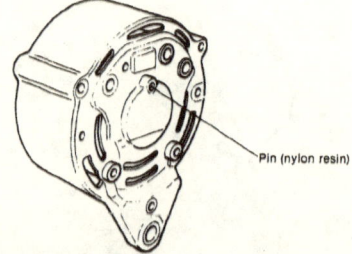

Pin (nylon resin)

(9) When (1)—(8) above are completed, the alternator is completely disassembled.

4-9 Inspection and adjustment
4-9.1 Diodes
(1) Diode short test

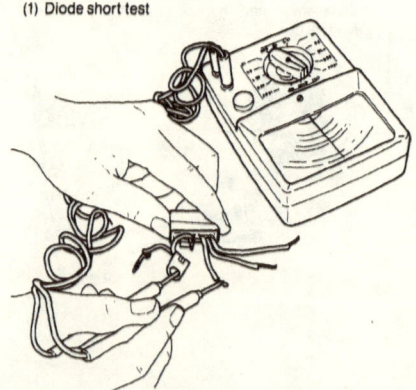

A set of 6 diodes and a set of 3 moulded diodes (field diodes) are used. The (+) diodes and (−) diodes of the six diode set conduct in opposite directions. (See the figure below.) Replace the diodes that conduct in both directions and the diodes that do not conduct in both directions.
Test for the continuity of each diode.

CAUTION: If a high voltage megger is used, a high voltage will be applied to the diode and the diode will be destroyed. Therefore, never test the diodes with a high voltage megger, etc.

(2) Replacement
1) Remove the cover.
2) Unsolder the diode assembly wiring. (CAUTION: Hold the diode with needle nose pliers so that the heat of the soldering iron is not transmitted to the diode.)
3) Remove the diode assembly mounting nut and bolt, and remove the diode ass'y.
Remove the nut and bolt holding the diode assembly in place, and then remove the diode assembly.

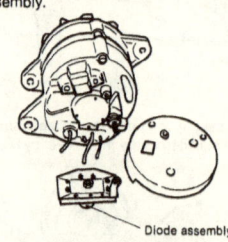

Diode assembly

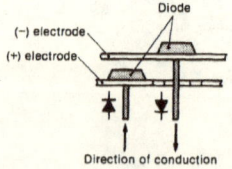

(−) electrode
(+) electrode
Diode
Direction of conduction

Chapter 10 Electrical System
4. Alternator

4-9.2 Rotor
(1) Slip ring wear
Because the slip rings wear very little, the diameter of the rings must be measured with a micrometer. Replace the rings (rotor assembly) when wear exceeds the maintenance standard by 1 mm.

mm (in.)

	Maintenance standard	Wear limit
Slip ring outside diameter	Ø31 (1.2205)	Ø30 (1.1811)

(2) Slip ring roughness
The slip ring should be smooth with no surface oil, etc. If the surface of the rings is rough, polish with #500 ~ #600 sandpaper, and if the surface is soiled, clean with a cloth dipped in alcohol.

(3) Rotor coil short test
Check the continuity between the rotor coil and slip ring with a tester. The resistance should be near the prescribed value.
If the resistance is extemely low, there is a layer short at the rotor coil; if the resistance is infinite, the coil is open. In either case, replace the rotor.

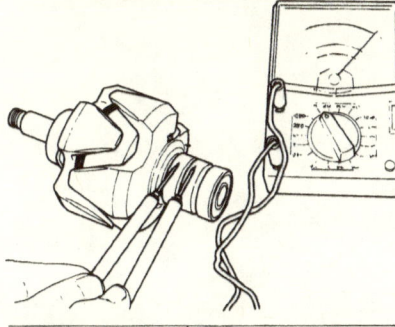

Resistance value:	Approx 3.83 ±0.15Ω (at 20°C)

(4) Rotor coil ground test
Check the rotor coil for grounding with a tester, or by checking the continuity between one slip ring and the rotor core or shaft.

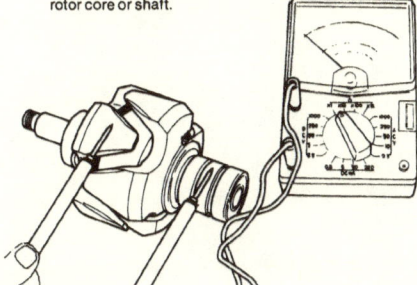

4-9.3 Stator coil
(1) Stator coil short test
Check the continuity between the terminals of the stator coil. Measure the resistance between the output terminals with a tester. The resistance should be near the prescribed value.
If the stator coil is open, indicated by infinite resistance, it must be replaced.

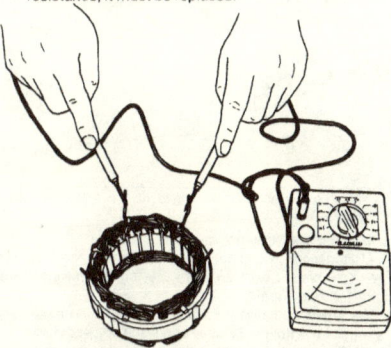

Resistance value:	Approx 0.128Ω (at 20°C) 2-phase resistance

(2) Stator coil ground test
Check the continuity between one of the stator coil leads and the stator core.
The stator coil is good if the resistance is infinite. If the stator core is grounded, indicated by continuity, it must be replaced.

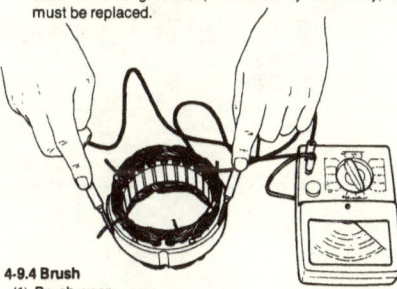

4-9.4 Brush
(1) Brush wear
Check the brush length.
The brush wears very little, but replace the brush if worn over the wear limit line printed on the brush.

Wear limit line (brush)

Chapter 10 Electrical System
4. Alternator

	mm(in.)	
	Maintenance standard	Wear limit
Brush length	14.5 (0.5709)	7.0 (0.2756)

(2) Brush spring pressure measurement
Measure the pressure with the brush protruding 2 mm from the brush holder, as shown in the figure. The spring is normal if the measured value is over 150 gr. Confirm that the brush moves smoothly in the holder.

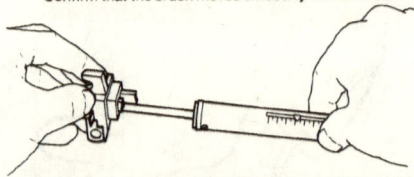

Brush spring strength	300 ±45g (0.562 ~ 0.761 lb.) (New brush)

(2) Output current measurement
  (a) Set the resistance of the variable resistor in the circuit in the figure to maximum, and drive the alternator after closing SW1 and SW2.
  (b) Increase the alternator speed to 5,000 rpm by adjusting the variable resistor, maintaining the voltage at 13 V.
  (c) Measure the deflection of the ammeter at this time.
  (d) An output current of 31 A is normal.
(3) Performance test precautions
  (a) Connect the alternator A terminal and battery (+) terminal, and the E terminal and battery (−) terminal with 2.5 m or less of wiring having a cross-sectional area of 8 mm² or more.
  (b) Check the wires for correct or loose connection.

4-10 Reassembly precautions
After inspection and servicing, reassemble the parts in the reverse order of disassembly, paying careful attention to the following items:
(1) When soldering the stator coil leads and diodes, hold them with needle nose pliers and solder quickly.
(2) Be sure that the insulation bushings, etc. are installed correctly when installing the terminal bolts and SR holder mounting screw.

4-11 Alternator performance test
4-11.1 Test equipment

Test equipment	Quantity	Specifications
Battery	1	12V
DC voltmeter	1	0 ~ 50V Range 0.5
DC ammeter	1	0 ~ 50A Range 1.0
Variable resistor	1	0 ~ 1Ω capacity: 1 kW
Switch	2	Switch capacity: 40 A

4-11.2 Performance test circuit

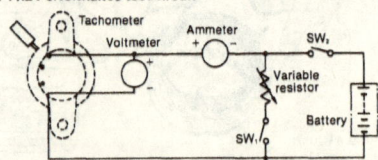

4-11.3 Performance test
(1) Speed measurement at 13 V (26 V rise speed)
  (a) Start the alternator slowly after opening SW1 and closing SW2.
  (b) After the alternator has reached a speed of approximately 500 rpm, open switch SW2.
  (c) Gradually increase the alternator speed while watching the voltmeter, and read the speed on the tachometer when the voltage reaches 13 V.
  (d) The speed at this time is 1,000 rpm or less, and is the 13 V rise speed.

Chapter 10 Electrical System
4. Alternator

SM/2QM15

4-12 Alternator troubleshooting and repair

(1) Failure to charge

Problem	Cause	Corrective action
Wiring, current	Open, shorted, or disconnected	Repair or replace
Alternator	Open, grounded, or shorted coil Terminal insulator missing Diode faulty	Replace Repair Replace
Transistor regulator	Transistor regulator faulty	Replace regulator

(2) Battery charge insufficient and discharge occurs easily

Problem	Cause	Corrective action
Wiring	Wiring shorted or loose, wiring thickness or length unsuitable	Repair or replace Replace
Generator	Rotor coil layer short Stator coil layer short; One phase of stator coil open Slip ring dirty V-belt loose Brush contact faulty Diode faulty	Replace Replace Clean or polish Retighten Repair Replace

(3) Battery overcharged

Problem	Cause	Corrective action
Battery	Electrolyte low or unsuitable	Add distilled water Adjust specific weight Replace
Transistor regulator	Regulator transistor shorted	Replace regulator.

(4) Current charge unstable.

Problem	Cause	Corrective action
Wiring	Wiring shorted at a break in the covering due to hull vibration or intermittent contact at break	Repair or replace
Alternator	Layer short Balance spring damaged Slip ring dirty Coil open	Replace Replace Replace Repair or replace

5. Alarm Circuit

5-1 Oil pressure alarm

If the engine oil pressure is below 0.2 ±0.1 kg/cm², with the main switch in the ON position, the contacts of the oil pressure switch are closed by a spring, and the lamp is illuminated through lamp → oil pressure switch → ground circuit system. If the oil pressure is normal, the switch contacts are opened by the lubricating oil pressure and the lamp remains off.

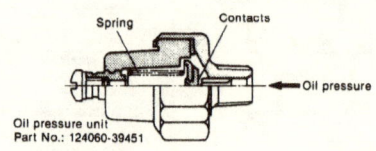

Oil pressure unit
Part No.: 124060-39451

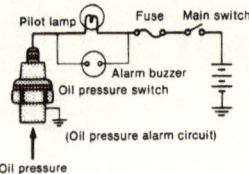

(Oil pressure alarm circuit)

Oil pressure unit specifications

Rated voltage	12 V
Operating pressure	0.2 ±0.1 kg/cm² (1.422 ~ 4.266 lb/in.²)
Lamp capacity:	5W

Inspection

Problem	Inspection item	Inspection method	Corrective action
Lamp not illuminated when main switch set to ON	1. Oil pressure lamp blown out	(1) Visual inspection	Replace lamp
		(2) Lamp not illuminated even when main switch set to ON position and terminals of oil pressure switch grounded	
	2. Operation of oil pressure switch	Lamp illuminates when checked as described in (2) above	Replace oil pressure switch
Lamp not extinguished while engine running	1. Oil level low	Stop engine and check oil level with dipstick	Add oil
	2. Oil pressure low	Measure oil pressure	Repair bearing wear and adjust regulator valve
	3. Oil pressure faulty	Switch faulty if abnormal at (1) and (2) above	Replace oil pressure switch
	4. Wiring between lamp and oil pressure switch faulty	Cut the wiring between the lamp and switch and wire with separate wire	Repair wiring harness

5-2 Cooling water temperature alarm

A water temperature lamp and water temperature gauge, backed up by an alarm in the instrument panel, are used to monitor the temperature of the engine cooling water. A high thermal expansion material is set on the end of the water temperature unit. When the cooling water temperature reaches a specified high temperature, the contacts are closed, and an alarm lamp and buzzer are activated at the instrument panel.

Water temperature switch

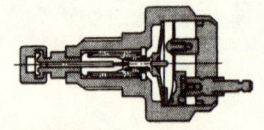

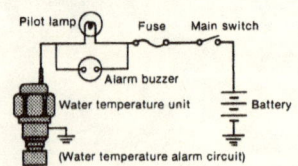

(Water temperature alarm circuit)

Operating temperature		Current capacity
ON	OFF	
60 ±2°	56 ±2°	DC12V. 7A

Pilot lamp: 12 V, 3 W
Alarm buzzer: 12 V, 1 W

Water temperature unit
Part No.: 46150-004530

Chapter 10 Electrical System
5. Alarm Circuit

SM/2QM15

The parts of the alarm circuit which must be checked are the open pilot bulb, fuse, and wiring. To check, disconnect the wiring at the water temperature unit side and ground the cord—the pilot lamp is normal if the pilot lamp illuminates. Moreover, be sure to check the operating temperature of the unit after replacing.

5-3 Alarm buzzer
The alarm buzzer sounds when the engine oil pressure, cooling water temperature, or charging becomes abnormal. The trouble source is indicated by illumination of the appropriate alarm lamp simultaneously with the sounding of the buzzer.

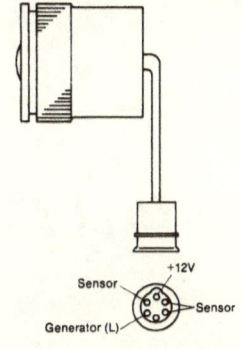

Type	WI1-02
Voltage	10 ~ 15V
Current drain	100mmA
Sound level	75dB(A) at 1m
Weight	0.2kg
	Part No.: 124070-91350

Normal operation is as follows:

	Alarm buzzer	Charge lamp	Oil pressure lamp	Water temperature lamp
Main switch ON, engine stopped	Alarm	Illuminated	Illuminated	Extinguished
Main switch ON, engine running	No alarm	Extinguished	Extinguished	Extinguished
Key switch OFF, engine stopped	No alarm	Extinguished	Extinguished	Extinguished

5-4 Tachometer
A tachometer that monitors ring gear speed and converts it to frequency to operate the meter is optional.
(1) Operating circuit

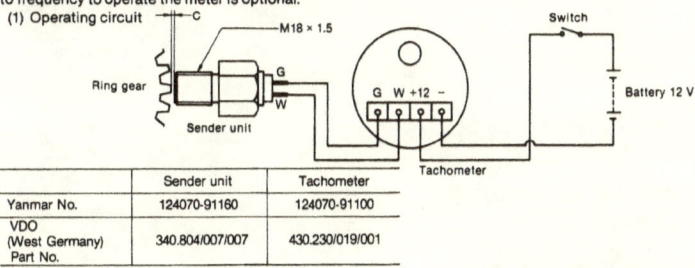

	Sender unit	Tachometer
Yanmar No.	124070-91160	124070-91100
VDO (West Germany) Part No.	340.804/007/007	430.230/019/001

(2) Sender unit sensitivity limits

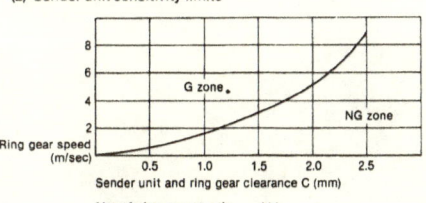

No. of ring gear teeth   114
Module   2.54
Tachometer frequency   6,650 Hz

(3) Alternator LR155-04 (Option)
The R terminal of the alternator can be used. Refer to CHAPTER 10 para. 4.6.
NOTE: Confirm the number of tachometer electrodes.

Wiring example

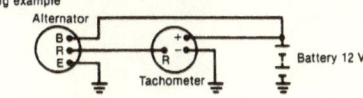

Printed in Japan
2F015A

CHAPTER 11
INSTALLATION AND FITTING

1. Propeller Selection 11-1
2. Engine Installation 11-2
3. Stern Equipment 11-6
4. Interior Piping and Wiring 11-10
5. Front Power Take-Off 11-15

1. Propeller Selection

1-1 Criteria for matching

When determining whether the propeller matches the operating requirements, the following criteria must be taken into consideration:

Output setting	15 HP/3,000 rpm
Injection timing	b TDC 27°
Injection pressure	160 ±10 kg/cm² (2133.5 ~ 2418 lb/in.²)

NOTE: Load shall be 100%

1-2 Propeller selection and shaft diameter

(1) Calculating vessel displacement

Since displacement represents the weight of the vessel, the vessel weight expresses the weight of the displaced water.

Calculating displacement by adding the weights of each part of the vessel is the most accurate method.

Hull weight	W1 (ton)
Engine	W2
Stern propeller	W3
Fuel, lubricating oil	W4
Battery	W5
Fishing gear	W6
Front power take-off	W7
Crew	W8
Other fittings	W9

Displacement Δ = W1 + W2 ... + W9

(2) Propeller and shaft diameter
- Propeller diameter and pitch (mm)

Number of blades	Stern opening area	Diameter × Pitch	
		Reduction ratio 2.14	Reduction ratio 2.83
3	0.36	360 × 250	430 × 320
2	0.23	380 × 230	460 × 280

- Propeller shaft diameter (mm)

Stainless steel SUS304	25	28
Bronze BS & M	25	28
Propeller rotation direction	Clockwise viewed from stern	

NOTE: Shaft diameter represents the shaft diameter safety limit. Therefore, a shaft smaller than the dimensions given in the table must not be used.

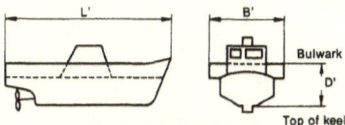

L' : Overall length (m)
B' : Maximum breadth (m)
D' : Overall depth (m)

NOTE: 1. Check the hull weight with the hull manufacturer or shipyard, or when unknown, calculate a criteria with the following equation.
- Light FRP vessel

$$W1 = L'm \times B'm \times D' \times \frac{CN'}{(0.06 \sim 0.09)} \text{ ton}$$

- Heavy FRP vessel or wood vessel

$$W1 = L'm \times B'm \times D' \times (0.09 \sim 0.12) \text{ ton}$$

Note that when D' is especially large because of a bulwark, etc., CN' will be 0.045 ~ 0.08.

2. The displacement may also be calculated from L, B, and D, but since the error is large for small vessels it should not be used.

2. Engine Installation

2-1 Engine room

The overall layout of the engine room is planned for easy inspection, servicing and handling of the engine, front power take-off and driven machinery.

Do not overlook the position and space of the fuel tank, battery and Kingston cock and their related piping, wiring and remote control cables in the engine room layout. Thoroughly study all the equipment and apparatuses to be installed, and consult the shipyard and make a paper plan to provide optimum engine room space.

The engine room conditions required to handle the engine will be covered below.

(1) Ventilation inside engine room
  Since an increase in the engine room temperature causes a reduction in the intake air volume and thus a drop in engine output, ventilation inside the engine room must be ample.
  - Dimensions and capacity with a ventilator installed
  - Dimensions and capacity with an intake duct installed
(2) Engine room height
  - The distance from the lubricating oil inlet at the top of the rocker arm cover to the ceiling must be great enough that lubricating oil can be easily added.
(3) Space must be sufficient to move the propeller shaft flange face toward the stern when disassembling the clutch, changing the gear, etc.

2-2 Engine bed

(1) Although the installation angle of the engine differs with the hull shape and engine installation position, it must be 8° or less when the vessel is cruising. If the tilt exceeds 8°, the output will decrease, the exhaust color will worsen without the speed rising, vessel speed will fall or the parts will wear abnormally, and oil consumption will increase.

(2) From the engine installation surface, the shape of the bottom must be such that there is no contact, as in the figure.

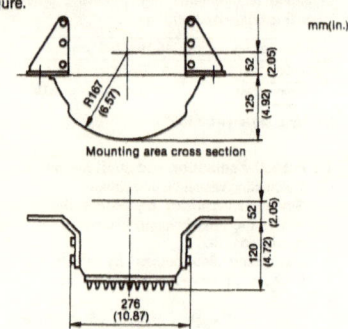

Mounting area cross section

Oil pan area cross section

(3) Sufficient space must be available for easy setting of the wrench to the reamer bolt on the propeller shaft joint.
(4) The bed must be constructed so that a wrench can be set at the bottom of the engine base to retighten the engine mounting bolts.
(5) Make the bed such that the propeller shaft and engine drive shaft are in a straight line.

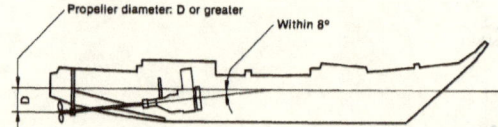

Chapter 11 Installation and Fitting
2. Engine Installation
_____SM/2QM15

2-3 Dimensions

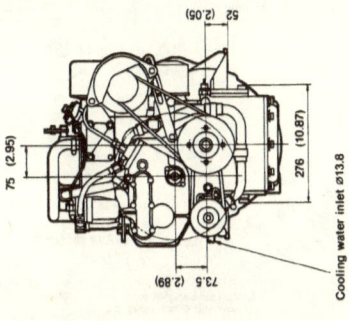

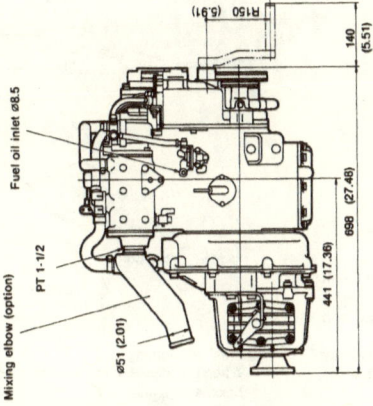

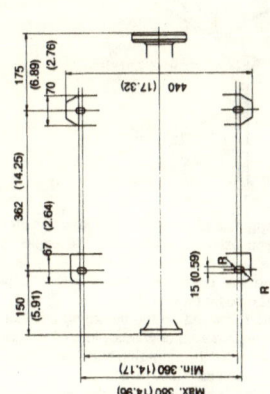

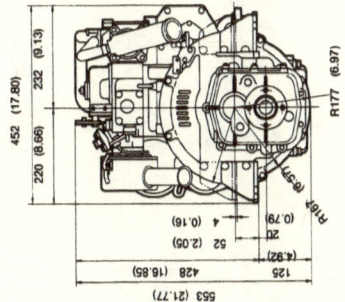

Chapter 11 Installation and Fitting
2. Engine Installation

2-4 Engine installation method
2-4.1 Fixed installation

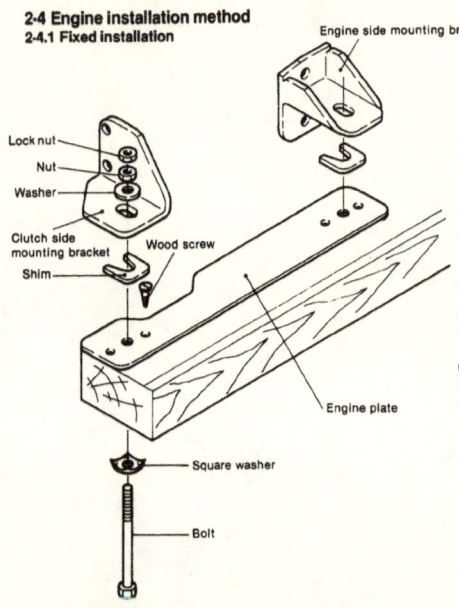

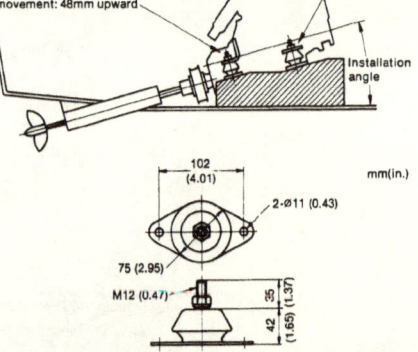

Part No: 124070 - 08340

(2) Fixed type flexible mounting — Must be centered with shims

Part No: 104271 - 08340

(1) If the engine bed is made of wood, use a steel engine plate and securely attach it to the engine bed with wood screws.
Machine the engine so that the engine plate and engine bed contact securely.
(2) Bite into the wood on the mounting bolt hull side by using a square washer with a width of at least 5 times the diameter of the mounting bolt.
Mounting bolt size: M12 ~ M14
(3) Adjust the shim between the engine plate and mounting bracket so that the propeller shaft and drive shaft are in a straight line.
Shim thickness: 0.2 ~ 1.0mm
(4) Tighten the mounting bolts uniformly. The bolts must not be tightened excessively at one side even when not centered. Two mounting nuts should be used so that there is no chance of the nuts working loose.

(3) Flexible coupling
When the engine is installed with flexible mountings a flexible coupling must always be used at the propeller shaft coupling.
NOTE: Install only after the drive shaft coupling and propeller shaft coupling have been centered.

2-4.2 Flexible mounting
(1) Ajustable type flexible mounting

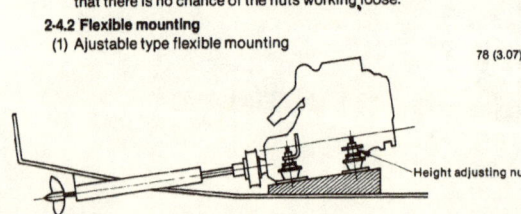

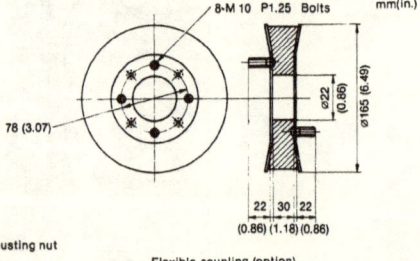

Flexible coupling (option)

Chapter 11 Installation and Fitting
2. Engine Installation

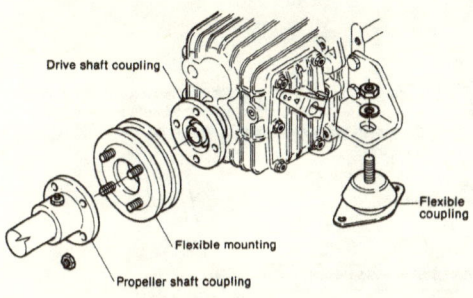

(a) Install a dial gauge on the propeller shaft coupling and measure the circumference versus drive shaft coupling center run-out (at four equally spaced points around the circumference).

(b) Then lock the drive shaft, turn the propeller shaft and dial gauge, and measure the outside periphery of the drive shaft and adjust to the value measured at (a) above.

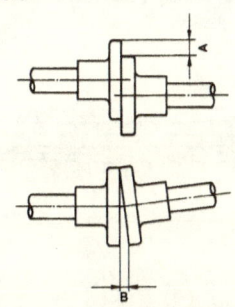

2-5 Centering
2-5.1 Coupling mating face measurement

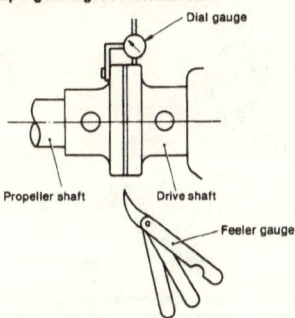

Coupling misalignment A	0.05 mm or less (0.002in.)
Coupling face run-out B	0.2 mm or less (0.0079in.)

2-5.2 After launching the vessel, check whether the drive shaft and propeller shaft are aligned.

Before installing the propeller shaft to the engine (intermediate shaft when there is an intermediate shaft), ascertain that the couplings of both shafts are centered. When the center of the engine is too high, adjust by cutting the engine bed, and when the engine is too high, adjust by inserting plates.

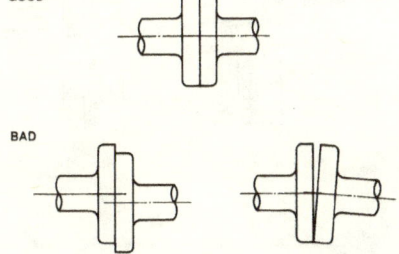

3. Stern Equipment

3-1 Stern tube installation

The bearing at the point at which the stern equipment passes through the hull is called the stern tube. The propeller shaft is supported by inserting lignumvitae (wood), cutless bearing (rubber) and other support materials. The propeller shaft is inserted into the stern tube and the bow end is connected to the intermediate shaft or drive shaft, while the propeller shaft is installed to the stern end taper.

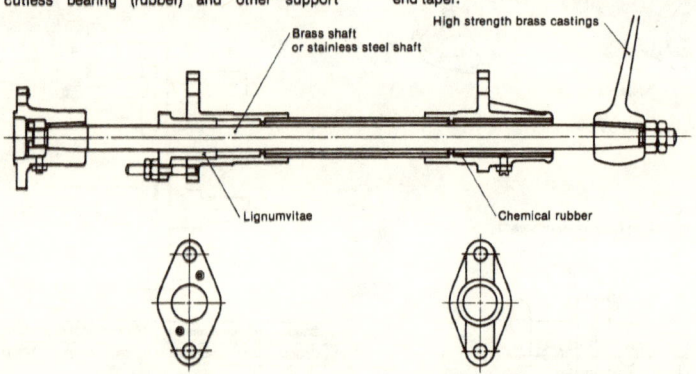

(a) Initial drilling
 Bore a 30 ~ 40 mm diameter temporary hole smaller than the stern tube through the hull as shown in the drawing

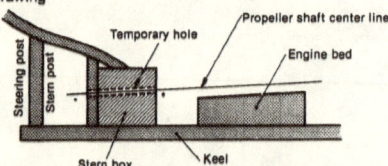

* Set the hole center, than drill

(b) Passing the centering line through the temporary hole
 Pass the centering line through the temporary hole and fasten one end to the steering post and the other end to the engine room wall as shown below (The line should be tight.)

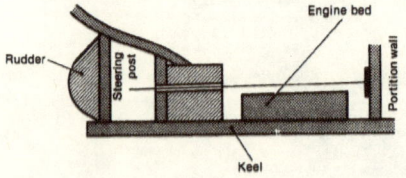

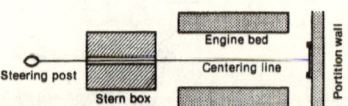

Make a parallel-cross frame (below) and attach it to the engine room wall. Then insert plate A, which carries the centering line, so that it is movable in all directions to allow correction of the line's position.
Fasten the line as illustrated in below [b] for easy removal. The empty hole in plate A (after the line is removed) permits pencil marking-off or center peep.

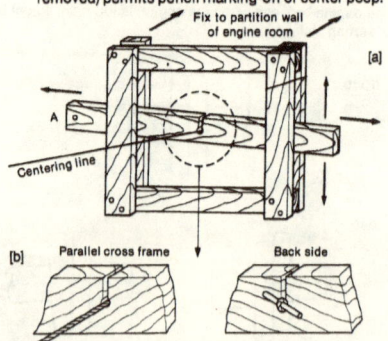

Chapter 11 Installation and Fitting
3. Stern Equipment

SM/2QM15

(c) Centering
Measure the dimensions between various points and the centering line and set the temporary position of the engine in accordance with the dimensions given in the drawing.
(1) Measure the dimension between the centering line and the top of the engine bed to determine the installation level and height of the crankshaft center line, then measure the clipping margins of the engine bed.
(2) Measure the dimensions between the centering line and the inside surface of the engine bed.
(3) At the flywheel and clutch, measure the dimensions between the centering line and the ship's bottom to check that the clutch case, engine oil pan, and flywheel clear the ship's bottom or sleepers.
(4) Then temporarily fix the centering line adjusting plate A.

NOTE 1: Since centering based on the stern tube hole is performed on land, ample engine bed chipping allowances under the center line must be provided to allow for possible distortion after launching.
NOTE 2: If the flywheel, oil pan or clutch case contact the ship's bottom or any sleeper, raise the shaft center. However, in this case, the engine installation angle must be no more than 8°.
NOTE 3: The engine should be installed on as horizontal a plane as possible. Remember, propeller efficiency is highest when the engine is horizontal.

(d) Final drilling
After temporary centering, mark off one stern tube hole on each side of the stern box based on the centering line, and then bore holes that exactly fit the stern tube (no play).

(e) Stern tube installation
(1) Remove the centering line, but either leave the frame of parallel crosses or mark off its center position on the front wall of the engine room
(2) Insert the stern tube, check for interference, and temporarily tighten.
(3) Centering for stern tube installation
 (a) Prepare a wooden block having a center hole covered with a thin tin plate.
 Hammer the block into the propeller side of the stern tube, obtain the center point with a compass and then make a small hole at this point with a nail or the line. Pass one end of the centering line through the hole and fasten the other end to the empty hole in plate A (3-1 (b)).

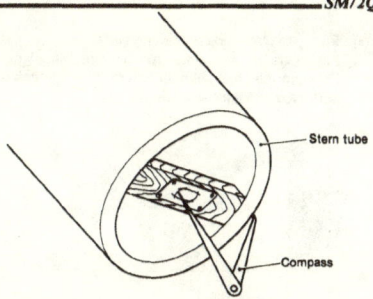

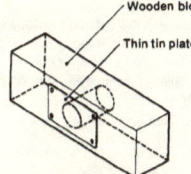

NOTE 1: The center deflection of the stern tube is 3 ~ 4 times greater at the front of the engine bed. Therefore, sufficient care must be exercised.
NOTE 2: If the stern tube holes are so large that stern tube play is excessive, tighten the stern tube to the correct position and mark that position so that the tube can be replaced correctly.
Check that the centering line is at the center of the stern tube at the inside flange. If not, center by moving either the stern tube or the centering line.

 (b) When centering the propeller side of the stern tube, the use of a centering jig with various outside diameters that fit the stern tube (below) will prove very convenient.

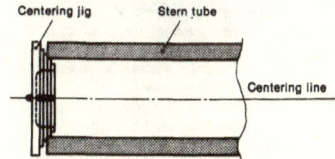

A tapered jig can be made for an infinite variety of stern tube inside diameters.

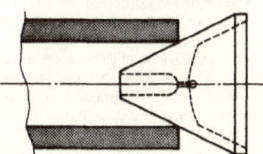

11-7

Chapter 11 Installation and Fitting
3. Stern Equipment

SM/2QM15

(4) Fitting of stern tube tightening surface
Pay careful attention to the rectangularity between the stern tube and stern tube tightening surface of the stern box when fitting.

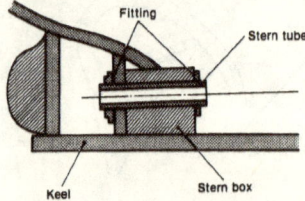

NOTE: If the stern tube and stern tube tightening surface of the stern box are not exactly rectangular, the stern tube will bend when tightened, causing overheating, seizing, abnormal lignumvitae wear and other troubles.

(5) Attaching the stern tube

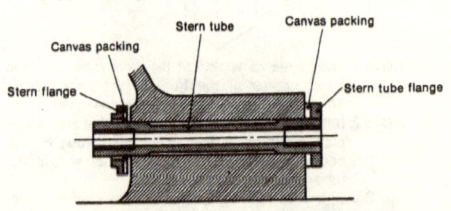

(a) Paint the outside of the stern tube with rust-preventive paint.
(b) Paint the stern tube flange and the surface of the stern box with white paint, and attach the canvas packings.
(c) Install the stern tube.
(d) Paint the outside of the stern post and the stern tube flange with white paint, and install the canvas packing and the stern flange.
Also paint the screw holes with white paint and tighten the screws.
(e) Attach the clamp for the stern tube chemical rubber tube and install the fastening wire.
(f) Drive in the coach screws to lock the inside and outside stern tube flanges and lock the stern flange nuts.

3-2 Propeller shaft installation
After fitting the stern tube packing gland to the propeller shaft, fit the propeller shaft to the stern tube by hand. Before fitting the propeller shaft to the stern tube, clean the interior of the stern tube and coat the lignumvitae with grease. When suspending the propeller shaft with a rope when inserting the shaft, the rope must not contact the rubber coil directly. Since propeller shaft insertion is performed at the narrowest part of the hull, be careful not to damage the brass coil and rubber coil. After inserting the propeller shaft, check the clearance between the stern tube and shaft while turning the shaft.
Insert the waterproof packing at the stern tube packing gland. Use braided string boiled in grease as the packing. Do not use a long coil, but rings cut one at a time, such as piston rings. When inserting the packing, the notches must alternate.
Tighten the packing uniformly while measuring the distance from the stern tube face to the gland face so that the packing gland is not tightened unevenly.

3-3 Propeller installation
(1) First, remove the shaft key, coat the shaft with red lead or bearing blue, fit the propeller shaft, and mark the position of the propeller on the brass coil. Then check the propeller shaft and propeller hole contact—if the contact is poor, correct. Poor contact and play during use will damage the key and key groove. After repairing, install the propeller and mark its position on the brass coil.
Then remove the propeller, insert the key on the shaft and fit and tighten the propeller. However, before this, check whether the marks made after repair match. If they do not, the key is contacting and must be removed and cut.

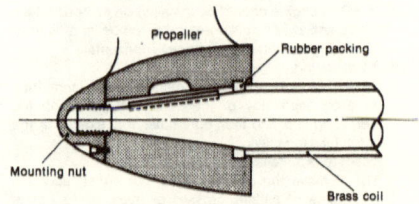

(2) Measuring the dimensions of the waterproofing rubber between the propeller shaft and propeller.

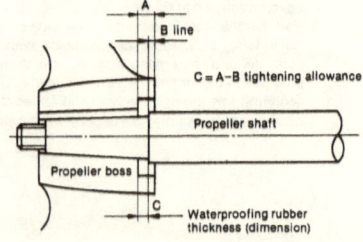

Chapter 11 Installation and Fitting
3. Stern Equipment

Insert the propeller onto the propeller shaft and mark the end of the propeller on the brass coil. The difference between the A dimension and B dimension in the figure is the waterproof rubber dimension, but a slight tightening allowance must be made.

(3) Propeller position
With the propeller installed, the ship's full speed will not be obtained if the spacing between the propeller and hull is not equal to, or greater than, the value given in the figure.
The position of the propeller section shaft center must be at least the diameter of the propeller from the surface of the water with the ship fully loaded.

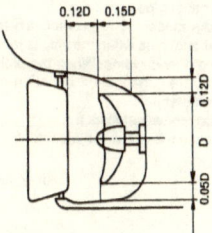

4. Interior Piping and Wiring

4-1 Exhaust pipe
4-1.1 Exhaust muffler installation

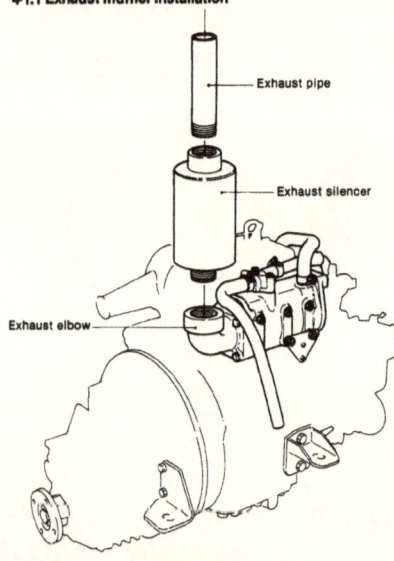

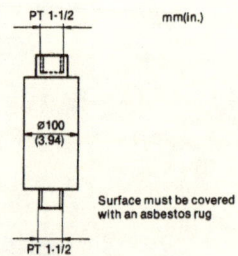

Surface must be covered with an asbestos rug

(1) Installation method and dimensions
- Install the exhaust silencer either directly to the exhaust elbow installed on the exhaust manifold or on the exhaust pipe.
- When the silencer is installed in the exhaust pipe, use an exhaust pipe socket.
- In the case of a horizontal exhaust, use a horizontal exhaust elbow.

(2) Precautions
1) Always use an exhaust elbow when the direction of the exhaust must be changed.
2) Clamp the pipe to the hull at suitable positions.
3) Decide the exhaust silencer installation position according to the structure of the hull, but since the silencer reaches a high temperature, it should protrude past the cabin.
4) When piping the exhaust, the prevention of heat damage and fire must be considered because the exhaust is hot. Always cover the surface of the exhaust pipe with a rug.
5) Take measures to prevent rain from entering the exhaust pipe when the ship is moored.
6) Avoid long piping. When the piping must be long and the change of direction large, use large diameter pipe.

4-1.2 Mixing elbow installation
(1) Installation method and dimensions
   1) L-type

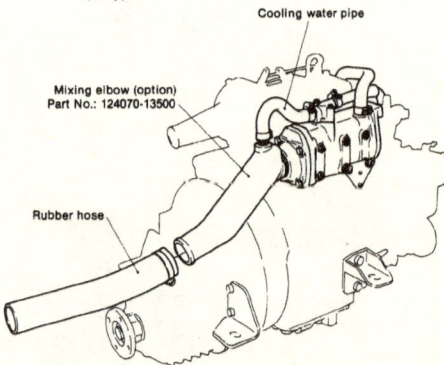

- Rubber hose connection dimensions

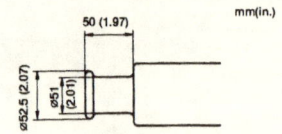

Rubber hose
Inside diameter: 50.8 mm
Outside diameter: 63 ~ 70 mm
Hose clip: 65 ~ 70 mm

Chapter 11 Installation and Fitting
4. Interior Piping and Wiring

2) U-type

Mixing elbow (option)
Part No.: 124070-13520

Joint (option)
Part No.: 104214-13580

Exhaust elbow

Rubber hose

Cooling water pipe (option)
Part No.: 104564-49210

• Rubber hose connection dimensions

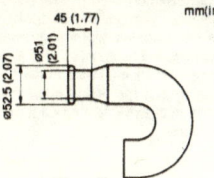

mm(in.)

Rubber hose dimensions
Inside diameter: 50.8 mm
Outside diameter: 63 ~ 70 mm
Hose clip: 65 ~ 70 mm

(2) Exhaust section installation   mm(in.)

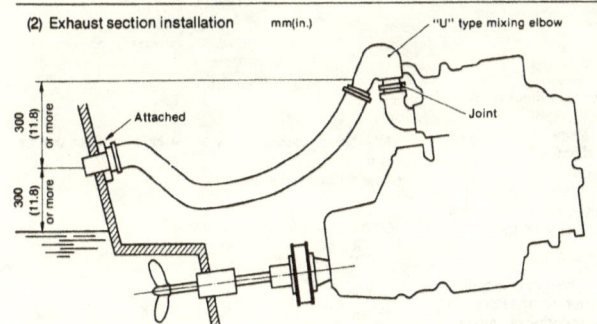

"U" type mixing elbow

Attached

Joint

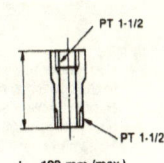

PT 1-1/2

PT 1-1/2

L = 100 mm (max.)

If different from the left, adjust the height by inserting the joint shown above

4-2 Cooling water pipe
4-2.1 Kingston cock
(1) Installation
- Determine the position of the Kingston cock by the position of the cooling water pipe and the direction of the cooling water pump inlet joint.
- Finish the contact face of the Kingston cock hole drilled in the ship's bottom by grinding.
- Install the cock using canvas on the outside of the hull and canvas or rubber packing on the inside.

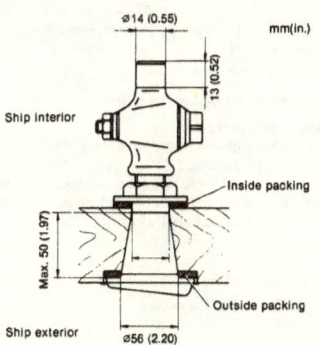

(2) Scoop strainer
The inlet section should have a double bottom to prevent troubles stemming from a lack of cooling water caused by sucking in of a vinyl sheet, etc., at the Kingston cock inlet port. Install the strainer so that the large area of the scoop strainer faces away from the direction of the ship's forward movement, as shown in the figure.

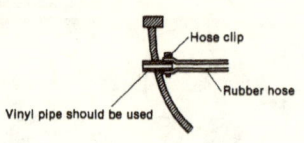
Vinyl pipe should be used

4-2.3 Bilge pipe piping precautions

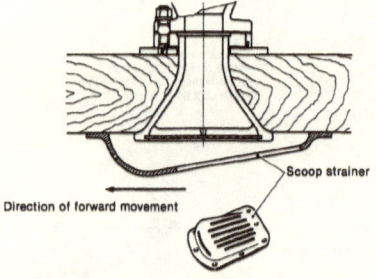

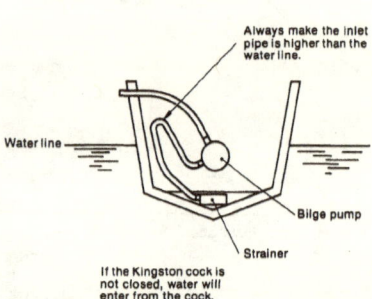
If the Kingston cock is not closed, water will enter from the cock.

(3) Piping
- Use rubber hose for piping from the Kingston cock to the cooling water pump.
  Rubber hose size: Inside diameter x outside diameter x length = 13 × 20 × ℓ (mm)
  Hose clip size: ⌀22 mm.

- The piping must be as straight as possible and bends must not be severe—radius must be 100mm or greater.

(4) When two Kingston cocks are used
When one of the Kingston cocks becomes clogged, operation can be switched to the other while the clogged cock is being cleaned, even during operation. In this case, use a 3-way cock for switching.

4-2.4 When cooling water outlet is lower than the water line
Always use a water lock.

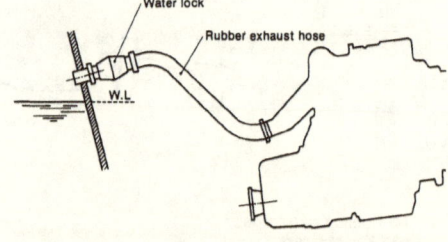

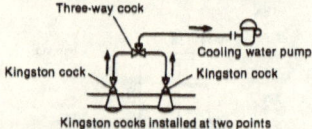
Kingston cocks installed at two points

4-2.2 Cooling water outlet pipe
(1) When a mixing elbow is installed, refer to the exhaust rubber hose piping section.
(2) When the mixing elbow is not used, connect a rubber hose to the cooling water outlet fixture so that the cooling water is purged directly from the ship.

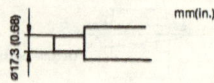

4-3 Fuel tank and fuel piping
4-3.1 Fuel tank
(1) Clean the interior of the fuel tank with light oil and install the tank to the hull.
(2) The fuel tank must be positioned so that fuel is easy to add, fuel level is easy to check, and draining is easy. Moreover, take engine maintenance and inspection into consideration when deciding fuel tank position.
(3) A fuel pump is installed as standard, but the fuel tank should be installed at the highest possible point as near the engine as possible.

Chapter 11 Installation and Fitting
4. Interior Piping and Wiring

(4) Fuel tank (option) details

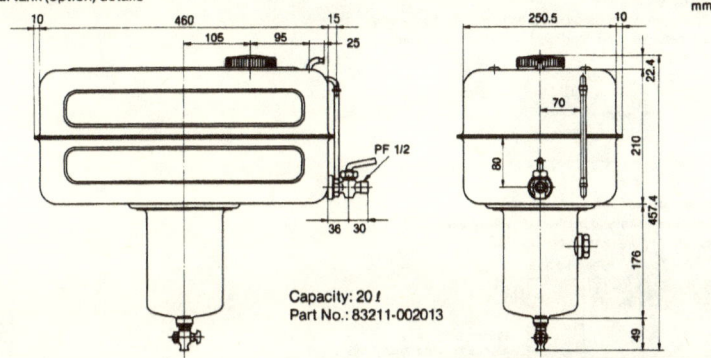

Capacity: 20 l
Part No.: 83211-002013

4-3.2 Fuel piping
(1) The hose must be as straight as possible.
    Minimum bend radius: 50mm
(2) Be careful that the fuel piping does not touch the exhaust pipe or other hot parts.
(3) Fuel pipe (option) details.

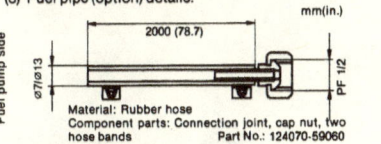

Material: Rubber hose
Component parts: Connection joint, cap nut, two hose bands
Part No.: 124070-59060

4-4 Electrical system
4-4.1 Battery installation and wiring
(1) Select a battery position which meets electrical wiring requirements.
    The battery must be positioned for easy checking of the electrolyte level.
(2) Install the battery on the battery mounting frame.
(3) Connect the wiring securely so that there is no voltage drop, and cover the terminals for protection.
(4) Select battery cables (battery—starter ground, battery—battery switch, battery switch—starter) having a total resistance of less than 0.002Ω.

4-4.2 Instrument panel
(1) Mounting dimensions

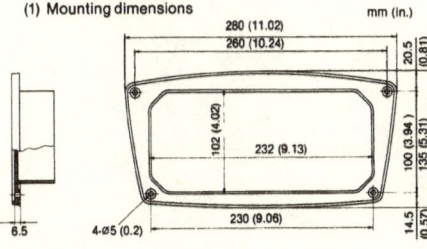

Drill the mounting holes and bolt holes in accordance with the instrument panel mounting diagram.
(2) Installation location and dimensions
The instrument panel should be installed in the cabin, but if it is installed outside, pay careful attention to the following points.
   1) Install in a location where there is no danger of the panel being splashed by sea water.
   2) When the instrument panel is installed where it may be splashed by sea water, install it in a recessed position or install a cover.

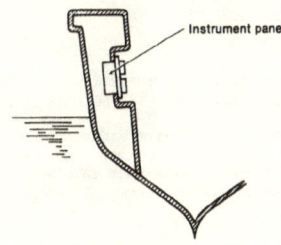

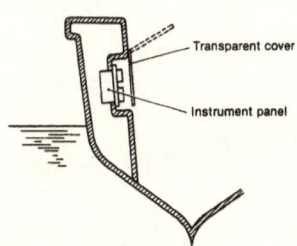

3) Installation angle
   The instrument panel must be installed at an angle of between 45° and 90° to prevent indicating errors.

4-5 Remote control

4-5.1 Remote control stand installation dimensions

(1) Morse one-handle remote control (MT)

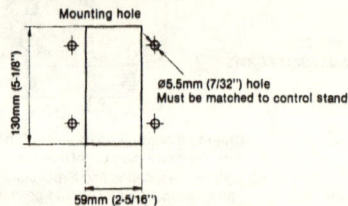

(2) Engine stop remote control decompression remote control

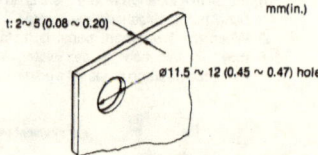

Common to both stop remote control and decompression remote control

4-5.2 Remote control cable precautions

The remote control push-pull cable must be as straight as possible. Numerous bends will increase the operating load and shorten the life of the cable.

5. Front Power Take-Off

Power to drive the deck machinery and small generator, pump, compressor, etc. can be taken from the front of the engine.
Power take-off capacity, drive system selection and the quality of installation centering have a considerable effect on the engine, and care must be exercised.

5-1 Front power take-off details
A crankshaft V-pulley is used as the front power take-off coupling.

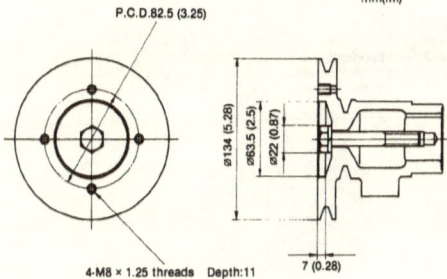

5-2 Front drive system
(1) A-system
   Belt drive system using one outside bearing

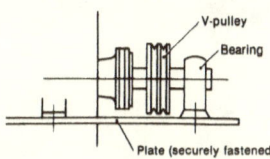

NOTE: Alignment must be within 0.05 mm.
(3) B-system
   Direct coupling to driven machine without belt drive

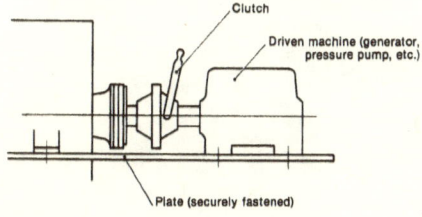

NOTE: Alignment must be within 0.05 mm.

(4) C-system
   Belt drive using two or more outside bearings

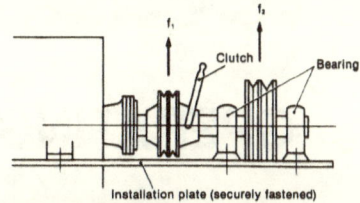

NOTE: 1. Maximum take-off output = f1 + f2
2. f1 must be less than output possible with "A" system.
3. Alignment = 0.05 mm or less
   Surface run-out = 0.05 mm or less

5-3 Front power take-off general precautions
(1) With belt drive, the belt tension must be adjusted so that an excessive load is not applied to the drive shaft.
(2) Since the possible take-off power depends on the drive system, it must be used within the allowable output range shown in the graph.
(3) The engine installation plate and driven machine installation plate must be made of steel, and securely fastened to the engine bed. Further, the bearing and driven machine must be centered and installed accurately.
(4) Pulleys and other rotating parts must be balanced.
(5) Since the engine will shake when flexible mountings are used for engine installation, a flexible coupling or universal joint must be used between the engine and the driven machine.

5-4 Front power take-off allowable output

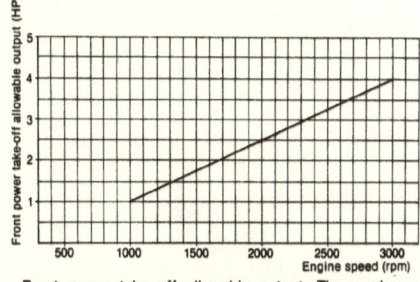

Front power take off allowable output: The maximum output for the A, B and C systems is given above.
Range connection: 1HP/1,000 rpm ~ 4HP/3,000 rpm
NOTE: Engine speed must be 1,000 rpm or greater for operation of the front drive.

CHAPTER 12
OPERATING INSTRUCTIONS

1. Fuel Oil and Lubricating Oil 12-1
2. Engine Operating Instructions 12-8
3. Troubleshooting and Repair 12-12

1. Fuel Oil and Lubricating Oil

Selection of and proper attention to fuel and lubricating oils have a substantial effect on engine performance, and are vital factors governing engine life.
The use of low quality fuel and lubricating oils will lead to various engine troubles. Yanmar diesel engines will display satisfactory performance and ample reliability if the fuel and lubricating oil recommended by Yanmar are used correctly. For the engine to display long-term high performance, sufficient knowledge of the properties of the fuel and lubricating oils and their selection, management and usage is necessary.

1-1 Fuel
1-1.1 Properties of fuel
Numerous kinds of fuels are used with diesel engines, and the properties and composition of each differ somewhat according to the manufacturer.
Moreover, the various national standards are introduced here for reference purposes.

1-1.2 Recommended fuels

Manufacturer	Brand name
Caltex	Caltex Diesel Oil
Shell	Shell Diesoline or local equivalent
Mobil	Mobil Diesel Oil
Esso	Esso Diesel Oil
British Petroleum	BP Diesel Oil

1-1.3 Fuel selection precautions
Pay careful attention to the following when selecting the fuel.

(1) Must have a suitable specific gravity
Fuel having a specific gravity of $0.88 \sim 0.94$ at 15°C is suitable as diesel engine fuel. Specific gravity has no relation to spontaneous combustibility, but does give an idea of viscosity and combustibility or mixing of impurities.
Generally, the higher the specific gravity, the higher the viscosity and the poorer the combustibility.

(2) Must have a suitable viscosity
When the viscosity is too high, the fuel flow will be poor, operation of the pump and nozzle will be inferior, atomization will be faulty and fuel combustion will be incomplete.
If the viscosity is too low, the plunger, nozzle, etc. will wear rapidly because of insufficient lubrication. Generally, however, the higher the viscosity, the lower the quality of the fuel.

(3) Cetane value must be high.
The most important indicator of fuel's combustibility is its cetane value (also represented by cetane index or diesel index). The cetane value is particularly important for fuels used in high-speed engines. The relationship among the cetane value, startability and firing delay is shown in the below figure. Firing delay becomes smaller and starting characteristics better as the cetane value becomes higher.

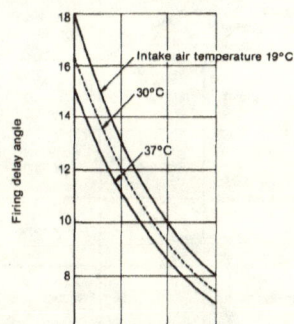

Relationship between cetane value and firing delay

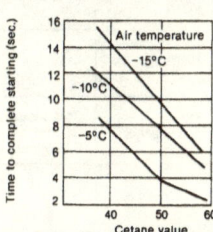

Cetane value and starting characteristic

The use of a fuel with an unsuitable cetane value will cause the following troubles:
1) Difficult starting.
2) Poor operation.
3) High combustion pressure and diesel knock.
4) Lower output and engine damage because of overheating caused by knocking.
5) Sticking of nozzles and exhaust valves.
6) Severe smoking, carbon build-up inside the engine, and oil contamination.
7) Deterioriation of the oil and excessive wear in the piston rings, ring grooves, and cylinder liner.

(4) The level of impurities must be low
1) Sulfur
With proper combustion sulfur in the fuel turns to nitrous acid gas (SO_2) and sulfuric anhydride (SO_3). When combustion is imperfect, it becomes sulfuric acid containing water that corrodes and wears the cylinder liners, pistons, exhaust valve and exhaust pipe.

Chapter 12 Operating Instructions
1. Fuel Oil and Lubricating Oil

SM/2QM15

Properties and compositions of fuel of various national standards

National standard / Properties and components		Japan JIS-K-2204-1965		U.S.A. ASTM-D975-74	U.K. BS-2689-70	
		Class No.1 light oil	Class No.2 light oil	No. 2D Diesel oil	Class A1	Class A2
Specific gravity	15/4°C	—	—	—	—	—
Kinetic viscosity	30°C cst	2.7 or more	2.5 or more	(∼ 5.2)	(∼ 7.5)	(∼ 7.5)
	37.8°C (100°F) cst	(2.3 or more)	(2.2 or more)	2.0∼4.3	1.6 ∼ 6.0	1.6 ∼ 6.0
Reaction		Neutral	Neutral	—	—	—
Flash point	°C	50 or more	50 or more	51.7 or more	55 or more	55 or more
Flow point	°C	−5 or less	−10 or less	−12 or less	—	—
Residual carbon	Weight %	(10% residual oil) 0.15 or less	(10% residual oil) 0.15 or less	0.35 or less	0.2 or less	0.2 or less
Moisture	Volume %	—	—	—	0.05 or less	0.05 or less
Ash	Weight %	—	—	0.01 or less	0.01 or less	0.01 or less
Sulfur	Weight %	1.2 or less	1.2 or less	0.5 or less	0.5 or less	1.0 or less
Cetane valve		50 or more	45 or more	40 or more	50 or more	45 or more
Sludge or sedimentation	%	—	—	0.05 or less	0.01 or less	0.01 or less
Distillation properties, temperatures at 90% distillation	°C	350 or below	350 or below	282.21 ∼ 338	357 or below	357 or below

Chapter 12 Operating Instructions
1. Fuel Oil and Lubricating Oil

2) Water content
   A high water content causes sludge, resulting in lower output, imperfect combustion and trouble in the fuel injection system.
3) Carbon content
   If the carbon content is high, carbon will remain inside the combustion chamber, causing accelerated cylinder liner and piston wear and corrosion of the pistons and exhaust valves.
4) Residual carbon (coke content)
   Coke becomes a carbide that sticks to the end of the nozzle, causing faulty injection. In addition, unburned carbon will build up on the pistons and liners, causing piston ring wear and sticking.

1-1.4 Simple methods of identifying fuel properties
(1) Fuel that is extremely odorous and smoky contains a large amount of volatile components and impurities.
(2) Fuel that emits little smoke when used in a lamp is of good quality.
(3) Fuel that emits a crackling sound when soaked in paper and ignited contains a high water content.
(4) If a transparent film of diesel oil is squeezed between two pieces of glass, the water content and impurities can be determined.
(5) If cracked by mixing with an equal amount of sulfuric acid in a glass tube, numerous black particles and impurities will appear. These are mainly carbon and resin.
(6) Discoloration of litmus test paper indicates the presence of acids.

1-1.5 Troubles caused by bad fuel
(1) Clogging of exhaust valve
   In addition to faulty compression, incomplete combustion, and high fuel consumption, a clogged exhaust valve will cause fuel to be mixed in the exhaust, leading to corrosion of the exhaust valve seat.
(2) Clogging of piston ring grooves
   Clogged piston ring grooves will cause accelerated cylinder liner and piston wear due to sticking rings, fuel gas blowback, faulty lubrication, incomplete combustion, high fuel consumption, contaminated lubricating oil, and combustion gas blowback.
(3) Clogged or corroded injection valve hole
   This will cause incomplete combustion and piston and liner wear, fuel injection mechanism wear, corrosion, and groove wear and corrosion.
(4) Sediment inside crankcase
   Since sediment in the crankcase is often mistakenly judges as coming from the lubricating oil, care must be taken in determining its true origin.

1-1.6 Relationship between fuel properties and engine performance

Fuel property	Starting characteristic	Lubrication characteristic	Smoke generation	Exhaust odor	Output	Fuel consumption	Clogging of combustion chamber
Firing Cetane value	Directly related—Starting characteristic improves as cetane value increases	Directly related—Lubrication improves as cetane value rises	Closely related—Smoke increases as cetane value decreases	Directly related—Decreased by increasing cetane value	Irrelevant	Related	Related—Decreased by reducing cetane value
Volatility 90% end point	No clear relationship	Related—Becomes poor when volatility is poor	Directly related—Increases as volatility decrease	No direct relationship	Irrelevant	Irrelevant	Related—Increases as volatility decreases
Viscosity	No clear relationship	Some relationship—Becomes poor when viscosity increases	Related—Increases as viscosity increases	No independent relationship	Irrelevant	Irrelevant	Related—Increases with viscosity
Specific gravity	Irrelevant	Irrelevant	Related—Increases as specific gravity increases	No independent relationship	Directly related—Associated with calorific value	Related—Associated with calorific value	Related—Depends on properties of engine
10% residual carbon	Irrelevant	Irrelevant	Related—Improves as residual carbon decreases	No independent relationship	Irrelevant	Irrelevant	Related—Decreases as residual carbon decreases
Sulfur				No independent relationship			
Flash point				No independent relationship			

Chapter 12 Operating Instructions
1. Fuel Oil and Lubricating Oil

1-1.7 Fuel handling precautions
(1) Fill the fuel tank after work to prevent condensation of water in the tank.
(2) Always use a tank inlet strainer. Water mixed in the fuel can be removed by removing the strainer quickly.
(3) Remove the plug at the bottom of the fuel tank and drain out the water and sediment after every 100 hours of operation, and when servicing the pump and nozzle.
(4) Do not use fuel in the bottom of the fuel tank because it contains large amounts of dirt and water.

1-2 Lubricating oil
Selection of the lubricating oil is extremely important with a diesel engine. The use of unsuitable lubricating oil will cause sticking of the piston rings, accelerated wear and seizing of the piston and cylinder liner, rapid wear of the bearings and other moving parts, and reduced engine durability. Since this engine is a high-speed engine, always follow the lubricating oil replacement interval.

1-2.1 Action of the lubricating oil
(1) Lubricating action: Builds a film of oil on each moving part reduce wear and its accompanying damage.
(2) Cooling action: Removes heat generated at moving parts by carrying it away with the lubricating oil flow.
(3) Sealing action: Maintains the air tightness of the pistons and cylinders by the oil film on the piston rings.
(4) Cleaning action: Carries away carbon produced at the cylinders as well as dust that has entered from the outside.
(5) Rustproofing action: Prevents corrosion by coating metal surfaces with a thin film of oil.

Various additives are added to the lubricating oil to assure that adequate performance is derived under the high-speed, high-load and other severe operating conditions met by modern diesel engines. While these additives differ with each manufacturer, commonly used additives include:
(1) Flow point reduction additive
(2) Viscosity index improvement additive
(3) Oxidation prevention additive
(4) Cleaning dispersant
(5) Lubrication additive
(6) Anticorrosion additive
(7) Bubble elimination additive
(8) Alkali neutralizer

1-2.2 Required lubricating oil conditions
(1) Must be of suitable viscosity
If the viscosity is too low, the oil film will be too thin and the lubricating action insufficient. If the viscosity is too high, the friction resistance will be increased and starting will become especially difficult.
(2) Viscosity change with temperature must be small
While the lube oil temperature goes from low at starting to high during operation, the viscosity change by temperature should be small. That is, the viscosity index should be high at all temperatures.
(3) Must have good lubricating capability
That is, it must coat to metal surfaces as a thin film. In other words, the lubricating oil must coat the metal surfaces so that metal-to-metal contact caused by breaking of the oil film at the top dead center and bottom dead center piston position does not occur, or that the oil film is not broken by collision, even at the bearings.
(4) Mixability with water must be low
Since water can mix with the oil because of the presence of cooling water in the engine, the emulsification of water and oil, which causes the oil to lose its lubricating properties, must be prevented.
(5) Must be neutral and difficult to oxidize
Since acids and alkalis corrode metal, the lubricating oil must be neutral. Moreover, since even a neutral oil will be oxidized easily by contact with the combustion gas, the oil must be stable with few oxidizing elements.
(6) Must withstand high heat and must evaporate or combust with difficulty
Oil must have a high flash point. If it is evaporated by heat or is not burned completely, carbon will be produced. This carbon is toxic.
(7) Must not contain any water or dirt and must have a low sulfur and coke content

1-2.3 Classification by viscosity

SAE No.	6°F (−17.8°C)		210°F (98.9°C)		Applicable temperature range (outside temperature)
	Saybolt universal viscosity (sec)	Dynamic viscosity (cst)	Saybolt universal viscosity (sec)	Dynamic viscosity (cst)	
5W	Under 4,000	Under 869	—	—	20°C or less
10W	6,000 ~ 12,000	1,303 ~ 2,606	—	—	
20W	12,000 ~ 48,000	2,606 ~ 10,423	—	—	
20	—	—	45 ~ 58	5.73 ~ 9.62	20°C ~ 35°C
30	—	—	58 ~ 70	9.62 ~ 12.93	
40	—	—	70 ~ 85	12.93 ~ 16.77	35°C or greater
50	—	—	85 ~ 110	16.77 ~ 22.68	

Chapter 12 Operating Instructions
1. Fuel Oil and Lubricating Oil

SM/2QM15

Since only the 98.9°C viscosity is stipulated for S.A.E. No. 20 ~ 50 oil in the table, and only the −17.8°C viscosity is stipulated for S.A.E. No. 5W ~ 20W oil, they are not guaranteed at other temperatures. On the other hand, S.A.E. No.10W viscosity is stipulated and oil having the viscosity equal to that of S.A.E. No.30 even at 98.9°C is called S.A.E. No.10W—30, or multigrade oil. Multigrade oil comprises S.A.E. No. 5W—20, 10W—30, and 20W—40. In arctic regions, oil from S.A.E. No. 20W to 10W—30 can be used.

1-2.4 SAE service classification and API service classification

SAE new classification (1970)	API service classification (1960)
CA	DG
CB·CC	DM
CD	DS

(1) DG grade: Used when deposits and engine wear must be controlled when the engine is normally operated at a light load using low sulfur fuel.
(2) DM grade: Used when the generation of deposits and wear caused by sulfur in the fuel is possible under severe conditions.
(3) DS grade: Used under extremely severe operating conditions or when excessive wear or deposits are caused by the fuel.

Classification	Engine service (API)
CA	Light duty diesel engine service: Mild, moderate operation diesel engine service with high-performance fuel, and mild gasoline engine service. The oil designed for this service was mainly used in the 1940s and 50s. This oil is for high performance fuel use and has bearing corrosion and high temperature deposit prevention characteristics.
CB	Moderate duty diesel engine service: Mild, moderate operation diesel engine service using low performance fuel requiring bearing corrosion and high temperature deposit prevention characteristics. Includes mild gasoline engine service. Oil designed for this service was introduced in 1949. The oil is used with high sulfur fuels and has bearing corrosion and high temperature deposit prevention characteristics.
CC	Moderate duty diesel engine service and gasoline engine service: Applicable to low supercharged diesel engines for moderate to severe duty. The oil designed for this service was introduced in 1961 and is widely used in trucks and agricultural equipment, construction machinery, farm tractors, etc. The oil features high deposit prevention characteristics in super-charged diesel engines, and rust, corrosion and low temperature sludge prevention characteristics in gasoline engines.
CD	Severe duty diesel engine service: Applicable to high-speed, high-output high supercharged diesel engines which are subjected to considerable wear and more deposits. This oil was introduced in 1955, and is used as a wide property-range fuel in high supercharged engines. It also has bearing corrosion and high temperature deposit prevention characteristics.

1-2.5 Fuel oil
SAE new classification CB grade or CC grade fuel having suitable viscosity for the atmospheric temperature must be used in this engine.

Chapter 12 Operating Instructions
1. Fuel Oil and Lubricating Oil

1-2.6 Recommended lubricating oils

Supplier	Brand Name	SAE No.			
		Below 10°C	10~20°C	20~35°C	Over 35°C
SHELL	Shell Rotella Oil	10W, 20/20W	20/20W	30 40	50
	Shell Talona Oil	10W	20	30 40	50
	Shell Rimula Oil	20/20W	20/20W	30 40	—
CALTEX	RPM Delo Marine Oil	10W	20	30 40	50
	RPM Delo Multi-Service Oil	20/20W, 10W	20	30	50
MOBIL	Delvac Special	10W	20	30	—
	Delvac 20W—40	20W—40	20W—40	—	—
	Delvac 1100 Series	10W, 20/20W	20/20W	30 40	50
	Delvac 1200 Series	10W, 20/20W	20/20W	30 40	50
ESSO	Estor HD	10W	20	30 40	—
	Esso Lube HD	—	20	30 40	50
	Standard Diesel Oil	10W	20	30 40	50
B.P. (British Petroleum)	B.P. Energol ICMB B.P. Energol DS-3	20W	20W	40	50

1-2.7 Engine oil replacement and handling

(1) Necessity of replacement

Since the engine oil is exposed to high heat during use and is mixed with air at high temperatures, it will oxidize and its properties will gradually change. In addition, its lubricating capabilities will be lost through contamination and dilution by water, impurities, and the fuel. Emulsification and sludge are produced by heat and mixing when the lubricating oil contains water and impurities, causing its viscosity to increase. Moreover, if the carbon in the cylinders enters the crankcase, the oil will turn pure black and the change in its properties can be seen at a glance. The continued use of deteriorated oil will not only cause wear and corrosion of moving parts, but will ultimately cause the bearings and cylinders to seize. Therefore, deteriorated oil must be replaced.

(2) Replacement period

Although the engine oil change interval differs with the engine operating conditions and the quality of the lubricating oil and fuel used, the oil interval should be change as follows when CB grade oil is used in a new engine:

1st time . . . . After approximately 20 hours of use
2nd time . . . . After approximately 30 hours of use
From 3rd time . . . After every 100 hours of use

Drain the old oil completely and replace it with new oil while the engine is still warm.

CAUTION: Never mix different brands of lubricating oil.

1-2.8 Adding oil

The crankcase and clutch case are not connected. For the crankcase, add one of the lubricating oils described in chapter 1.2.6. For the clutch case, add the lubricating oil described below. Be sure not to mix up the oils.

Supplier	Kinds
SHELL	DEXRON
CALTEX	TEXAMATIC FLUID
MOBIL	ATF220
ESSO	ATF
B.P.	AUTRAN DX

Chapter 12 Operating Instructions
1. Fuel Oil and Lubricating Oil

(1) Remove the clutch case clutch and head cover filler plug (engine), and fill with specified lubricating oil up to the top marks on the respective dipsticks. (Oil levels must not drop below the lower marks on the dipsticks.)

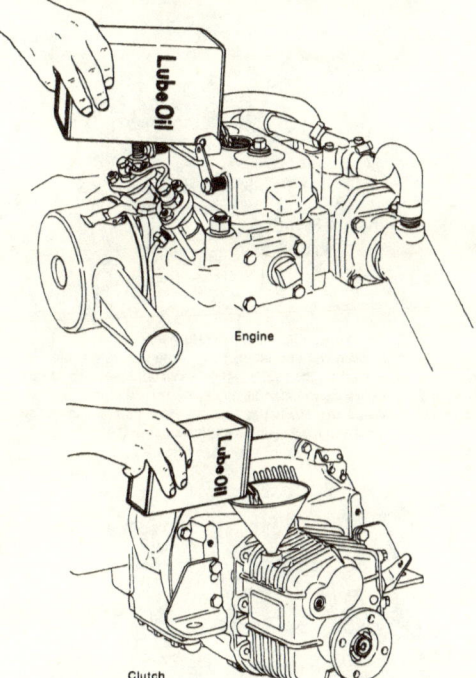

Engine

Clutch

(2) Since it takes sometime for these oils to flow completely into the clutch case and oil pan, wait for 2 ~ 3 minutes after filling before checking the oil levels. Moreover, check the oil while the ship is afloat.

1-2.9 Oil capacity
Lubricating oil capacity at an engine mounting angle (rake) of 8° is given below.

Crankcase	2.5ℓ	1.0ℓ
Clutch case	0.7ℓ	—

- Check the crankcase oil level by completely inserting the dipstick. Check the clutch case oil level without screwing in the cap.
The oil levels must be between the upper and lower limit marks on both dipsticks.

2. Engine Operating Instructions

2-1 Preparations before starting
2-1.1 Fueling up
(1) Check the fuel level in the fuel tank and add fuel if necessary.
Fuel consumption for 10 hour/day operation is given below.

14 HP/3,000 rpm	Approx. 26 l
15 HP/3,000 rpm	Approx. 30 l

(2) Remove water and dirt collected in the bottom of the tank using the fuel tank drain cock.
(3) Add clean fuel to the tank.
Since dirt and water sink to the bottom of the fuel drum, do not turn the drum upside down and do not pump the fuel from the bottom of the drum.

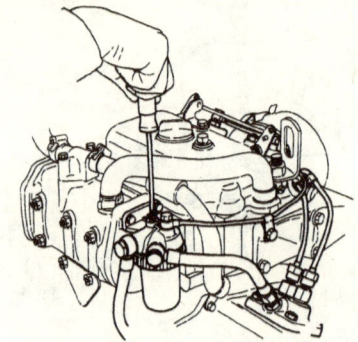

2-1.2 Adding lubricating oil
(1) Check the oil level with the dipstick, and add oil, if necessary, to bring the level up to the to mark of the dipstick.
The level must neither be too low nor too high.
(2) The crankcase and clutch case require different oil. Check both and add oil separately, being careful not to mix the oils.
(3) Since the crankcase oil flows into the crankcase through the camshaft and valve chambers, wait 2 ~ 3 minutes before checking its level.

2-1.3 Lubricating each part
(1) Lubricate each pin of the remote control lever.

2-1.4 Checking fuel priming and injection
(1) Operate the priming lever of the fuel pump.
(2) Set the regulator handle to the full speed position and check for injection sound by turning the engine over several times.
(3) If there is no fuel injection sound, bleed the air from the fuel system.

2-1.5 Bleeding the fuel system
Since the presence of air in the fuel system anywhere between the fuel tank and the injection valve will cause faulty fuel injection, always bleed the air from the system when the fuel system is disassembled and reassembled.

Bleeding the fuel system
(1) Open the fuel tank cock.
(2) Bleed the air from the fuel filter.
Loosen the air bleeding plug at the top of the fuel filter body and operate the manual handle of the fuel pump until no more bubbles appear in the fuel flowing from the filter.
Then install and tighten the air bleeding plug.

(3) Bleed the air from the fuel return pipe.
Loosen the connector bolt of the fuel return pipe installed on the fuel injection valve, and bleed the air by operating the manual handle of the fuel pump.
Bleed the air in the No.1 cylinder (timing gear case side) and No.2 cylinder (clutch side), in that order.

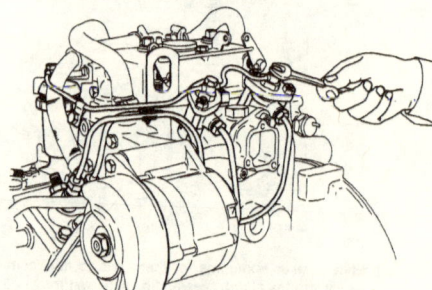

(4) Bleed the air from the fuel injection pipe.

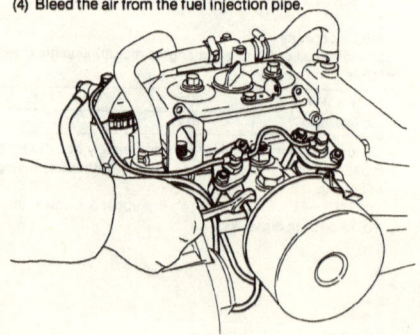

Chapter 12 Operating Instructions
2. Engine Operating Instructions

_____ SM/2QM15

Loosen the nipple on the fuel injection valve side, set the regulator handle to the operating position and the decompression lever to the decompression position, and crank the engine. When no more bubbles appear in the fuel flowing from the end of the injection pipe, retighten the nipple.

(5) Check injection.
After bleeding the air, set the regulator handle to the operating position, set the decompression lever to the decompression position, and crank the engine. When fuel is being injected from the injection valve, an injection sound will be heard and you can feel resistance if you place your hand on the fuel injection pipe. This check must not be performed more than two or three times since overchecking will flood the combustion chamber with fuel, and faulty combustion will occur at starting.

2-1.6 Checking for abnormal sounds by cranking

(1) Set the regulator handle to the STOP position, release the compression of the engine by setting the decompression lever, and crank the engine about 10 times to check for abnormal sounds.
(2) Crank the engine with the starting handle or starter motor.
(Always turn the engine in the proper direction of rotation.)

2-1.7 Checking the cooling system

(1) Open the Kingston cock.
(2) Check for bending and cross-sectional deformation of the cooling water inlet pipe.
(3) Set all water drain cocks to the CLOSED position.

2-1.8 Checking the remote control system

(1) Check that the remote control handle operates correctly.
(2) Check that the engine stop remote control operates smoothly.

2-1.9 Checking the electrical system

(1) Check the battery electrolyte level and add distilled water if low.
(2) Turn the battery switch on, set the main switch to the ON position, and check if the oil pressure lamp and charge lamp are illuminated and if the alarm buzzer sounds when the engine is stopped.
(The charge lamp should be on while the engine is stopped and should be off while the engine is running.)

2-1.10 Checking appearance and exterior

(1) Check for loose or missing bolts and nuts.
(2) Check for loose or disconnected piping and hoses.
(3) Check that there are no tools or other articles near rotating parts or on the engine.

2-2 Starting and warm-up
2-2.1 Starting

(1) Starting procedure
Pull the neutral knob and set the control lever to the MEDIUM SPEED position.

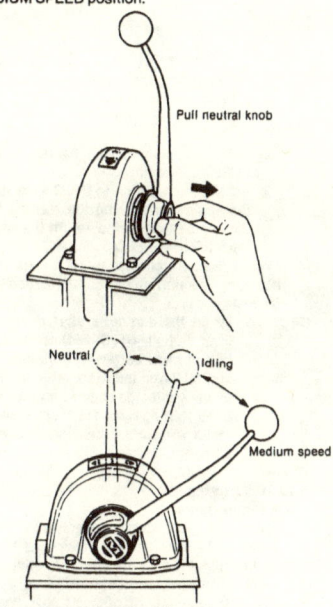

(2) Set the main switch to the ON position.
The alarm buzzer will sound.
(3) Push the starting button to start the engine.
Release the start button after the engine has started.
(4) When the engine has started, the alarm lamps and buzzer will go off.
If the lamps or buzzer stay on, immediately stop the engine and check for trouble.

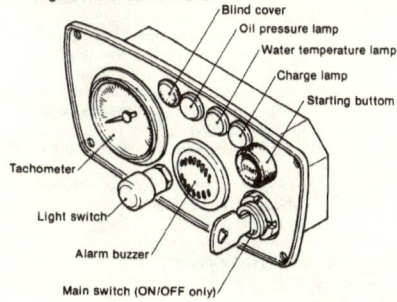

Printed in Japan
2F015A

Chapter 12 Operating Instructions
2. Engine Operating Instructions _____ SM/2QM15

(2) Starting in cold weather
  1) Pull the neutral knob, and set the control lever to the HIGH SPEED position.

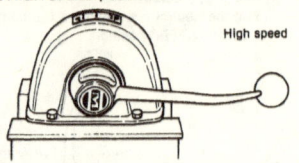
High speed

  2) Set the decompression handle to the DECOMPRESSION position.
  3) Set the main switch to the ON position and start the engine by pushing the starting button. After the engine has started, return the control lever to the MEDIUM SPEED position.
  *When the control lever is set to the HIGH SPEED position, injection timing is automatically delayed to facilitate starting.
  CAUTION: When the engine is started with the control lever in the HIGH SPEED position, the starting button must be released immediately and the control lever must be returned to the idling position after the engine has started.
  If the starting button is not released, the starter motor will overrun, causing it to be damaged or burnt out.

2-2.2 After starting
(1) Warm-up operation
  The engine must not be suddenly operated at full load immediately after starting. Warm up the engine for about 5 minutes after starting by running the engine at about half speed, and begin full load operation only after the temperature of each part has risen to a uniform value. Neglecting to warm up the engine will result in:
  1) Seizing of the piston and liner due to sudden neat expansion of the piston.
  2) Burning of piston rings and seizing of bearings/bushings because of insufficient lubrication.
  3) Faulty intake and exhaust valve seat contact and shortening of the life of each part due to sudden heating.

  Warm-up time (no-load operation)
  1,000 ~ 1,200 rpm 3 minutes
  1,600 ~ 1,800 rpm 2 minutes
  CAUTION: Do not run the engine at full speed for 50 hours after installation to assure proper break-in.
(2) Checking after starting
  Check the following with the clutch in the NEUTRAL position:
  1) Meters and lamps on the instrument panel
    • Check that all alarm lamps are off (1,000 rpm or higher).
    • Alarm buzzer must be off.
  2) Cooling water discharge state
    (Check that the cooling water temperature reaches 45 ~ 55°C before beginning operation.)
  3) Check for abnormal sounds and heating.
  4) Check for oil and water leakage from piping.
  5) Check the state of lubrication of the valve arms.

2-3 Operation
If warm-up operation is normal, engage the clutch and begin normal operation. Check the following during operation and stop the engine and take suitable corrective action if there are any abnormalities.

2-3.1 Checks during operation
(1) Oil pressure
  Check that the lubricating oil pressure and operating oil pressure lamps are off.
  Lubricating oil pressure during operation: 3.0 ~ 3.5 kg/cm^2
(2) Cooling water
  Periodically check whether water is being discharged from the cooling water outlet pipe.
  If the cooling water is being discharged intermittently or if only a small amount of water is being discharged during high speed operation, immediately stop the engine and check if air is being sucked into the cooling system, the impeller of the water pump is abnormal, or the water pipes and Kingston cock are clogged.
  Cooling water temperature during operation: 45 ~ 55°C.
  Check that the water temperature alarm lamp is off.
(3) Fuel
  Check the fuel level in the fuel tank and add fuel before the tank becomes too low. If the fuel level is low, air will enter the fuel injection system and the engine will stop.
(4) Charging
  Check that the charge lamp is off.
  If the charge lamp is still on even when the engine is run at 1,000 rpm or above, the charging system is faulty and the battery is not being charged.
(5) Temperature of each part
  At full power operation, the surface temperature of each engine part is about 50 ~ 60°C and hot to the touch. If engine temperature is too high, the oil will be used up, the propeller shaft will not be centered, or other troubles may occur.
(6) Leakage and abnormalities
  Check for water leakage, oil leakage, gas leakage, loose bolts, abnormal sounds, abnormal heating, and vibration.
(7) Exhaust color
  Black exhaust smoke indicates that the engine is being overloaded and that the lives of the intake and exhaust valves, piston rings, cylinder liners, and injection nozzle will be shortened. Do not run the engine for long periods when it is being exhausted.
(8) Abnormal sounds, abnormal heating
  When abnormal sounds or abnormal heating occur during operation, immediately stop the engine and check for trouble.

2-3.2 Operating precautions
(1) Always set the battery switch and main switch to the ON position during operation.
(2) Do not touch the starting button during operation. Operation of the starter motor pinion will damage the gears.
(3) Since the ship will resonate and vibrate at a certain speed, depending on the structure of the hull, do not operate it at that speed.
(4) Always set the clutch to the neutral position and wait for the propeller to stop rotating before raising the propeller shaft (if hoisting type stern gears are installed).
(5) Do not suddenly apply a full load to the engine or operate it at full load for long periods.

2-4 Stopping
2-4.1 Stopping procedure
(1) Before stopping, put the clutch in NEUTRAL and run the engine at approximately 1,000 rpm for about 5 minutes.
(2) Before stopping, temporarily raise the speed to the rated speed to blow out residue in the cylinders. Then stop the engine by pulling the engine stop lever to cut the fuel.

2-4.2 Stopping precautions
(1) Do not stop the engine with the decompression lever. If the engine is stopped with the decompression lever, fuel will remain in the combustion chamber and abnormal combustion will occur when the engine is started again, perhaps damaging the engine.
(2) If the engine is stopped immediately after full-load operation, the temperature of each part will rise suddenly, leading to trouble.

2-4.3 Inspection and procedures after stopping
(1) Always close the Kingston cock after the engine is stopped.
Water may enter because of a faulty water pump, etc.
(2) In cold weather, the cooling water should always be drained after engine use to prevent freezing. There are water drain cocks on the cylinders and the exhaust manifold. (Drain the water after the engine has cooled.)
(3) Check for oil leakage and water leakage, and repair as required.
(4) Check for loose bolts and nuts, and repair as required.

2-5 Storage when moored for an extended period
(1) Securely close engine room windows and doors so that rain and snow cannot enter.
Also plug the exhaust outlet since water that enters the cylinder from the exhaust pipe will be compressed when the engine is started, causing serious trouble.
(2) The ship may also sink because of water leakage at the stern tube stuffing box packing. This can be prevented by tightening the packing.
(3) Change the lubricating oil before cranking the engine.
(4) Wipe off each part and coat with oil to prevent rusting of the engine exterior.
(5) Coat the regulator handle stand and each link with a thin film of lube oil or grease.
(6) Run the engine once a week to lubricate each part. This will prevent rusting of the bearings, pistons, and cylinder liners.

2-6 Emergency stop
(1) Loosen the fuel valve high-pressure pipe to release the fuel.
(2) Pull the decompression lever (decompression mechanism) so that compression is not applied to the combustion chamber.
(3) Block the air intake port so that air does not enter the combustion chamber.

3. Troubleshooting and Repair

If trouble occurs in the engine, the engine must be immediately stopped or run at low speed until the cause of the trouble is located.
If even extremely small troubles are not detected and corrected early, they can lead to serious trouble and even to disaster. Detecting and correcting troubles quickly is extremely important.

3-1 Troubles and corrective action at starting

Trouble	Cause	Corrective action
Flywheel fails to rotate correctly	(1) Battery not charged (2) Starter motor faulty (3) Moving parts seized (4) Lubricating oil viscosity too high	1) Recharge battery 2) Diassemble and repair starter motor 3) Inspect and repair 4) Replace with lubricating oil of suitable viscosity
Starter motor rotates, but engine fails to start	(1) Fuel not injected, or injection faulty	1) Prime and bleed air from fuel lines 2) Inject fuel through injection valve and replace needle if required 3) Clean fuel filter 4) Check operation of fuel pump, plunger, plunger spring, and delivery valve, and replace if required 5) The remote control system or governor is faulty, so check if fuel is cut off, and adjust if required
	(2) Fuel injection timing incorrect	1) Check if alignment mark of timing gear is aligned
	(3) Compression pressure low	1) Lap valves when air tightness of intake and exhaust valve is poor 2) Replace cylinder head packing if gas is leaking 3) Clean or replace piston rings when sticking occurs 4) Readjust timing when intake and exhaust valve closing is considerably slow
	(4) Drop in compression ratio	1) Replace piston pin bearing and crank pin bearing if worn 2) Replace piston rings if worn

Chapter 12 Operating Instructions
3. Troubleshooting and Repair

SM/2QM15

3-2 Troubles and corrective action during operation

Trouble	Cause	Corrective action
Engine stops suddenly	(1) Fuel injection cut off due to trouble in the governor or governoring system (2) Air in fuel tank (3) Air in fuel system (4) Piston, bearing, or other moving parts seized	1) Inspect, and repair or replace 2) Add fuel 3) Bleed air 4) Inspect and repair or replace the parts
Speed decreases unexpectedly	(1) Governor maladjusted (2) Overload (3) Piston seized (4) Bearing seized (5) Fuel filter clogged (6) Fuel injection pump or injection valve sticking Dirt in fuel pump delivery valve (7) Air in fuel system (8) Water in fuel	1) Adjust 2) Lighten the load (Check propeller system and power take-off system) 3) Stop the engine, and repair or replace 4) Stop the engine, and repair or replace 5) Clean the fuel filter 6) Stop the engine, and repair or replace 7) Prime and bleed air 8) Drain the fuel tank and fuel filter Add fuel if insufficient
Exhaust color is bad	(1) Load unsuitable (2) Fuel injection timing off (3) Fuel unsuitable. (4) Injection valve faulty (5) Intake and exhaust valve adjustment faulty (6) Intake and exhaust valves leaking. (7) Output of cylinders uneven (8) Injection pressure too low (9) Precombustion chamber melted	1) Adjust the load (Check propeller system and power take-off system) 2) Adjust injection timing 3) Change the fuel type 4) Test injection and replace valve if required 5) Adjust valve head clearance 6) Lap or grind valves 7) Check the fuel injection pump and injection valve and replace if necessary 8) Set injection pressure to 160 kg/cm^2 with shims 9) Replace the precombustion chamber...Perform item (1) above
Full load operation impossible	(1) Fuel filter clogged (2) Fuel pump plunger worn	1) Check and replace filter element 2) Replace plunger and barrel as a set
Output of cylinders uneven	(1) Air in fuel pump or fuel line (2) Water in fuel (3) Fuel injection volume uneven (4) Fuel injection timing uneven (5) Intake and exhaust valves sticking (6) Injection valve faulty	1) Prime and bleed air from the fuel pump and fuel lines 2) Drain the fuel tank and fuel filter and add fuel 3) Check and adjust injection volume 4) Check and adjust injection timing 5) Disassemble and clean 6) If nozzle is clogged, clean; Replace nozzle if necessary If the needle is sticking, inspect and replace

Chapter 12 Operating Instructions
3. Troubleshooting and Repair   *SM/2QM15*

3-2 Troubles and corrective action during operation

Trouble	Cause	Corrective action
Engine knocks	(1) Bearing clearance too large (2) Connecting rod bolt loose (3) Flywheel bolt, coupling bolt loose (4) Injection timing faulty (5) Too much fuel injected because of faulty fuel pump or injection nozzle	1) Inspect, and repair or replace parts 2) Check and retighten 3) Check and retighten or replace bolt as required 4) Check and adjust 5) Check fuel injection pump and injection nozzle and replace if required
Engine oil pressure low	(1) Lubricating oil leakage (2) Bearing, crankpin bearing clearance too large (3) Oil filter clogged (4) Oil regulator valve loose. (5) Oil temperature high; cooling water flow insufficient (6) Lubricating oil viscosity low (7) Excessive gas leaking into crankcase	1) Check engine interior and exterior piping, replenish oil 2) Check clearance, and replace bearing if necessary 3) Check and replace filter element 4) Check and readjust oil pressure 5) Check oil pump, and replace if necessary 6) Replace with oil having a high viscosity index 7) Check pistons, piston ring, and cylinder liners and replace if necessary
Lubricating oil temperature too high	(1) Cooling water flow insufficient (2) Excessive gas leaking in to crankcase (3) Overload	1) Check water pump 2) Check piston rings and cylinder liners 3) Lighten the load
Cooling water temperature high	(1) Air sucked in with cooling water (2) Cooling water flow insufficient (3) Cooling system dirty (4) Thermostat faulty	1) Check water pump inlet side pipe connections 2) Check water pump 3) Flush cooling system with cleaner 4) Replace thermostat
Propeller shaft rotates even when clutch is in neutral position	(1) Neutral position adjustment faulty (2) Friction plate seized (3) Steel plate warped	1) Reset neutral position adjusting bolt 2) Check and repair 3) Repair or replace
Ahead, neutral, astern switching faulty	(1) Clutch face seized (2) Moving parts, lever system malfunctioning (3) Remote control system malfunctioning	1) Replace 2) Readjust 3) Repair or replace
Abnormal heating	(1) Clutch slipping because of overload operation (2) Bearing damaged (3) Excessive oil (4) Oil deteriorated	1) Reduce load 2) Replace. 3) Check oil level and adjust to prescribed level 4) Replace oil
Abnormal sound	(1) Gear noise caused by torsional vibration (2) Gear backlash excessive	1) Avoid high speeds 2) Replace

CHAPTER 13

DISASSEMBLY AND REASSEMBLY

1. Disassembly and Reassembly Precautions 13-1
2. Disassembly and Reassembly Tools 13-2
3. Other 13-7
4. Disassembly 13-8
5. Reassembly 13-16
6. Tightening Torque 13-25
7. Packing Supplement and Adhesives 13-27

DISASSEMBLY AND REASSEMBLY

This chapter covers the most efficient method of disassembling and reassembling the engine. Some parts may not have to be removed, depending on the maintenance and inspection objective. In this case, removal is unnecessary and disassembling in accordance with this section is not required.

However, if you follow the disassembly and reassembly procedures, adjustment methods, and precautions described in this chapter, you should be able prevent subsequent troubles and a loss in engine performance after reassembly. The engine must be test-run to confirm that the engine is functioning properly and delivering full performance.

Since this chapter does not cover detailed disassembly and reassembly procedures for each part, refer to pertinent chapters for details.

1. Disassembly and Reassembly Precautions

(1) Record the parts that require replacement, and replace them with new parts during reassembly.
Be careful not to reassemble with the old parts.

(2) Do not forget adhesives and packing agents for sealing during reassembly.
Packing of the specified quality and packing agents matched to the packing material must be used.

(3) Arrange the disassembled parts into groups, such as individual cylinders, intake and exhaust, etc.
No.1 cylinder: Flywheel side
No.2 cylinder: Gear case side

(4) The prescribed tightening torque must be observed when tightening bolts and nuts. Moreover, since the strength of the bolts and nuts depends on their material, be sure to use the correct bolts and nuts at their proper places.

Special bolts, nuts .... Head cover, rod bolts, flywheel, etc.
Strong bolts .... Bolts marked (7) (JIS.7T)
Common bolts, nuts ... Unmarked (JIS.4T)

In addition, check the disassembly and reassembly precautions for each engine model.

2. Disassembly and Reassembly Tools

The following tools are necessary when disassembling and reassembling the engine. These tools must be used according to disassembly process and location.

Name of tool	Part number	Illustration mm(in.)	Application
Wrench	28110-100130	10 × 13	
Wrench	28110-170190	17 × 19	
Wrench	28110-220240	22 × 24	
Gasoline Feeder	28210-000150		
Screwdriver	104200-92350		
Piston ring compressor	101300-92140	22 (0.87), 80 (3.15), 26 (1.02)	Piston insertion guide

Chapter 13 Disassembly and Reassembly
2. Disassembly and Reassembly Tools

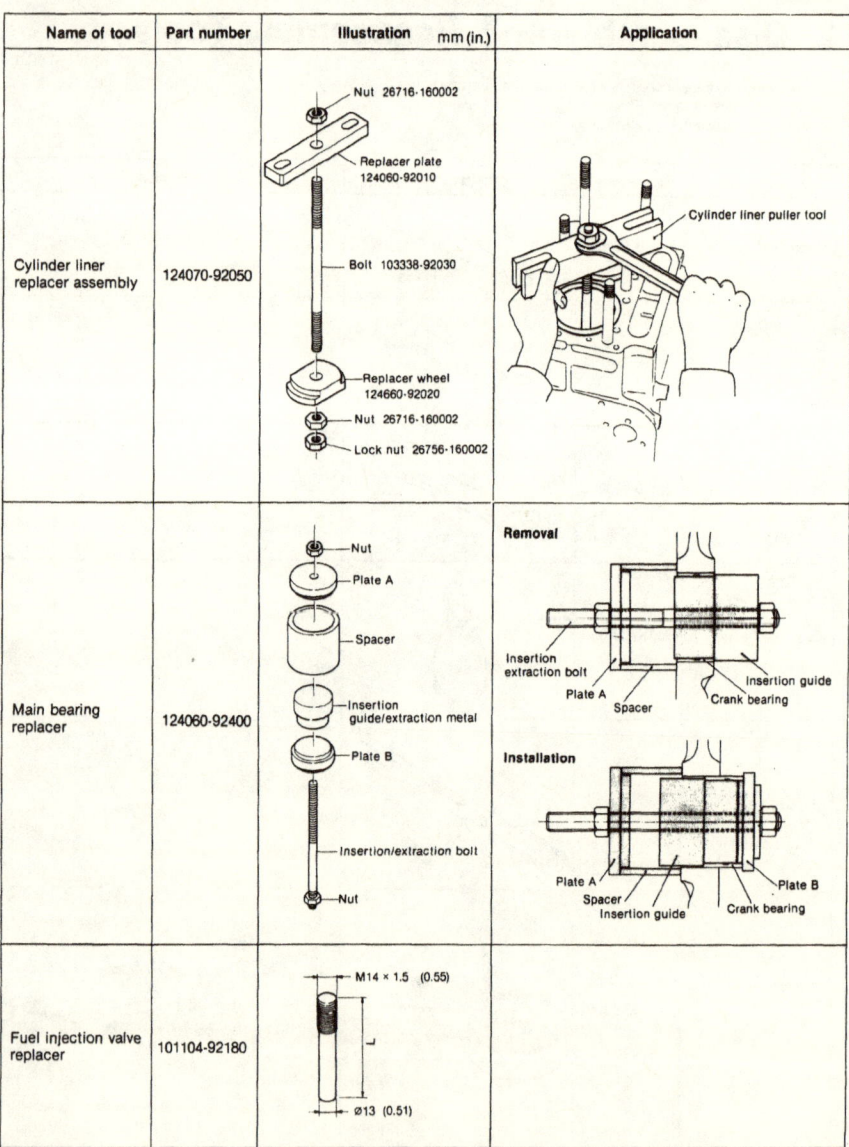

Chapter 13 Disassembly and Reassembly
2. Disassembly and Reassembly Tools

Name of tool	Part number	Illustration mm (in.)	Application
Valve lapping handle	28210-000031		
Valve lapping powder	28210-000070		
Feeler gauge	28312-150750		
Lubricating oil No. 2 filter case remover			
Piston pin insertion/ extraction tool		12 (0.47) 20 (0.79) 75 (2.95) 22 (0.87)	
Connecting rod small end bushing insertion/extraction tool		23 $^{0}_{-0.025}$ (0.905 ~ 0.906) 20 (0.79) 50 (1.97) 25 $^{0}_{-0.2}$ (0.976 ~ 0.984)	

Chapter 13 Disassembly and Reassembly
2. Disassembly and Reassembly Tools

── SM/2QM15

Name of tool	Part number	Illustration mm (in.)	Application
Intake and exhaust valve insertion/ extraction tool		6.5 (0.26); 40 (1.6); 100 (4); 11 (0.43)	
Output shaft nut wrench	177099-09010	Ø55; 230; 45	
Output shaft coupling lock	177099-09020	290; Ø100	Output shaft nut wrench / Output shaft coupling lock. For removing and tightening the output shaft nut.
Puller cradle	177095-09170	Ø29; 17	Cradle / Pulley puller. For removing the output shaft when using a pulley puller.
Pulling support	177099-09030	Ø100; 12; 33	Hammer / Output shaft / Pulling support. For removing the needle bearing inner race, thrust collar and thrust bearing of the output shaft (forward gear side).

Chapter 13 Disassembly and Reassembly
2. Disassembly and Reassembly Tools
_____ SM/2QM15

Name of tool	Part number	Illustration mm (in.)	Application
Plate for spring retainer	177095-09070	⌀80, 80	For removing and installing the plate spring, retainer and circlip of the large gears (forward and reverse). Labels: Plate spring, Circlip, Plate spring retainer, Vice.
Assembly spacer	177090-09010	⌀80, 20	For determining the thickness of the adjusting plate. Labels: Bearing inner race, Spacer, Assembly spacer.
Inserting tool	177095-09020	⌀45, 250	For installing the spacer and needle bearing inner race of the output shaft. (reverse small gear side). Labels: Inserting tool, Driving plate, Pressure plate, Forward large gear.
Inserting tool	177099-09040	⌀38, ⌀45, 100	For installing the thrust bearing and thrust collar (reverse large gear side). Labels: Inserting tool, Reverse large gear, Shift ring, Forward large gear.

13-6

3. Other

Supplementary packing agent

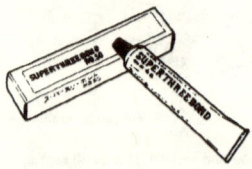

Type	Use
"Three Bond 3B8-005"	White. Since "Three Bond 3B8-005" is a nonorganic solvent, it does not penetrate asbestos sheet made principally or completely of asbestos. Always use it for gray asbestos sheet packing for complete oiltightness. When "Three Bond 3B8-005" is difficult to obtain, use silicone nonsolvent type "Three Bond No. 50."
"Three Bond No. 50"	Grey. Silicone nonsolvent type liquid packing. Semidry type packing agent coated on mating faces to prevent oil and gas leakage. Does not penetrate asbestos sheet and assures complete oiltightness.
"Three Bond No. 1"	Reddish brown. Paste type wet viscous liquid packing. Ideal for mating faces which are removed but reinstalled. Particularly used to prevent water leakage and to prevent seizing of bolts and nuts.

The surface to be coated must be thoroughly cleaned with thinner or benzene and completely dry. Moreover, coating must be thin and uniform.

Products of Three Bond Co., Ltd.

Paint

Color spray

Metallic Ecole Silver is used entirely on this engine.

Wipe off the surface to be painted with thinner or benzene, shake the spray can well, push the button at the top of the can and spray the paint onto the surface from a distance of 30 ~ 40 cm.

Paint

Type
White paint
(Mixed oil paint)

Usage point
Cylinder liner insertion hole

Use
Paint parts that contact the cylinder body when inserting the cylinder liner to prevent rusting and water leakage.

Yanmar cleaner

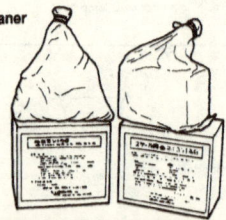

Cooling passage cleaner is made by adding one part "Unicon 146" to about 16 parts water (specific gravity ratio). To use, drain the water from the cooling system, fill the system with cleaner, allowing it to stand overnight (10 ~ 15 hours). Then drain out the cleaner, fill the system with water, and operate the engine for at least one hour.

NEJI LOCK SUPER 203M: a locking agent for screws

For coating on screws and bolts to prevent loosening, rusting, and leaking. To use, wipe off all oil and water on the threads of studs, coat the threads with screw lock, tighten the stud bolt, and allow to stand until the screw lock hardens. Use screw lock on the oil intake pipe threads, oil pressure switch threads, fuel injection timing shim faces, and front axle bracket mounting bolts.

Chapter 13 Disassembly and Reassembly
4. Disassembly
SM/2QM15

4. Disassembly

4·1 Open the cooling water drain cocks and drain the cooling water.
Cylinder body water drain cock
Exhaust pipe water drain cock

(2) Speed remote control cable and bracket
(3) Engine stop remote control cable and bracket
(4) Decompression remote control cable

4·4 Disconnect the electrical wiring.
(1) Alternator wiring
(2) Starter motor wiring

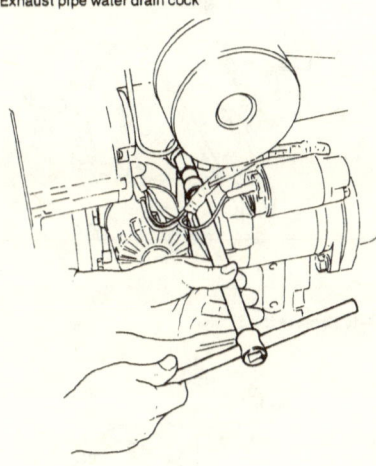

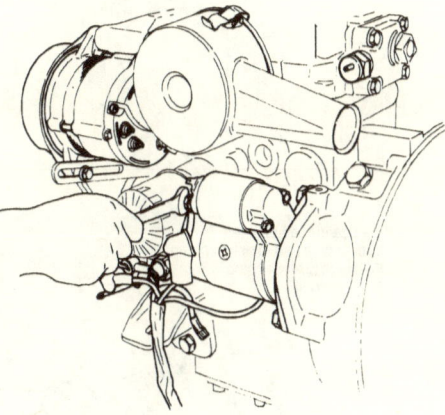

4·2 Drain the lubricating oil.
(1) Engine side
Insert a suction tube into the dipstick hole and pump out the oil with a waste oil pump (option).

(3) Water temperature switch wiring
(4) Oil pressure switch wiring
(5) Tachometer sensor wiring

4·5 Disconnect the cooling water inlet pipe and bilge pipe.
NOTE: Always close the Kingston cock.

4·6 Remove the air intake silencer.
Remove the intake silencer clip and the filter element. Then remove the set screw and the body.

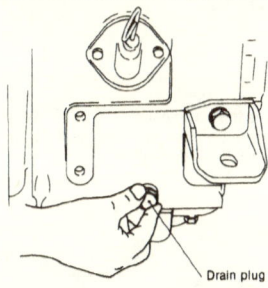

Drain plug

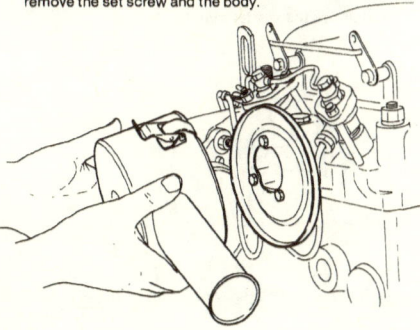

(2) Clutch side
Pump out the oil from the filler/dipstick hole using a waste oil pump or remove the drain plug at the bottom stern side of the crankcase and drain the oil.

4·3 Disconnect the remote control cables.
(1) Clutch remote control cable and bracket

Printed in Japan
2F015A

Chapter 13 Disassembly and Reassembly
4. Disassembly

_SM/2QM15_

4-7 Disconnect the fuel piping.
(1) Fuel tank to feed pump

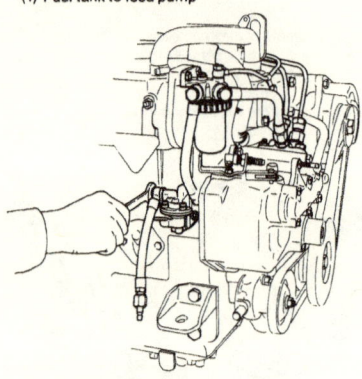

(2) Feed pump to fuel filter
(3) Fuel filter to fuel injection pump
(4) Fuel high pressure pipe
(5) Fuel return pipe

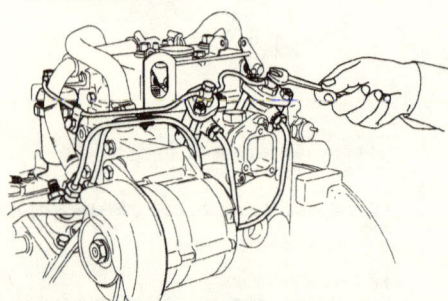

4-8 Remove the starter motor.

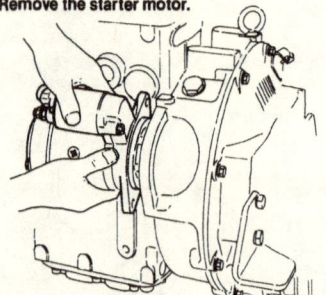

4-9 Remove the alternator
(1) Loosen the adjusting bolt and remove the V-belt.
(2) Remove the alternator and bracket.

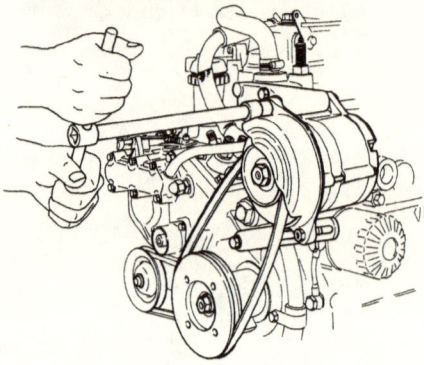

4-10 Remove the oil filter.

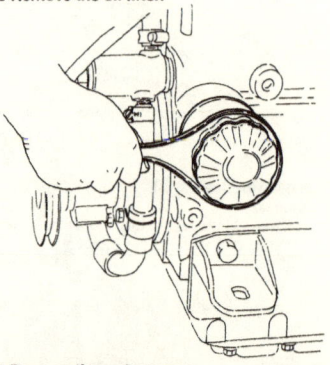

4-11 Remove the water pump.
(1) Disconnect the hose between the water pump and cooling water cylinder inlet joint.

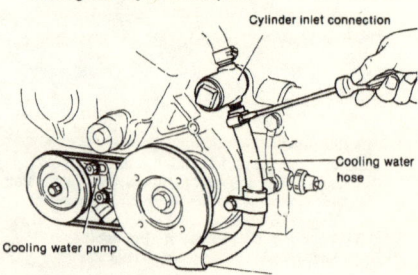

Printed in Japan
2F015A

Chapter 13 Disassembly and Reassembly
4. Disassembly

SM/2QM15

(2) Loosen the water pump mounting bolts, remove the V-belt by sliding it toward the crankshaft side, and remove the water pump.

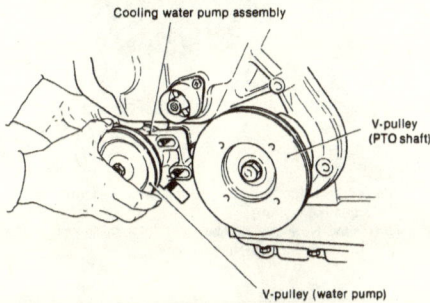
Cooling water pump assembly
V-pulley (PTO shaft)
V-pulley (water pump)

4-12 Remove the rocker arm chamber.

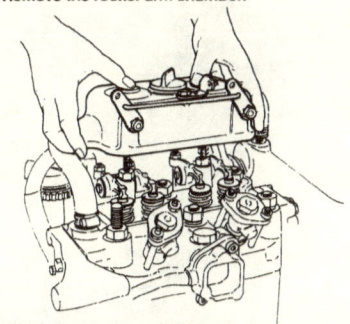

4-13 Remove the exhaust manifold.
(1) Disconnect the cooling water bypass hose at the cylinder inlet joint side.
(2) Disconnect the water inlet pipe at the cylinder head outlet side.
(3) Remove the exhaust manifold together with the fuel filter.

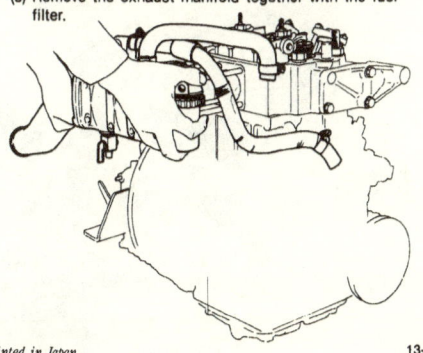

4-14 Remove the rocker arms.
(1) Remove the rocker arm ass'y.

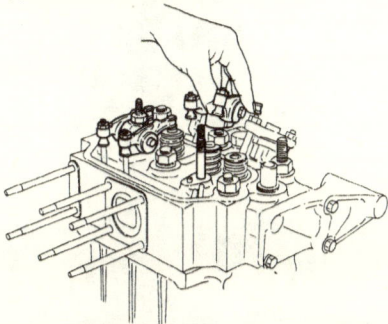

(2) Pull the push rods.

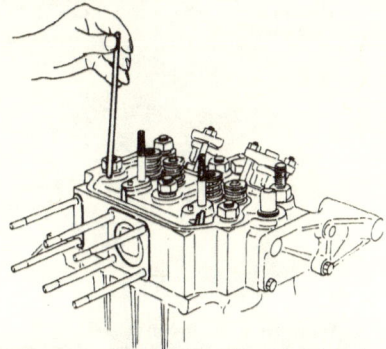

(3) Remove the cotter pins of the intake and exhaust valve springs.
NOTE: Arrange the parts by cylinder no., intake and exhaust.

4-15 Remove the cylinder head.
(1) Remove the breather pipe:

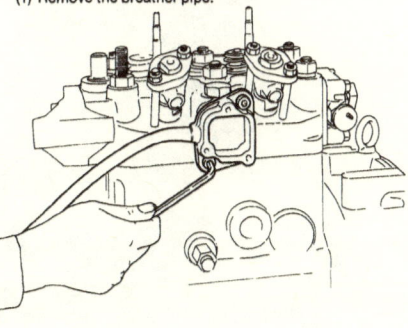

Printed in Japan
2F015A

13-10

Chapter 13 Disassembly and Reassembly
4. Disassembly

SM/2QM15

(2) Remove the cylinder head nuts in the prescribed order, and remove the cylinder head.

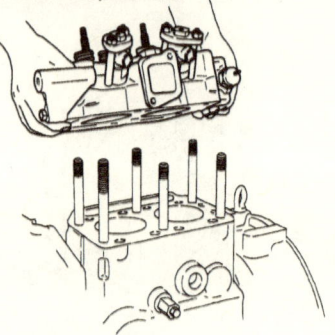

(3) Remove the gasket packing.
NOTE: Clearly identify the front and back of the gasket packing.

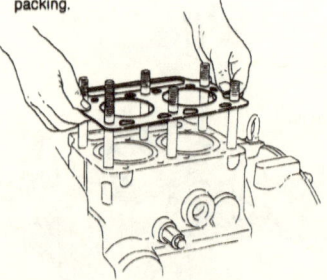

4-16 Remove the crankshaft pulley.
Remove the crankshaft pulley end nut and remove the V-pulley.

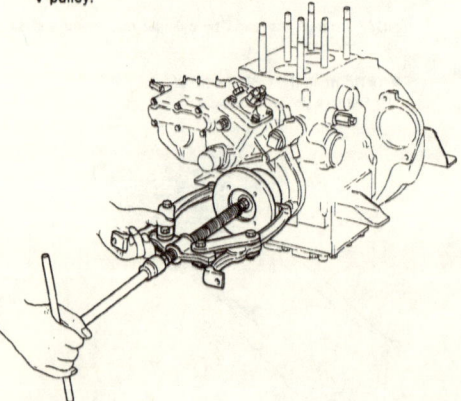

4-17 Remove the injection pump.
(1) Remove the governor cover and the regulator spring.

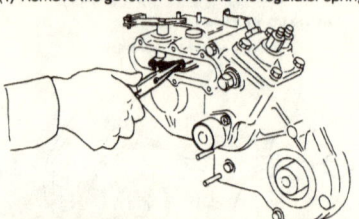

(2) Remove the injection pump and injection timing adjustment shims.
CAUTION: Note the number and total thickness of the timing adjustment shims.

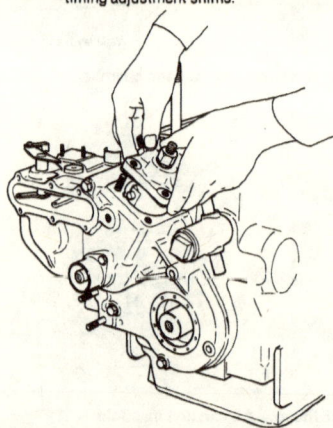

4-18 Remove the timing gear chamber.
(1) Remove the gear case.

Printed in Japan
2F015A

13-11

Chapter 13 Disassembly and Reassembly
4. Disassembly

_____ SM/2QM15

(2) Remove the governor gear.

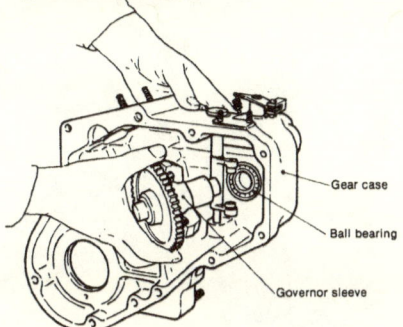

- Gear case
- Ball bearing
- Governor sleeve

4-19 Remove the clutch assembly
Loosen the mounting flange bolts and remove the clutch assembly.

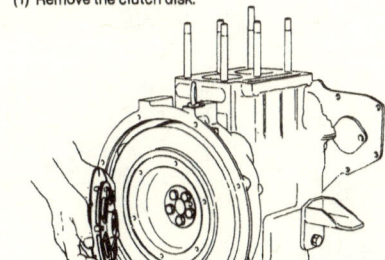

- Flywheel housing
- Damper disk
- Clutch assembly

4-20 Remove the flywheel.
(1) Remove the clutch disk.

(2) Remove the flywheel.

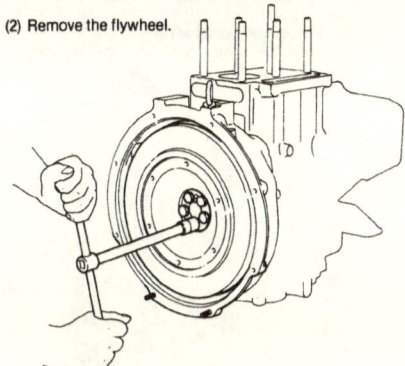

4-21 Remove the flywheel housing.

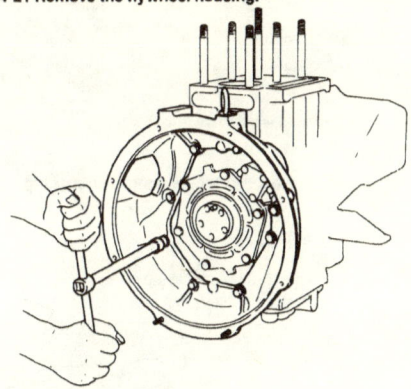

4-22 Remove the feed pump.

4-23 Remove the lubricating oil dipstick together with the flange.

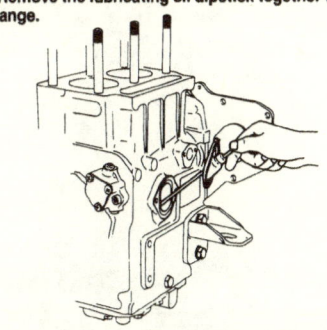

Printed in Japan
2F015A

13-12

Chapter 13 Disassembly and Reassembly
4. Disassembly

4·24 Remove the camshaft gear.
(1) Remove the camshaft end nut and remove the fuel cam.
(2) Remove the intermediate idle gear.

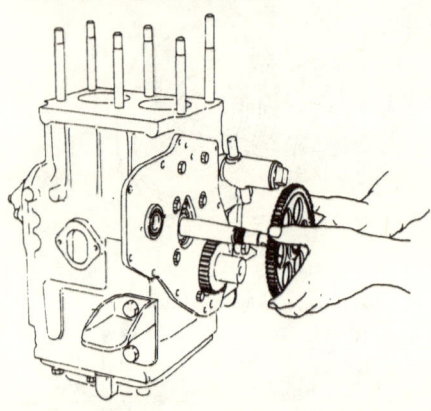

(3) Remove the camshaft gear.

4·25 Remove the gear case flange and packing.

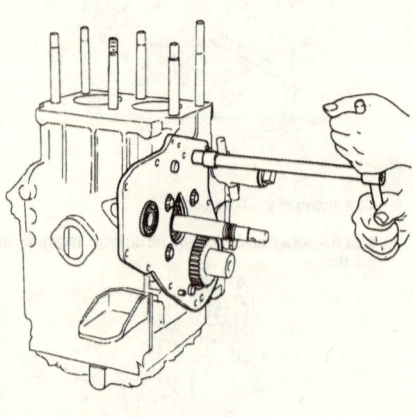

4·26 Remove the crankshaft gear.

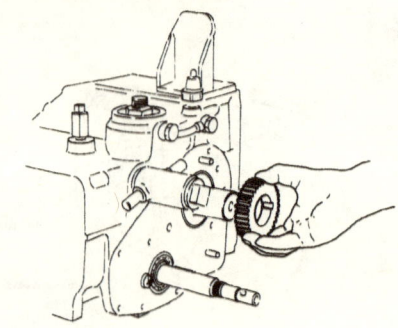

4·27 Turn the engine onto its side.
(1) Remove the engine feet or the camshaft side.
(2) Turn the cylinder block over so that the camshaft side is on the bottom.

4·28 Remove the oil pan and the oil intake pipe.

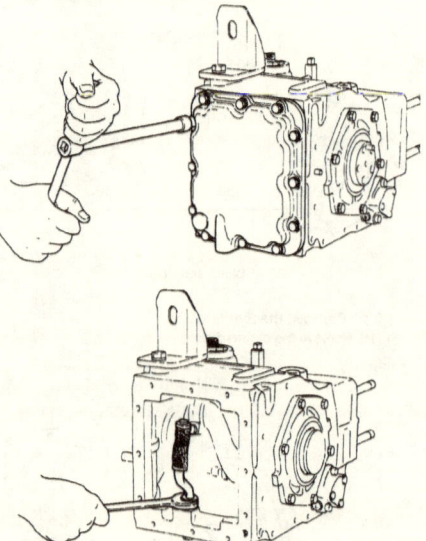

Chapter 13 Disassembly and Reassembly
4. Disassembly

4-29 Remove the piston connecting rod assembly.
(1) Set the piston to bottom dead center and remove the connecting rod bolts.

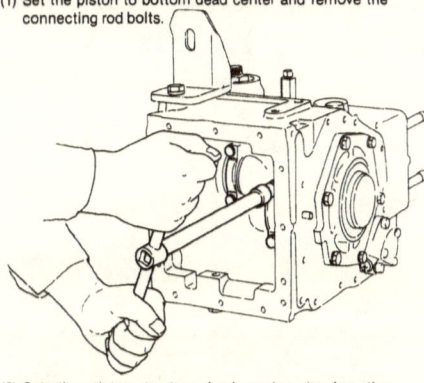

(2) Set the piston to top dead center, turning the crankshaft so that the connecting rod does not separate from the crank pin. Pull out the piston connecting rod assembly by pushing the large end of the rod with a pusher.

4-30 Remove the main bearing housing.
(1) Remove the main bearing housing bolt and remove the main bearing housing by threading the housing bolt into the extracting hole.

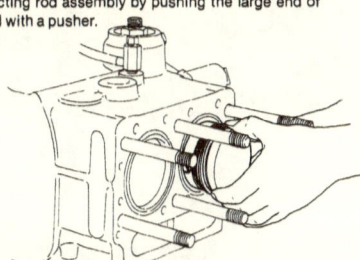

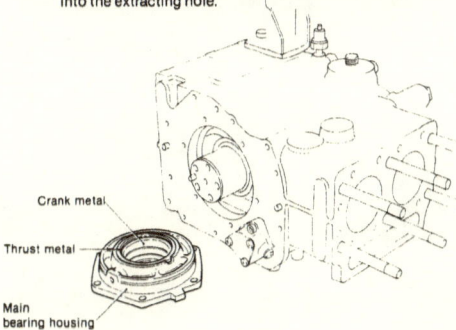

(2) Remove the thrust metal.

4-31 Pull the crankshaft.
(1) Pull the crankshaft.
(2) Remove the thrust metal.

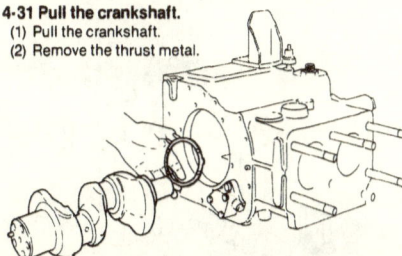

4-32 Remove the oil pump.

4-33 Remove the camshaft.
(1) Remove the oil pressure switch and the engine feet on the intake side. Then turn the engine over so that the intake side is on the bottom (the cylinders are upside-down).
(2) Remove the camshaft bearing set screw.

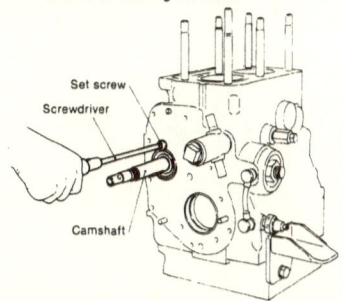

Chapter 13 Disassembly and Reassembly
4. Disassembly

(3) Check that all the tappets are separated from the cam, and pull the camshaft out by tapping it from the lube oil pump side.

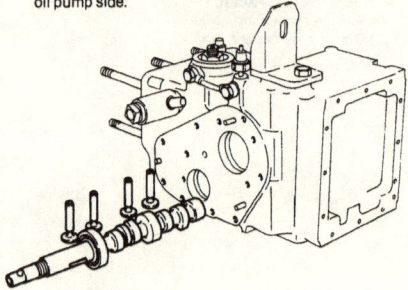

4-34 Remove the tappets.
NOTE: Arange the removed tappets in cylinder no. and intake and exhaust groups.

4-35 Remove the liners.
Set the engine upright and pull the liners with a liner puller.

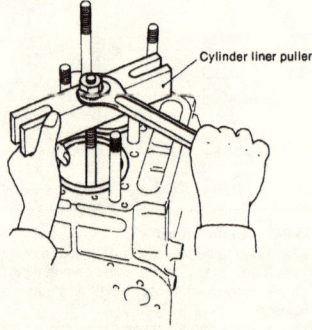

Cylinder liner puller

5. Reassembly

5-1 Assemble the cylinder liners.
(1) Remove any rust from the cylinder block where it contacts the cylinder liners and clean the rubber packing grooves.
(2) Insert new rubber packing into the cylinder block grooves.
(3) Coat the outside periphery of the liners with waterproofing paint.
(4) Insert the liners into the cylinder block, making sure to check that the cylinder liner protrusion is correct.

5-3 Insert the camshaft.
(1) Coat the camshaft bearing section with oil and insert the camshaft into the cylinder blockry tapping the shaft end with a wooden mallet.

NOTE: Be careful not to damage the groove in the end of the shaft.

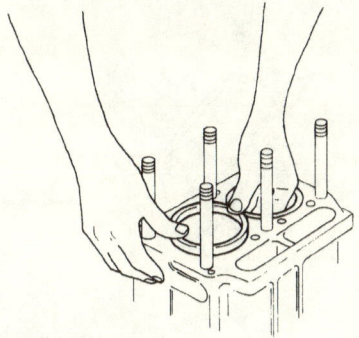

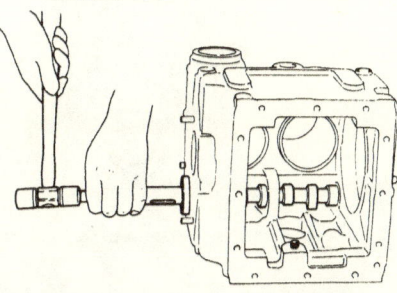

(2) After inserting the camshaft, check that it rotates smoothly before tightening the camshaft bearing set screw.
Tightening torque: 2 kg-m (14.5ft-lb)

5-2 Insert the tappets.
(1) Turn the cylinder block over or turn it upside down so that the intake side is on the bottom.
(2) Coat the tappets with oil and insert into the tappet holes.

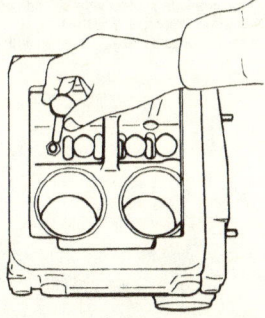

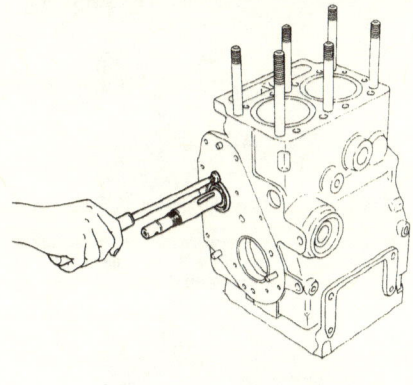

NOTE: Assemble the tappets at their original positions, paying careful attention to the cylinder numbers and intake and exhaust groupings.

5-4 Install the crankshaft.

(1) Coat the cam gear side thrust metal with oil and install.

CAUTION: Install so that the thrust metal oil groove is at the crankcase side, being careful not to damage the tab.

(2) Insert the crankshaft.

5-5 Install the main bearing housing.

(1) Replace the packing.
(2) Install the thrust metal to the main bearing housing so that the oil groove in the thrust metal is facing the crankcase. (Coat with grease or oil.)

(3) Coat the oil seal section with oil.
(4) Insert the main bearing housing and tighten.
 Tightening torque: 2.5 kg-m (18ft-lb)
(5) Check that the crankshaft rotates smoothly.
(6) Measure the crankshaft side gap, and adjust it to the prescribed value by the thickness of the packing.
 Crankshaft side gap: 0.1 ~ 0.2 mm
 (0.00394 ~ 0.0078 in.)

5-6 Install the lube oil pump.

Fit the end of the oil pump shaft on the slit in the end of the camshaft and tighten.

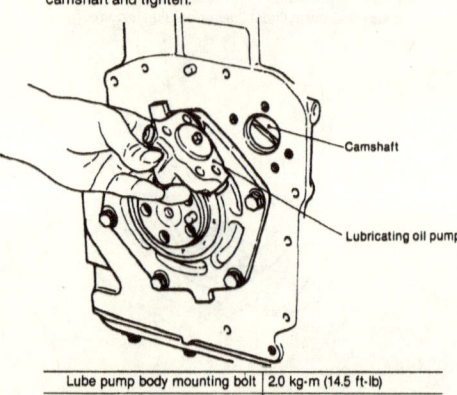

| Lube pump body mounting bolt | 2.0 kg-m (14.5 ft-lb) |
| Lube pump cover mounting bolt | 0.8 kg-m (5.8 ft-lb) |

5-7 Assemble the piston and connecting rod assembly.

(1) Coat the crankpin section with oil and position so that the insertion side crank is at the top.
(2) Coat the piston and crankpin bearing with oil.

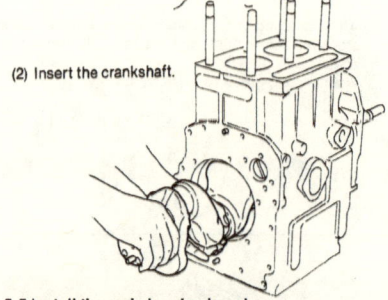
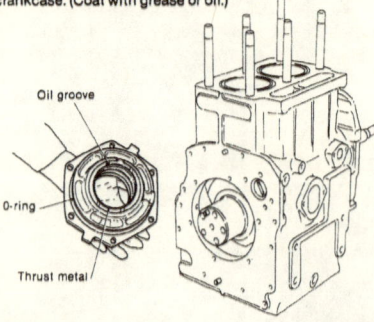

Chapter 13 Disassembly and Reassembly
5. Reassembly

(3) Position the piston rings so that the gaps are 180° apart, being sure that there is no gap at the side pressure section.

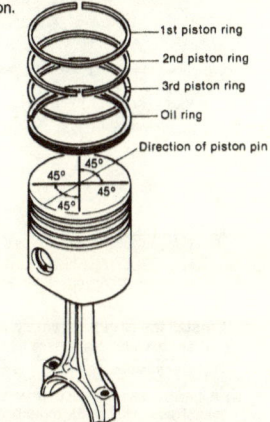

(4) Insert the piston connecting rod assembly so that the side of the connecting rod big end with the identification number is on the exhaust side.
Install the piston rings with a piston ring inserter.

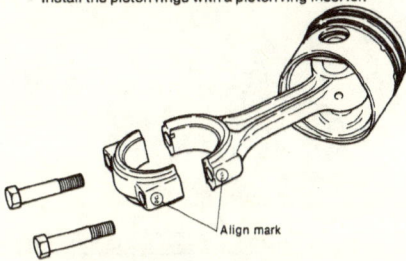

(5) After the connecting rod large end contacts the crankpin, push the piston crown down slowly to turn the crankshaft to bottom dead center.

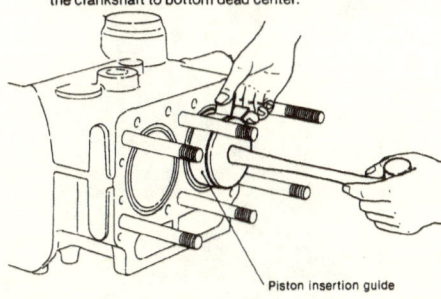

(6) Align the connecting rod cap and connecting rod large end matching mark and tighten the connecting rod bolts.
CAUTION: 1. Be careful to tighten the connecting rod bolts evenly.
2. Coat the bolt threads and washer face with oil.

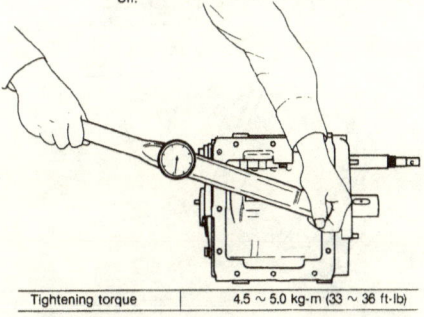

Tightening torque	4.5 ~ 5.0 kg-m (33 ~ 36 ft-lb)

(7) Measure the side clearance.

Side clearance	0.25 ± 0.1 mm (0.0059 ~ 0.0137 in.)

(8) Check that the crankshaft rotates smoothly.

5-8 Install the lubricating oil intake pipe.
Coat the threads with "Screw Lock Super 203M", screw the pipe in and lock with the nut.

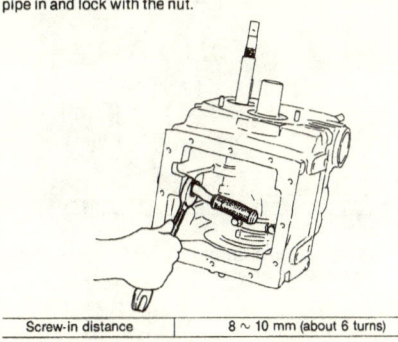

Screw-in distance	8 ~ 10 mm (about 6 turns)

Chapter 13 Disassembly and Reassembly
5. Reassembly

SM/2QM15

5-9 Install the engine bottom cover (oil pan)
(1) Change the packing.
(2) Install the bottom cover.

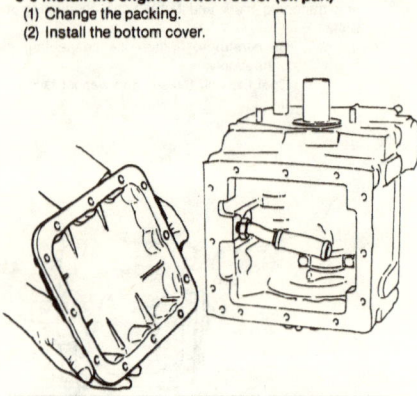

Tightening torque	2.5 kg·m (18 ft·lb)

5-10 Install the mounting flange.
(1) Set the engine upright.
(2) Align the positioning pins and tighten the flange.

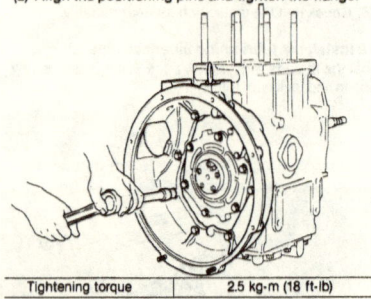

Tightening torque	2.5 kg·m (18 ft·lb)

5-11 Install the flywheel.
(1) Align the reference pins.

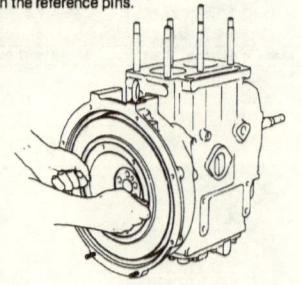

(2) Install the flywheel.

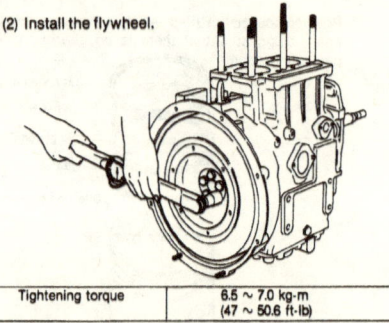

Tightening torque	6.5 ~ 7.0 kg·m (47 ~ 50.6 ft·lb)

NOTE: After tightening, check the end run-out.

5-12 Install the clutch assembly.
(1) Install the clutch disc on the flywheel.

Tightening torque	2.5 kg·m (18 ft·lb)

(2) Align the disc and input shaft spline, and install the clutch assembly on the mounting flange.

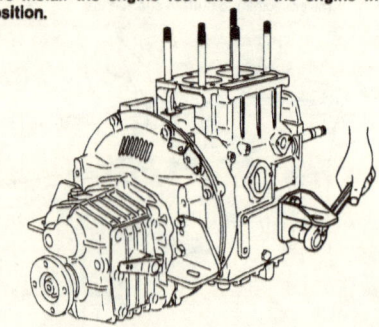

Tightening torque	2 ~ 2.5 kg·m (14.5 ~ 18 ft·lb)

5-13 Install the engine feet and set the engine in position.

Chapter 13 Disassembly and Reassembly
5. Reassembly

(1) Dipstick flange and dipstick
(2) Fuel pump
(3) Oil pressure switch

5-14 Install the gear case flange.
(1) Replace the packing.
(2) Coat both sides of the packing with "Three Bond 3B8-005".
(3) Tighten the gear case flange.

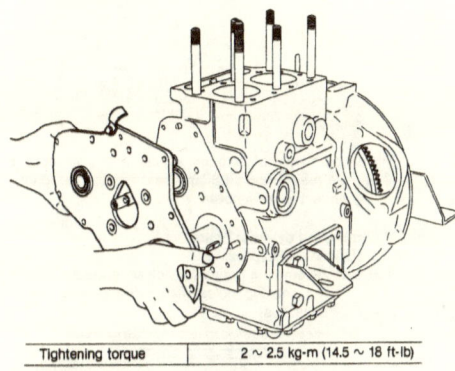

| Tightening torque | 2 ~ 2.5 kg·m (14.5 ~ 18 ft·lb) |

5-15 Assemble the camshaft gear and fuel cam.
(1) Coat the shaft hole of the camshaft gear with oil and insert the gear.
(2) Coat the shaft hole of the intermediate gear with oil and insert the gear.
(3) Coat the fuel cam with oil and insert the cam by aligning the "0" mark opposite the camshaft gear.

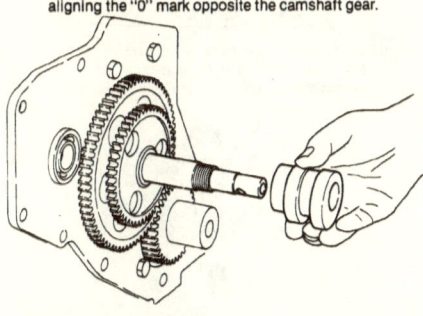

(4) Tighten the camshaft end nut.

| Tightening torque | 10 kg·m (72.3 ft·lb) |

5-16 Assemble the crankshaft gears.
(1) Coat the crankshaft section and the inside of the gear with oil.
(2) Align the matching marks of the camshaft gear and the crankshaft gear and insert the crankshaft gear.

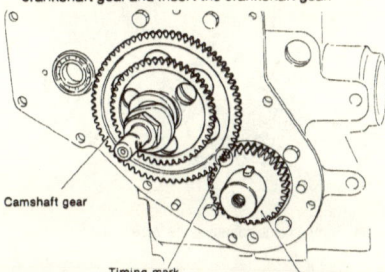

Camshaft gear

Timing mark Crankshaft gear

(3) After inserting the crankshaft gear, check the backlash.

| Backlash | 0.08 ~ 0.16 mm (0.0031 ~ 0.0062 in.) |

5-17 Install the timing gear case.
(1) Coat both sides of the new packing with "Three Bond 3B8-005" and install.
(2) Insert the governor gear shaft, aligning it with the hole in the gearcase flange, and temporarily tighten.

5-18 Install the crankshaft V-pulley.
(1) Coat the crankshaft V-pulley and the inside of the oil seal with oil.
(2) Insert and tighten the V-pulley, making sure that the lip of the oil seal is not distorted.

| Tightening torque | 6.5 kg·m (47 ft·lb) |

5-19 Tighten the timing gear case.

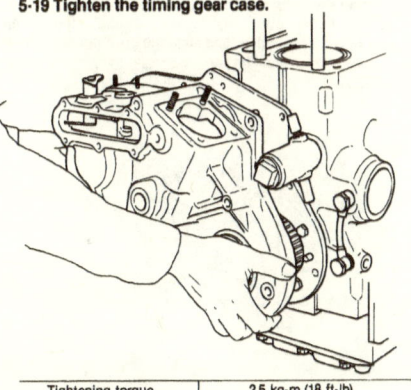

| Tightening torque | 2.5 kg·m (18 ft·lb) |

5-20 Install the water pump.
(1) Install the V-belt to the crankshaft V-pulley and install the water pump.

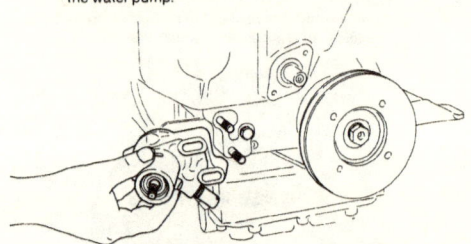

(2) Tighten while adjusting the V-belt tension.

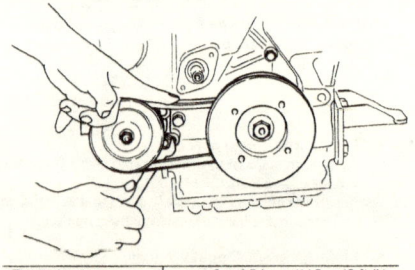

Tightening torque	2 ~ 2.5 kg-m (14.5 ~ 18 ft-lb)

(3) Install the water pipe (pump to cylinder inlet joint).

5-21 Install the fuel injection pump.
(1) Remove grease from both sides of the fuel injection timing adjustment shims with thinner, and coat the shims with "Screw Lock Super 203M."
(2) Insert the pump by looking through the pump adjustment window, and align the governor No. 2 lever and rack connecting part.

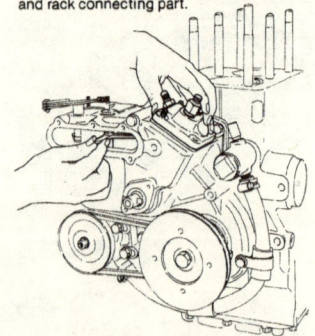

(3) Tighten the fuel pump.

Tightening torque	2.0 ~ 2.5 kg-m (14.5 ~ 18ft-lb)

(4) Install the regulator spring.

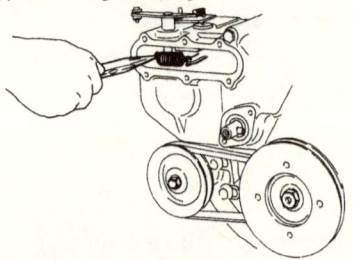

(5) Coat both sides of the pump adjustment cover packing with "Three Bond 3B8-005" and install the pump adjustment window cover.

5-22 Install the cylinder head.
(1) Install the gasket packing.
CAUTION: Be sure the front and back are correct and that the packing holes match the cooling water passages.

The side between cylinders is the cylinder head side.

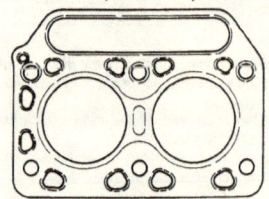

(2) Insert the cylinder head, being careful not to damage the threads of the tightening bolts, and tighten the nuts in the tightening sequence.

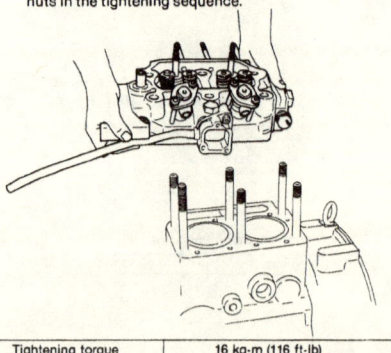

Tightening torque	16 kg-m (116 ft-lb)

Chapter 13 Disassembly and Reassembly
5. Reassembly

Cylinder head tightening sequence

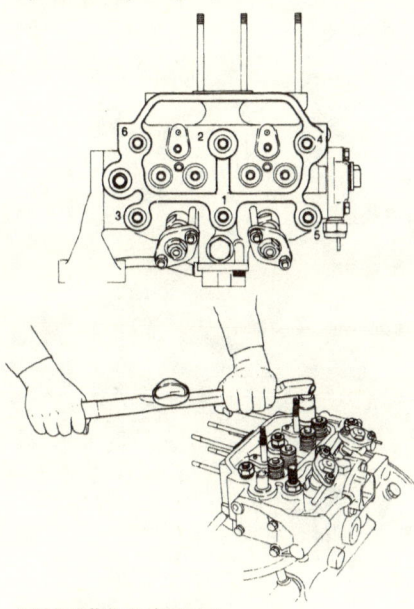

5-23 Install the rocker arms.
(1) Install the push rods on the tappets.

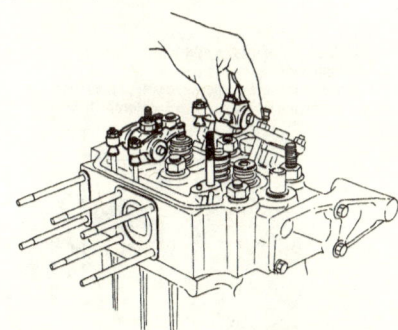

(2) Coat the inside of valve spring retainer with oil.
(3) Install the rocker arm mount and tighten the nut.

Tightening torque	3.7 kg·m (27 ft-lb)

CAUTION: 1. Loosen the valve head clearance adjusting screw in advance.
2. Check that the arm moves smoothly.

(4) Adjust the intake and exhaust valve head clearance and lock with the nut.

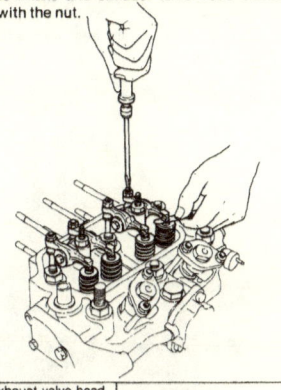

Intake and exhaust valve head clearance (engine cold):	0.2 mm (0.008 in.)

5-24 Install the rocker arm cover.

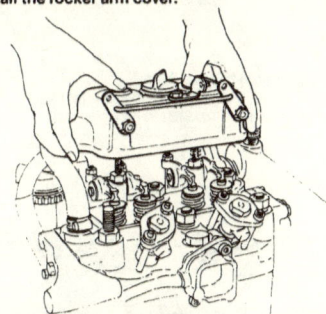

5-25 Install the exhaust manifold.
(1) Install the exhaust manifold.

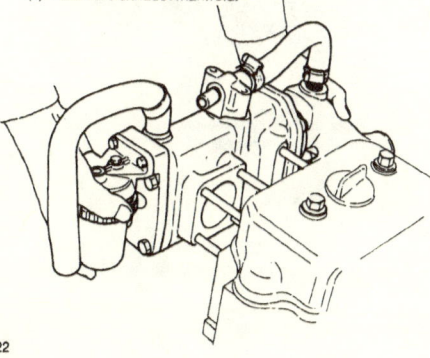

Chapter 13 Disassembly and Reassembly
5. Reassembly

SM/2QM15

(2) Install the cooling water bypass hose to the cylinder inlet joint.
(3) Install the cooling water inlet hose to the cylinder head outlet joint.

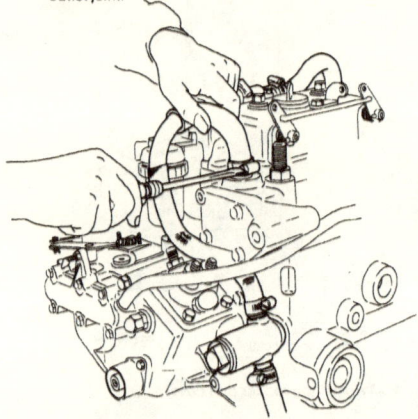

5-26 Install the fuel pipe.
(1) Install the feed pump to fuel filter pipe.
(2) Install the fuel filter to fuel injection pump pipe.

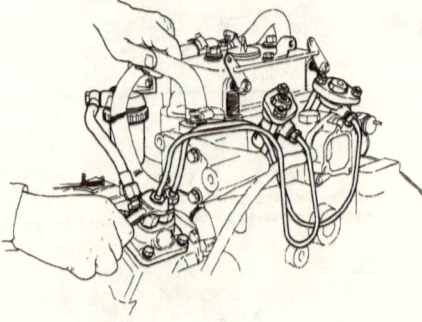

(3) Install the fuel high pressure pipe.
(4) Install the fuel return pipe.

5-27 Install the starter motor.

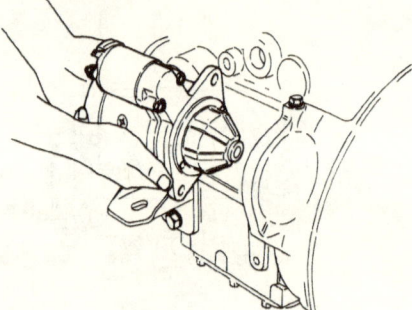

5-28 Install the oil filter.

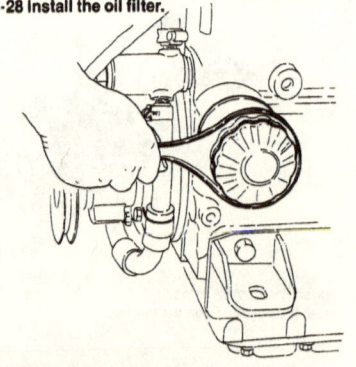

5-29 Install the intake silencer.
(1) Install the breather pipe.
(2) Install the intake silencer cover to the intake port.
(3) Install the intake silencer and tighten it with the clip.

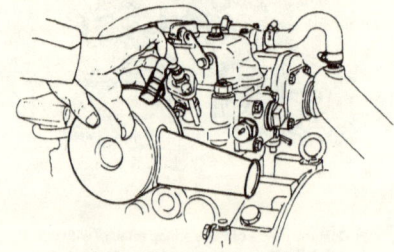

Chapter 13 Disassembly and Reassembly
5. Reassembly
_____SM/2QM15

5-30 Install the alternator.
(1) Install the alternator to the bracket.

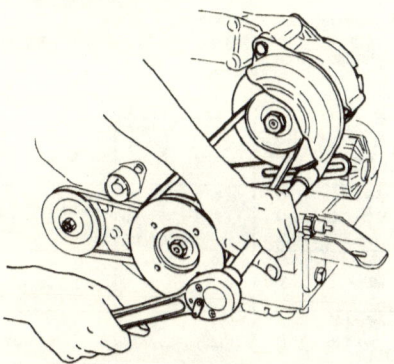

(2) Install the V-belt and tighten the adjusting bolt while adjusting the V-belt tension.

5-31 Connect the electrical wiring.

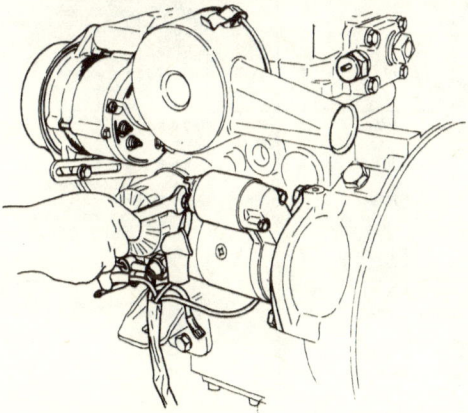

5-32 Install the remote control cables.

5-33 Connect the interior piping.

6. Tightening Torque

The bolts and nuts used in this engine employ ISO general metric threads stipulated in JIS (Japanese Industrial Standards). Pay careful attention to the thread dimensions when replacing bolts and nuts.
Tighten the bolts and nuts to the tightening torque given in the table below.

6-1 Main bolt and nut tightening torque.

Location	Bolt/nut	Thread diameter X pitch (mm)	Width across flats (mm)	Quantity	Tightening torque (kg-m)	Remarks
Cylinder head	Cylinder head tightening nut	M14 × 1.5	22	6	15 ~ 16	Coat with molybdenum dioxide
	Rocker arm support nut	M10 × 1.25	17	2	3.5 ~ 4.0	
	Exhaust manifold nuts	· M8			2.0 ~ 2.5	
Timing gear	Timing gear case mounting bolt	M8 × 1.25	13	10	2.0 ~ 2.5	
	Camshaft end nut	M20 × 1.5	30	1	10	
Cylinder block	Mounting flange bolt	M8 × 1.25	13	8	2.5	
	Bottom cover bolt	M8 × 1.25	13	12	2.0 ~ 2.5	
	Oil pressure switch mounting	PT 1/8	27	1	1.0	Coat with "Three Bond 3B8-005"
Crankshaft, pistons	Main bearing housing bolt	M8 × 1.25	13	6	2 ~ 2.5	
	Connecting rod bolt	M9 × 1.0	13	4	4.5 ~ 5	Coat with molybdenum dioxide
	Crankshaft V-pulley bolt	M12 × 1.25	19	1	6.5	
	Flywheel bolt	M10 × 1.25	17	6	7.0 ~ 7.5	Coat with molybdenum dioxide
Cooling system	Water temperature sender bolt	PT 3/8	27	1	1.0 ~ 1.5	"Three Bond 3B8-005"
	Anticorrison zinc mounting	M25 × 2.0	22	2	5 ~ 6	
	Cooling water inlet joint	PT 3/4	—	1	5 ~ 10	Must be coated with screw lock and positioned.
	Water pump body bolt	M8 × 1.25	13	2	2.5	
Fuel system	Nozzle nut	M20 × 1.5		2	10	
	Delivery valve holder	M18	17	2	4.0 ~ 4.5	
Clutch system	Clutch housing nut	M10 × 1.5	17		4.5	
	Clutch mounting bolt	M8 × 1.25	13	8	2.0	
	Output shaft coupling tightening nut	M24	—	1	9.5	
	Shaft coupling bolt	M10 × 1.5	17	4	4.5	

Chapter 13 Disassembly and Reassembly
6. Tightening Torque

6-2 General bolt and nut tightening torque
(1) Hex bolts

Thread diameter	Width across flats	Tightening torque, kg·m	
		4T bolts	7T bolts
M5 × 0.2	9	0.2 ~ 0.3	0.3 ~ 0.5
M6 × 1.0	10	0.4 ~ 0.7	0.8 ~ 1.2
M8 × 1.25	13	1.0 ~ 1.6	2.0 ~ 3.0
M10 × 1.5	17	1.8 ~ 3.0	3.7 ~ 5.2
M12 × 1.25	19	3.5 ~ 5.5	7.5 ~ 10.0

(2) Pipe joint bolts

Thread diameter	Width across flats	Tightening torque, kg·m
M8 × 1.25	13	1.2 ~ 1.7
M12 × 1.25	17	2.5 ~ 3.0
M14 × 1.5	19	4.0 ~ 5.0
M16 × 1.5	22	5.0 ~ 6.0

Chapter 13 Disassembly and Reassembly
7. Packing Supplement and Adhesives

7. Packing Supplement and Adhesive Application Points

The packing used in this engine is asbestos sheet sealed at both mating faces.
Be sure to use the correct supplement in accordance with the below table.

Location	Packing (coated)	Packing agent and adhesive
Cylinder head	Both sides of cylinder head side cover packing	"Three Bond No. 4"
	Cylinder head top and bottom casting sand hole plug	
	Rocker arm chamber packing (rocker arm chamber side)	
	Both sides of cylinder head gasket packing	"Three Bond No. 50"
	Intake and exhaust manifold bolt threads	"Screw Lock Super 203M"
	Exhaust manifold stud bolt thread	"Screw Lock Super 203M"
	Rocker arm support stud bolt	
	Cooling water outlet joint threads	
Timing gear	Both sides of timing gear case packing	"Three Bond 3B8-005"
	Both sides of fuel injection timing adjustment shims	"Screw Lock Super 203M"
	Both sides of governor chamber packing	"Three Bond 3B8-005"
	Governor drive shaft bearing cover packing	
Cylinder block	Both sides of oil pan packing	"Three Bond 3B8-005"
	Outside surface of cylinder liner	White paint
	Cooling water pipe joint threads	"Three Bond No. 20"
	Lubricating oil suction pipe threads	"Screw Lock Super 203M"
	Lubricating oil intake pipe blind plug threads	
	Oil pressure regulator valve threads	
	Oil pressure switch threads	"Three Bond 3B8-005"
	Cylinder head bolt stud	
	Mounting flange face	
	Lube oil pump face	
	Both sides of bushing shell packing	
	Both sides of dipstick flange packing	
	Both sides of fuel pump packing	
Crankshaft, piston	Crankshaft V-pulley key groove tightening section	"Three Bond 3B8-005"
	Connecting rod bolt threads	
Cooling system	Both sides of water pump packing	"Three Bond No. 2"
	Both sides of water pump packing	"Three Bond No. 4"
	Anticorrosion zinc flange threads	
	Water temperature switch threads	
	Water drain joint (cylinder, exhaust pipe)	
Clutch system	Mounting flange face	
	Clutch housing face	

CHAPTER 14
INSPECTION AND SERVICING

1. Periodic inspection and servicing 14-1

1. Periodic Inspection and Servicing

Periodic inspection and servicing is necessary to keep the engine in top condition at all times.
The routine inspection period depends on engine application and usage conditions, fuel and lubricating oil quality, engine handling, etc., and cannot be definitely stated. However, a general guideline will be given here. The relationship between inspection and maintenance activities and operating time is given below.
Refer to pertinent inspection sections of this manual for details.
1. Perform inspection at the operating times given below, and quickly correct any defects found.
2. Before reusing disassembled parts, check that they are in good condition.

1-1 Routine inspection

○ Inspection   ◎ Parts replacement

Item	Description	Daily	Every 50 hours	Every 100 hours	Every 300 hours	Every 500 hours	Every 1,000 hours
Fuel system	Fuel tank level check and filling	○					
	Fuel filter cleaning		○				
	Fuel filter element replacement			◎			
	Injection valve / Injection timing check					○	
	Injection pump / Injection spray inspection					○	
	Injection pump / Main part disassembly and inspection						○
	Fuel feed pump / Disassembly and inspection						○
Lubrication system	Engine side / Oil pan oil level check and replenishment	○					
	Engine side / Oil change			○			
	Engine side / Oil filter change		◎ (1st time)		◎ (from 2nd time)		
	Clutch side / Oil level check and replenishment	○					
	Clutch side / Oil change		○ (1st time)		○ (from 2nd time)		
Cooling system	Thermostat inspection				○		
	Cooling water discharge condition	○					
	Anticorrosion zinc inspection				○		
	Water pump / Water pump drive belt tension adjustment				○		
	Water pump / Water pump disassembly and inspection					○	
Engine proper	Bolt retightening	After operation or 50 hours after restarting					
	Intake and exhaust valve head clearance adjustment				○		
	Combustion chamber cleaning				○		
	Intake and exhaust valve lapping					○	
	Piston disassembly and piston ring inspection					○	
	Bearing and rod bolt inspection					○	
Remote control	Cable inspection and adjustment				○		
Intake and exhaust system	Intake silencer element cleaning			○			
	Mixing elbow interior inspection				○		
Electrical system	Alarm lamps and alarm buzzer	○					
	Battery electrolyte level check and replenishment	○					
	Alternator drive belt tension adjustment					○	
	Main switch and starting button inspection					○	
Piping	Rubber pipe inspection and replacement	Should be replaced every 4 years					
Others	Flexible mount and flexible coupling	Should be replaced every 4 years					

Chapter 14 Inspection and Servicing
1. Periodic Inspection and Servicing

1-2 Routine maintenance and inspection procedures
Only the most common maintenance items will be described here. Refer to the pertinent chapters of this manual for details on various parts and workshop service.

1-2.1 Daily maintenance
(1) Oil level check
Check the engine and clutch oil levels with the dipsticks, and add oil up to the top mark. Oil level must not be allowed to fall below the bottom mark.

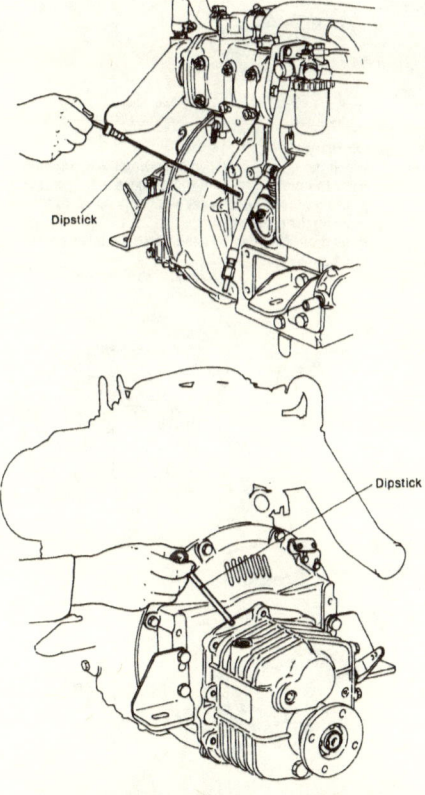

(2) Draining the cooling water
The cooling water will freeze in cold weather, causing faulty operation and cracking of the cylinders, cylinder head, and exhaust manifold. Therefore, always drain the water from the engine after use if the engine must sit in freezing weather.

Drain positions
(1) Cylinder block intake side drain cock

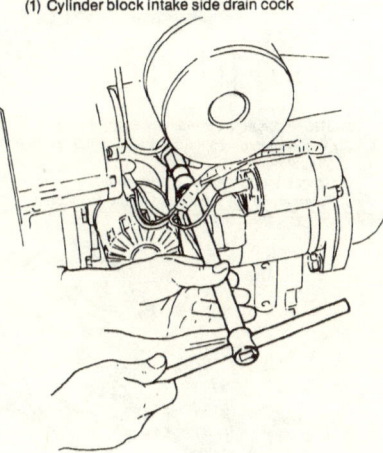

(2) Exhaust manifold bottom drain cock

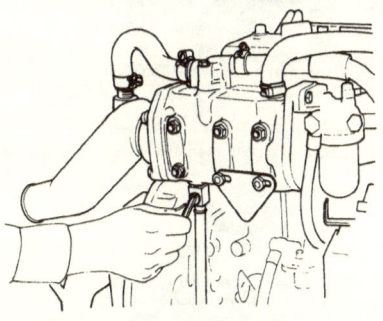

	Crankcase	Clutch case
Dipstick	Cylinder block exhaust side	Top of clutch case (filling plug with dipstick)
Filler	Top of rocker arm cover	

CAUTION: Use different lubricating oils for the engine and clutch.

1-2.2 Maintenance every 50 engine hours
(1) Clean the fuel filter
Close the fuel tank cock and remove the bowl of the fuel filter, then clean the inside of the bowl and the filter element. After reinstalling the bowl and element, open the fuel tank cock and bleed the air from the fuel system.

Chapter 14 Inspection and Servicing
1. Periodic Inspection and Servicing

SM/2QM15

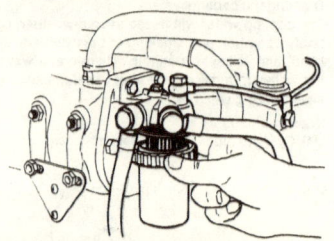

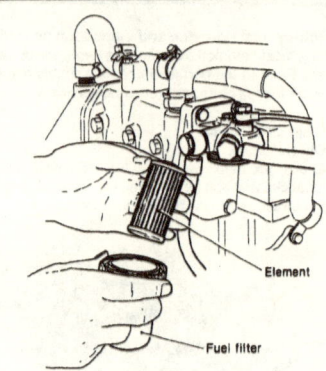
Element
Fuel filter

CAUTION: Change the element every 100 hours.
(2) V-belt tension adjustment (every 100 hours after 2nd adjustment)
Check the tension of the water pump drive V-belt and alternator drive V-belt, and adjust as required.

(2) Oil change
While the engine is still warm, pump the lubricating oil from the crank case and clutch case with a waste oil pump and refill both cases with new oil up to the top mark on the dipstick.
If the drain plug can be used, drain the oil by removing the drain plug.

Oil evacuation pump (accessory)

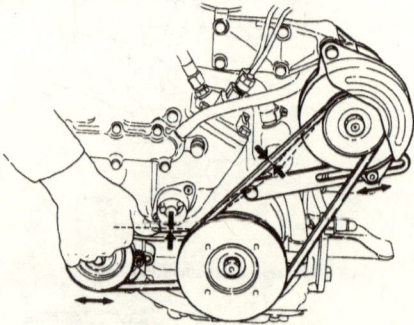

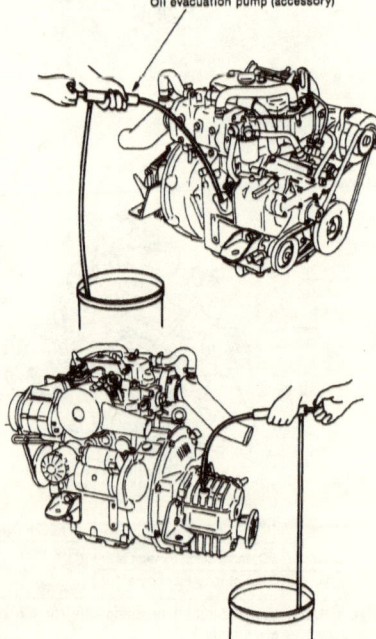

V-belt tension
(Pushed with a force of 10 kg (22 lb))

Water pump	8 ~ 12 mm (0.315 ~ 0.472 in.)
Alternator	10 ~ 15 mm (0.394 ~ 0.591 in.)

(3) Tightening bolts (Every 100 hours after the 2nd tightening
Check the engine mounting bolts, cylinder head bolts, gear case bolts, and the bolts of other main parts and tighten as required.
(Refer to the bolt tightening torque table.)

1-2.3 Maintenance every 100 engine hours
(1) Fuel filter element replacement
Close the fuel tank cock, remove the fuel filter bowl and replace the element and clean the inside of the bowl. After reinstalling the element and bowl, open the fuel tank cock and bleed the air from the fuel system.

Chapter 14 Inspection and Servicing
1. Periodic Inspection and Servicing

1-2.4 Maintenance every 300 engine hours
(1) Thermostat inspection
Remove the cooling water outlet flange on the top of the exhaust manifold and remove and inspect the thermostat.

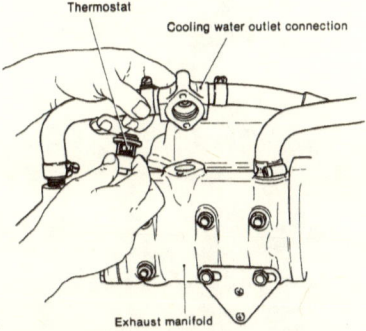

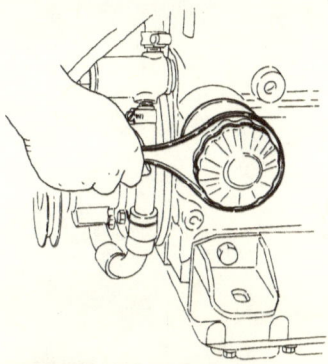

(2) Intake and exhaust valve adjustment
Remove the rocker arm chamber and check the intake and exhaust valve head clearance with a feeler gauge. Adjust if not within the prescribed limit.
(Refer to the cylinder head chapter of this manual for a description of the adjustment method.)

1-2.5 Maintenance every 500 engine hours
(1) Anticorrosion zinc replacement
Disassemble the clutch side cylinder head side cover and cooling water cylinder inlet joint and replace the anticorrosion zinc.

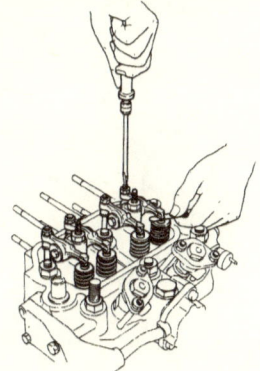

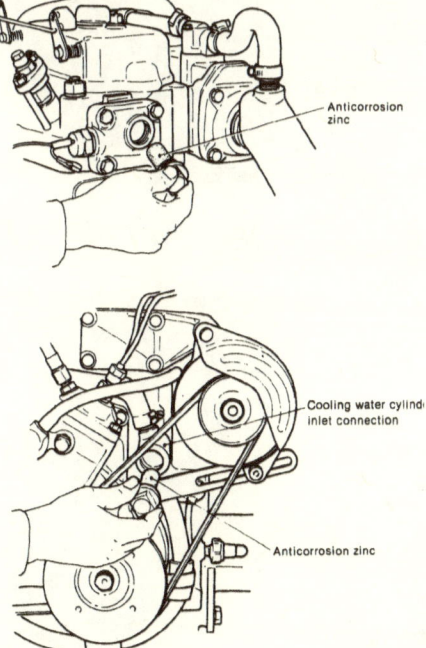

(3) Oil filter replacement
Change the oil filter every 300 hours or after the warning lamp comes on due to low oil pressure. Since the oil filter is a cartridge type, the element and case are replaced together.

www.ingramcontent.com/pod-product-compliance
Lightning Source LLC
Chambersburg PA
CBHW021706230426
43668CB00008B/743